What's Right with Macroeconomics?

Cournot Centre

Series Editor: Robert M. Solow, *Institute Professor Emeritus, Massachusetts Institute of Technology, USA, Co-founder and Chairman of the Cournot Foundation, Paris, France*

Conference Editor: Jean-Philippe Touffut, *Director of the Cournot Centre, Paris, France*

What's Right with Macroeconomics?

Edited by

Robert M. Solow

Institute Professor Emeritus, Massachusetts Institute of Technology, USA, Co-founder and Chairman, Cournot Foundation, Paris, France

Jean-Philippe Touffut

Director, Cournot Centre, Paris, France

THE COURNOT CENTRE SERIES

Edward Elgar

Cheltenham, UK • Northampton, MA, USA

Published by
Edward Elgar Publishing Limited
The Lypiatts
15 Lansdown Road
Cheltenham
Glos GL50 2JA
UK

Edward Elgar Publishing, Inc.
William Pratt House
9 Dewey Court
Northampton
Massachusetts 01060
USA

A catalogue record for this book
is available from the British Library

Library of Congress Control Number: 2012941927

ISBN 978 1 78100 739 6 (cased)
      978 1 78100 744 0 (paperback)

Typeset by Servis Filmsetting Ltd, Stockport, Cheshire
Printed and bound by MPG Books Group, UK

Contents

Figures and tables

FIGURES

TABLES

Contributors

Wendy Carlin is Professor of Economics at University College London, a Research Fellow of the Centre for Economic Policy Research (CEPR) and a Fellow of the European Economics Association. She is a member of the Expert Advisory Panel of the UK's Office for Budget Responsibility (OBR) and co-managing editor of *Economics of Transition*. Her research focuses on macroeconomics, institutions and economic performance, and the economics of transition.

Jean-Bernard Chatelain is Professor of Economics at the Sorbonne Economic Centre (Université Paris 1 Pantheon Sorbonne) and Co-director of the CNRS European Research Group on Money, Banking and Finance. His research interests include growth, investment, banking and finance, applied econometrics and statistical methodology.

Giancarlo Corsetti is Professor of Macroeconomics at Cambridge University (previously at the European University Institute [EUI], Rome, Bologna and Yale University). He is a consultant for the European Central Bank, programme director at the Centre for Economic Policy Research (CEPR), member of the European Economic Advisory Group at the CESifo (Munich Society for the Promotion of Economic Research) at the University of Munich, and co-editor of the *Journal of International Economics*. His main fields of interest are international economics, open-economy macroeconomics and the economics of currency areas.

Giovanni Dosi is Professor of Economics and Director of the Institute of Economics at the Sant'Anna School of Advanced Studies in Pisa. His major research areas include economics of innovation and technological change, industrial organization and industrial dynamics, theory of the firm and corporate governance, economic growth and development.

Giorgio Fagiolo is Associate Professor of Economics at the Sant'Anna School of Advanced Studies, Pisa, and holds a tenured position at the Institute of Economics and the Laboratory of Economics and Management. His research interests include agent-based computational economics, complex networks, evolutionary games, industrial dynamics, and economic methodology.

Robert J. Gordon is Stanley G. Harris Professor in the Social Sciences at Northwestern University, a Research Associate of the National Bureau of Economic Research (NBER), a Research Fellow of the Centre for Economic Policy Research (CEPR) and of the OFCE (French Economic Observatory, Sciences Po) in Paris. His research interests span macroeconomic studies of inflation, unemployment, and both short-run and long-run productivity growth as well as microeconomic work on price index bias and the value of new products.

Paul De Grauwe is Professor of European Political Economy at the London School of Economics. He is director of the Money, Macro and International Finance Research Network of the CESifo (Munich Society for the Promotion of Economic Research) at the University of Munich, and a research fellow at the Centre for European Policy Studies in Brussels. He was a member of the Belgian parliament from 1991 to 2003. His research interests are international monetary relations, monetary integration, theory and empirical analysis of foreign-exchange markets, and open-economy macroeconomics.

Mauro Napoletano is Senior Economist at the OFCE (French Economic Observatory, Sciences Po) in Paris and Sophia-Antipolis, France. He is an affiliated research fellow of the Laboratory of Economics and Management (LEM) in Pisa and of the SKEMA Business School in Sophia Antipolis. His research interests include the study of economic models with heterogeneous agents in macroeconomics, the empirical analysis of economic time series, and industrial dynamics.

Xavier Ragot is a Researcher at the CNRS (the French National Center for Scientific Research) and an Associate Professor at the Paris School of Economics. He was senior economist at the Bank of France from 2008 to 2011. He also served as chief economist of the French Agency for Industrial Innovation. His main field of interest is monetary economics and fiscal policy. His research focuses on liquidity issues, using the tools of incomplete market theory and the computation of equilibria.

Andrea Roventini is Assistant Professor of Economics at the University of Verona, Italy. He is an affiliated research fellow of the Laboratory of Economics and Management (LEM) at the Sant' Anna School of Advanced Studies in Pisa, Italy, and of the OFCE (French Economic Observatory, Sciences Po) in Paris and Sophia-Antipolis. His major research areas include agent-based computational economics, business cycles, applied macroeconometrics, and the statistical properties of micro-economic and macroeconomic dynamics.

Robert M. Solow is Institute Professor Emeritus of Economics at the Massachusetts Institute of Technology. He received the Bank of Sweden Prize in Economic Sciences in Memory of Alfred Nobel in 1987 for his contributions to economic growth theory. He is Robert K. Merton Scholar at the Russell Sage Foundation, where he is a member of the advisory committee for the Foundation's project on the incidence and quality of low-wage employment in Europe and the USA. Co-founder of the Cournot Centre, he is also co-founder of the Cournot Foundation.

Xavier Timbeau is Director of the Forecast and Analysis Department of the OFCE (French Economic Observatory, Sciences Po). He teaches macroeconomics and environmental economics at Supélec and Sciences Po, Paris. His main research interests include unemployment and inflation estimations, the economic outlook for the eurozone, the real-estate market, as well as public accounts and intangible assets.

Jean-Philippe Touffut is Co-founder and Director of the Cournot Centre. His research interests include probabilistic epistemology and the exploration of evolutionary games from neurological and economic perspectives.

Volker Wieland is Professor of Monetary Theory and Policy in the House of Finance at Goethe University of Frankfurt and a Founding Professor of the Institute for Monetary and Financial Stability. He is also a research fellow of the Center for Economic Policy Research in London, a member of the CEPR's Euro Area Business Cycle Dating Committee, advisory editor of the *Journal of Economic Dynamics and Control* and programme director for Central Banking and Monetary Economics at the Center for Financial Studies in Frankfurt.

Preface

This volume is one of a series arising from the conferences organized by the Cournot Centre, Paris. These conferences explore contemporary issues in economics, with particular focus on Europe. Speakers, along with other participants and members of the audience, are drawn from backgrounds in academia, business, finance, labour unions, the media and national or multinational governmental and non-governmental agencies.

The first versions of these revised and edited texts were delivered at the fourteenth conference of the Cournot Centre, 'What's Right with Macroeconomics?', held in Paris on 2 and 3 December 2010.

The term 'North Atlantic Crisis', as coined by Willem Buiter and Hans-Helmut Kotz, refers to the financial crisis that began in 2007 and has grown into an economic crisis. Although the authors often call it a 'world' or a 'global' crisis, we would like to remind readers that it is first and foremost 'North Atlantic', affecting most heavily the United States and the European Union.

Acknowledgements

Our heartfelt thanks go to Therrese Goodlett and Lucia Scharpf. From the organization of the conference to the preparation of the manuscript, they have enabled this work to see the light of day under the best possible conditions. Very special thanks also go to Richard Crabtree for the English edition. A film of the whole conference is available on the Cournot Centre's website: www.centrecournot.org.

About the series

Professor Robert M. Solow

The Cournot Centre is an independent, French-based research institute. It takes its name from the pioneering economist, mathematician and philosopher Antoine Augustin Cournot (1801–77).

Neither a think-tank nor a research bureau, the Centre enjoys the special independence of a catalyst. My old student dictionary (dated 1936) says that catalysis is the 'acceleration of a reaction produced by a substance, called the *catalyst*, which may be recovered practically unchanged at the end of the reaction'. The reaction we have in mind results from bringing together (a) an issue of economic policy that is currently being discussed and debated in Europe and (b) the relevant theoretical and empirical findings of serious economic research in universities, think-tanks and research bureaux. Acceleration is desirable because it is better that reaction occurs before minds are made up and decisions taken, not after. We hope that the Cournot Centre can be recovered practically unchanged and used again and again.

Notice that 'policy debate' is not exactly what we are trying to promote. To have a policy debate, you need not only knowledge and understanding, but also preferences, desires, values and goals. The trouble is that, in practice, the debaters often have only those things, and they invent or adopt only those 'findings' that are convenient. The Cournot Centre hopes to inject the findings of serious research at an early stage.

It is important to realize that this is not easy or straightforward. The analytical issues that underlie economic policy choices are usually complex. Economics is not an experimental science. The available data are scarce, and may not be exactly the relevant ones. Interpretations are therefore uncertain. Different studies, by uncommitted economists, may give different results. When those controversies exist, it is our hope that the Centre's conferences will discuss them. Live debate at that fundamental level is exactly what we are after.

There is also a problem of timing. Conferences have to be planned well in advance, so that authors can prepare careful and up-to-date texts. Then a publication lag is inevitable. The implication is that the Cournot Centre's conferences cannot take up very short-term issues of policy. Instead, a balancing act is required: we need issues that are short-term enough so that they are directly concerned with current policy, but long-term enough so that they remain directly relevant for a few years.

I used the words 'serious research' a moment ago. That sort of phrase is sometimes used to exclude unwelcome ideas, especially unfashionable ones. The Cournot Centre does not intend to impose narrow requirements of orthodoxy, but it does hope to impose high standards of attention to logic and respect for facts. It is because those standards are not always observed in debates about policy that an institution like the Cournot Centre has a role to play.

OTHER BOOKS IN THE COURNOT CENTRE SERIES

2004. *The Future of Economic Growth: As New Becomes Old*
Robert Boyer

2003. *Institutions, Innovation and Growth: Selected Economic Papers*
Edited by Jean-Philippe Touffut
Contributors: Philippe Aghion, Bruno Amable, with Pascal Petit, Timothy
Bresnahan, Paul A. David, David Marsden, AnnaLee Saxenian, Günther
Schmid, Robert M. Solow and Wolfgang Streeck

Introduction: passing the smell test

Robert M. Solow and Jean-Philippe Touffut

What is the relevance of macroeconomics today? The crisis that has been raging since 2007 has spread to economic theories, and it might seem that it is no longer possible to do macroeconomics as before. But what version of macroeconomics was at fault here? Macroeconomic questions have not really changed: they examine growth and fluctuations of the broad national aggregates (national income, employment, inflation, investment, consumer spending or international trade). How are these fundamental aggregates determined, and how differently should we think about them? The economic world is too complex to be thought about 'raw', so the use of a model to answer these questions helps make deductions and justify conclusions. It is easier, then, to perceive what beliefs they have been based on, and to challenge them. Economic concepts are not built to be put on a computer and run.[1] It is thus all the more important to point out fragility or recklessness wherever it appears. If intuition does not suffice to reject the hypothesis and reasoning, then experimentation must confirm our instincts: does it pass the smell test?

Economists do not directly perceive the concreteness of their world, but engage in diverse manoeuvres that seek to prepare that world for investigation. Using various abstractions and omissions, they build models to describe simple imaginary stage sets. Models are constructed rather than discovered; they are socially built because scientific work is an intrinsically social activity. If economic models of human interactions are socially constructed by economists, the social world is not constructed by the modelling practices of economists. It is from this standpoint that the authors of this volume offer to take stock of their discipline, with all its variety, from ancient to modern macro, or vice versa.

Since the late 1970s, a majority of macroeconomists have focused on developing what they call the 'modern macroeconomics of business cycle fluctuations'. Until the world entered a crisis initiated by subprime mortgage defaults, excessive leveraging followed by deleveraging, output and employment meltdowns and destruction of perceived wealth, there was a common belief that macroeconomic truth had been discovered. A

1

consensus had emerged about models that combined new-classical market clearing with the New-Keynesian contribution of sticky prices and other frictions. Along the way, contributions to this current had concluded that the great moderation of macroeconomic volatility in the 1984–2007 period was a positive side effect of their analysis. Neither the proponents of 'modern macro' nor the adherents of Keynesian ideas anticipated the crisis in advance (although there were exceptions, and mostly on the Keynesian side).

This book is consequently neither a programme of intellectual conservatism nor a nostalgic manifesto. Its discussion of the past, current or future state of macroeconomics is not a matter of being for or against a model. It does not argue that sounder economic reasoning will imply abandoning the use of formal mathematical analysis. Models provide a formal summary of how one experiences the economy: there is a set of variables, and the logical relationships between them represent economic processes. They make it easier to see how strong the assumptions must be for an argument to be valid, and how different conclusions depend on slight deviations in specific assumptions. How well they do that depends on how closely the assumptions resemble the world we live in. Economics is not the physics of society, and policy advisers cannot apply economics the way engineers use physical models.[2] History has shown that economic analysis should result in a collection of models contingent on circumstances, and not in a single, monolithic model for all seasons.

Our focus here is the relevance of contemporary macroeconomic ideas, which implies going back to the hypotheses and the causalities that founded the discipline. Fundamental macro still appeals to economists in its early versions. If you wake any economist in the middle of the night, our bet is that he or she would automatically think according to early macro, whether you choose to call it '1978-era macro' as Robert Gordon,[3] 'primeval macro' as Paul Krugman,[4] or 'eclectic Keynesianism' as Robert Solow. Old-fashioned macro remains a useful tool for carrying out practical policy analysis. At times like the present, when the (world) economy is clearly suffering from almost universal shortage of demand, policy analysis has little need of 'micro-founded' intertemporal maximization. The quasi-static goods–bonds–money model respects the essential added-up constraints and represents the motives and behaviour of individuals in a sensible way, without containing any superfluous moving parts.[5]

Old-fashioned macro can even help us think about the relationships between markets and how the whole system fits together, not only producing two goods, but multiple goods where some pairs of goods might be substitutes or complements. Three decades of rational expectations, equilibrium business cycles, the new economy, or rescue plans have nonetheless shown that debates about the actual state of affairs are always informed, sometimes implicitly, by old-fashioned macro. Although the traditional framework has remained the basis for most discussion, it has increasingly been pushed out of universities and research centres. As expressed in journals, conferences and speeches, 'modern macro' has become dominant.

Throughout the book, the contributors recurrently wonder in what ways this modern version belongs in 'macro'. Focus on individual preferences and production functions misses the essence of macro fluctuations, the coordination failures and the macro externalities that convert interactions among individual choices into constraints that prevent workers from optimizing working hours and firms from optimizing utilization, production and sales. By definition, modern macroeconomic models exclude involuntary unemployment (except through wage rigidities) and possess perfect capital markets; they fail to reproduce the observed dynamics of the economy with reasonable parameters. They had nothing useful to say about anti-recession policy, because they had built into implausible assumptions the impossibility of a crisis. They concluded that there was nothing for macroeconomic policy to do.

On the policy front, the precision of the model created the illusion that a minor adjustment in the standard policy framework could prevent future crises. With the economy attached to a highly leveraged, weakly regulated financial system, such reasoning and consequential inaction have proved unfounded. And the approach was no less false in earlier recessions that followed different patterns. If many economists have been led astray by reliance on certain categories of formal models, the consequences of such oversights have not only been methodological, but have challenged the legitimacy of the profession. This book wants to help expand the conversation on realism in macroeconomics. The contributors do not want the same answer for everything; they are looking for as many answers as there are questions.

In Chapter 1, Xavier Timbeau describes the contemporary challenge of economics by putting into perspective the criticisms of modern macroeconomics. Why do so many publications have so little to say about the crisis? Is this a failure of modern economic research in general, or specifically that of the dominant theory? The crisis has represented a profound violation of its world view, and has challenged many of its axioms. How can one determine a permanent income in such an event? How can one imagine companies going through the crisis independently of their balance sheet structure? How can one believe that people have reliable knowledge about the future when governments are embarking on massive stimulus packages? It becomes impossible to defend unrealistic axioms in the face of such overwhelming questions. The crisis has shown that uncertainty is radical, and the heterogeneity of agents is central to human activity. These two elements interact, and one cannot analyse the economy without taking into consideration the nature of expectations. The crisis invites us to re-evaluate experimentation: it does not involve choosing the most realistic model out of a set of models, knowing that even the most realistic one is not credible.

A systematic comparative approach to macroeconomic modelling is proposed by Volker Wieland in Chapter 2, with the objective of identifying policy recommendations that are robust to uncertainty. By examining multiple structural macroeconomic models, he evaluates their likely impact if applied. Wieland suggests organizing a level playing field on which models can compete and empirical benchmarks – which the models must satisfy to stay in the race – can be determined. The breadth of the models covered makes it possible to compare vintage and more recent Keynesian-style models for a given country or cross-country comparison between the United States, the euro area and some small open economies. Whatever the case, the assessment concerns standard New-Keynesian dynamic stochastic general equilibrium (DSGE) models and DSGE models that also include some financial or informational frictions. In the latter case, the agents are so clever that they even know the model in which they are being studied. The result is that the models' forecasts perform differently from one period to another. In recession times, no single model dominates the others. By construction, models are in fact incapable of forecasting crises. This was not only true for the 2008–09 period, but also for the four preceding ones. Even a thorough construction of the financial sector, with the inclusion of learning and beliefs, can only make a crisis conceivable, and possibly understandable.

From the perspective of an international economist, in Chapter 3, Giancarlo Corsetti carries out an admittedly biased review of emerging issues in macroeconomics. This involves judging the vitality of different macroeconomic currents based on questions that the crisis is forcing us to address. How are shocks transmitted? What is the role of financial channels in magnifying shocks or in translating financial disturbances into real ones? What is the extent of misallocation at the source? Corsetti concentrates on the opposition between liquidity runs versus policy/market distortions. Both must be overcome theoretically as much as politically: it is a question of guarantees versus market discipline, implying the removal or correction of policy. A highly stylized model discusses over-borrowing and exchange rate misalignments as general features of economies in which financial markets are incomplete. How can one build the framework in which the international dimensions of the crisis, ranging from global imbalances, to fiscal crisis and cross-border contagion, have so far typically been analysed as independent phenomena rather than as parts of the same process?

In Chapter 4, Jean-Bernard Chatelain lays out the historical conditions of how models are adopted and re-evaluated. Research results shape people's beliefs, and policy advice based on economic theories shapes economic policies. These in turn shape the economy. People's beliefs and economic facts are connected through mechanisms of self-fulfilment and self-defeat. In 'modern macro', models give a complete description of a hypothetical world, and its actors are assumed to understand the world in the same way it is represented in the model. When the complete economic systems happen to resemble experience, they are so pared down that everything about them is either known, or can be made up. Although fundamental to contemporary macroeconomics, questions such as (a) the impact of banking leverage, (b) interbank liquidity, (c) large shocks, (d) fire sales and (e) systemic crisis have consequently remained dangerously unaddressed. If weakly regulated financial sectors can be integrated into the models and the efficient capital market hypothesis can be rejected, then economists must investigate beyond macroeconomic policies. They will have to examine the interplay between innovative macroeconomic strategies and feasible banking and financial regulatory policy at the micro level, as well as political economy issues.

If the crisis has set a major challenge for alternative theories, those which link micro-behaviour with aggregate dynamics have a major advantage. In Chapter 5, Giovanni Dosi and his colleagues develop an evolutionary model, which goes back to basic Keynesian issues. The model first examines the processes by which technological change affects macro variables, such as unemployment, output fluctuations and average growth rates. The model then deals with the way endogenous, firm-specific changes in the supply side of the economy interact with demand conditions. Finally, the chapter explores the possible existence of long-term effects of demand variations. Is long-term growth only driven by changes in technology, or does aggregate demand affect future dynamics? Are there multiple growth paths whose selection depends on demand and institutional conditions?

In Chapter 6, Paul De Grauwe tackles the subject of strong growth followed by sharp declines. His model, written in the behavioural vein, is compared to a DSGE model where agents experience no cognitive limitations. De Grauwe's hypothesis forces agents to use simple rules to forecast output and inflation, and rationality is introduced by assuming a learning mechanism that allows for the selection of those rules. What information is available to the agents? When and how do they correct their beliefs? Are their expectations the same during periods of growth and periods of crises? In the DSGE model, large booms and busts can only be explained by large exogenous shocks. Price and wage rigidities then lead to wavelike movements of output and inflation. Thus, booms and busts are explained exogenously. Although it does not introduce financial markets and the banking sector, the behavioural model provides an endogenous explanation of business cycle movements. The inflation targeting regime turns out to be of great importance for stabilizing the economy in both models. In the behavioural model, this follows from the fact that credible inflation targeting also helps to reduce correlations in beliefs and the ensuing self-fulfilling waves of optimism and pessimism. Its conclusion is meaningful: strict inflation targeting cannot be an optimal policy.

Among the numerous rival research programmes, what were the criteria, and which programmes were adopted? In Chapter 7, Xavier Ragot provides an original perspective by placing himself in the position of the laboratory mouse, whose trajectory itself is the subject of observation. Within this framework, he endeavours to formalize Keynesian intuitions. The benchmarks of economic research have themselves been under debate: should they be able to reproduce past historical data, make better predictions than the others, or make fewer mistakes, and over what time horizon? A considerable simplification in the modelling strategy has clearly been decisive. In the dominant current, it has reduced macroeconomics to microeconomics, with one sole agent and one good. Ragot evaluates how the questions of information and frictions on the markets have challenged or reinforced the programme. New questions, however, are still being posed inside the community of economists. Like lab mice, researchers look for the cheese without knowing which labyrinth they were put in, and they may find themselves at a loss if the cheese is suddenly moved. The effervescence in the work produced by economists has not been on a par with the issues at stake. A new research programme and perhaps a new paradigm are needed, Ragot believes, and the cheese may have to wait a long time if the mice are in the wrong maze.

In the round table discussion that concludes this volume (Chapter 8), Wendy Carlin recalls the experience of the euro. The eurozone's first decade was celebrated as a success, before it was swiftly followed by a major crisis. Beneath the surface of the successful achievement of inflation close to target and a modest output gap for the eurozone as a whole, the diverse performance of its members reflected the failure of countries to implement stabilization policy at the national level in response to country-specific shocks. The macroeconomic apparatus at stake in Europe was not simply a powerful modelling tool, and its methods and recommendations may not have been at the service of building and improving the policy regime. It has rather dictated or defined those things. Fundamentally, good models of the leverage cycle need to be built to incorporate distributional effects. If a process is underway of moving to a new macroeconomic paradigm and policy regime, in what ways will it contain the seeds of the next crisis?

Robert J. Gordon takes an American perspective to clarify the co-existence of the Great Depression, the Japanese lost decade(s) and the Great Moderation followed by the Great American Slump. From the structure of shocks and propagation mechanisms, what can be learned from history about shocks? What are the propagation mechanisms that are essential to explaining this history? To answer these questions, Gordon points out, just as the other contributors to this book, that economists must not be too parsimonious: their 'models must be as simple as possible, but not more so'.[6]

NOTES

1. Lucas, R. (1988), 'On the mechanics of economic development', *Journal of Monetary Economics*, **22**(1), July, 3–42.
2. Among the pioneers who developed mathematical modelling for the social sphere, Augustin Cournot (1801–77) affirmed the mathematization of social phenomena as an essential principle. He made clear, however, that economics could not be constructed as an axiomatically based hard science, and that the scientific approach for understanding how society functions should not lead, in and of itself, to policy recommendations.
3. Gordon, R.J. (2009), *Is Modern Macro or 1978-era Macro more Relevant to Understanding the Crisis?*, Contribution to the International Colloquium on the History of Economic Thought, Sao Paulo, Brazil, 3 August.
4. Krugman, P. (2012), 'There is something about macro', MIT course, available at: http://web.mit.edu/krugman/www/islm.html.
5. Krugman, P. (2012), 'The macro wars are not over', *The New York Times*, 23 March.
6. Quote from Albert Einstein by Robert Solow during the round table.

1. The fireman and the architect

Xavier Timbeau[1]

INTRODUCTION

The disaster film *The Towering Inferno* (1974) is set in a newly constructed tower. The architect, played by Paul Newman, has devised a sophisticated security system that makes this tower perfectly safe, despite its great height and elegant design. Through greed, however, the building contractors and the architect's associates have not followed the requirements and recommendations of the architect. Since the technical specifications have not been respected, the tower is going to become a death trap. Boldness becomes arrogance, and the folly of man leads to a tragic fate. When the fire breaks out, the first reaction is to blame the security system for being defective. The design of the tower is so remarkable, however, that a fire is quite simply impossible, and the monitoring system is really only there to reassure the sceptics. A second character then comes on the scene. This is the fire chief, played by Steve McQueen. For him, no design is infallible, however advanced it may be. Each fire is unique, and must be fought, at the risk of his life, in this case because 150 people are trapped at the top of the tower and need to be saved.

We can use this story as a metaphor for the crisis we are currently in. The architects designed a new world, which they believed to be infallible. All previous achievements paled into insignificance beside the audacity of this architecture. But then, either because certain people, motivated by their own self-interest and cupidity, perverted the initial plan to such an extent that they turned it into a death trap, or because it is naive to believe that any design can be infallible, the defects, as always, came out in the end: the catastrophe occurred. And then the fire fighters were called out to try to remedy the situation, or at least to limit the damage.

Since it started in August 2007, the economic crisis has wrought havoc in our world. The repercussions are still being felt. And for those endeavouring to think about and understand how economies work, it represents an inescapable challenge. It is not possible to carry on doing macroeconomics as before. Like the Great Depression of the 1930s, the 'Great

Recession', as it is now called, has sent shock waves through the hushed circles of economists.

That is all the more so, since, just before the crisis, contemporary macroeconomics had reached a new consensus. A new synthesis, between the New Classicists and the New Keynesians, had produced a dominant corpus, driving alternative approaches into the shadows. This new synthesis enjoyed numerous successes, mainly after the collapse of the post-war Keynesian approach (the *trente glorieuses* in France) and the demise of the Bretton Woods system in 1971. The stagflation of the end of the 1970s completed the failure of Keynesian stimulus and the Phillips curve and cast doubts on the effectiveness of the welfare state. This provided a great opportunity for the classical counter-attack, set in motion long before by economists such as Milton Friedman. The success of the fight against inflation, followed by a golden period of triumphant globalization when strong, stable growth coexisted with low inflation, confirmed the new-found domination of the classicists.

The recent period has seen a reconciliation between the New Classicists and the supporters of a less irenic view of the market. This has allowed macroeconomics to make a leap forward, through a new synthesis, comparable to the one formed during the 1950s, of which Paul Samuelson was one of the initiators. George Akerlof (2007) has proposed a summary of this new synthesis based on five fundamental laws – five neutralities that shape macroeconomists' vision of the world.

But according to Akerlof, this synthesis is not satisfactory: the five fundamental laws of macroeconomics may structure the intellectual field, but they divert attention from the important questions. The crisis adds malaise to this doubt. One could accuse modern macroeconomics of failing to provide either the theoretical or the measuring instruments capable of predicting the crisis. But this criterion *à la* Friedman is not pertinent. One cannot reject a theory for failing to predict something that is impossible to predict. On the other hand, modern macroeconomics also fails to help us understand the crisis. Can this new synthesis be amended, or must we, with Akerlof, argue for new theoretical foundations?

THE ARCHITECTS AND THE BEATING HEART OF MODERN MACROECONOMICS

At the beginning of 2007, Akerlof delivered the presidential address at the 108th meeting of the American Economic Association. The paper on which his speech was based, 'The missing motivation in macroeconomics' (2007), drew partly on previous works written with Rachel Kanton.

Akerlof's paper was ambitious, arguing that current macroeconomics is at a dead end and setting out a brand new programme of research. Akerlof calls for the introduction of sociology and institutions into economics; he suggests that the fundamental hypotheses of economic behaviour (rationality) should be dismissed in favour of a behaviouralist approach, and he challenges – which is of particular interest to us here – the main 'results' of modern macroeconomics. Thus, according to Akerlof, five propositions (or results) constitute the beating heart of modern macroeconomics, built on and in contradiction to the Keynesian legacy – in other words, the macroeconomics born out of the ruins of the Great Depression. Borrowing from the tradition of physics, these results are defined as neutralities, with the status of fundamental laws (of realistic axioms) just like the conservation of matter.

Akerlof and the 'Missing Motivation'

The five neutralities listed by Akerlof are the following.

1. The independence of current income and current consumption (the life-cycle permanent income hypothesis). This result follows from the intertemporal choice of representative individuals with no financing constraints. So long as they are identified as temporary components, shocks to their current income will not cause any change in their level of consumption. Consumption is determined by intertemporal optimization, and there is no reason why it should be related to current income.
2. The Modigliani–Miller theorem (1958), or the irrelevance of current profits to investment spending. For the producer, this is the equivalent of the permanent income theory for the consumer. Investment choices, under a set of strict hypotheses, only depend on fundamental parameters, that is to say the marginal profitability of the investment in question. The structure of the balance sheet, the size of the firm, current demand and the average productivity of capital have no influence on the behaviour of the firm.
3. Ricardian equivalence or the neutrality of public debt. Developed by Robert Barro in a famous article (Barro, 1974), Ricardian neutrality affirms, under a series of hypotheses, that the budget deficit is no more than an accounting trick, which has no real or nominal influence on the macroeconomic equilibrium. Economic agents, or rather, the representative agent, see today's public debt as tomorrow's taxes. Private saving then compensates for public dissaving, and the only thing that matters is the national savings rate, the sum of public and private

saving. This result is founded on one noteworthy hypothesis, namely dynastic or intergenerational utility (when making current choices, people take into account the future utility of their descendants).

4. Natural rate theory. According to this result, there is no trade-off in the long run[2] between inflation and unemployment; consequently, inflation is not a real phenomenon and only depends, ultimately, on expected future inflation. Unemployment only has an impact on real wages, and this is the mechanism (more or less fast) whereby the economy returns to equilibrium, where equilibrium is defined by the natural rate of unemployment, or in less 'naturalistic'[3] approaches, by equilibrium unemployment.

5. Market efficiency, especially in capital markets. The latter are efficient because there is no information in the prices allowing to predict future returns any better than they have already been predicted. The hypothesis here is that all possible trade-offs have already been exploited. Fama (1970) is a central reference for this result. Robert Lucas and Thomas Sargent (1978) proposed a macroeconomic version of it. Since none of the agents can know the future better than the others do, there is no possibility of any macroeconomic 'trade-off', and in particular no possibility of short-term economic management. This theory, also known as the Rational Expectations hypothesis, entails that economic fluctuations are optimal reactions to irreducible, exogenous shocks. At best, using business cycle policy as a response to such shocks is ineffective (if the economic agents are not surprised by the policy), and at worst it exacerbates the volatility of the economy.

Akerlof's synthesis provides us with a matrix that we can apply to the different works and currents of research in modern, 'mainstream'[4] macroeconomics. Of course, there are other paradigms of macroeconomics, drawing on institutionalism, behaviourism, evolutionism and many other heterodoxies. But one must recognize the hegemony of mainstream macroeconomics in the realms of education, academia, international institutions, national administrations and the places of economic decision making. One of the strengths of the dominant macroeconomic approach is that these five neutralities are references around which a large number of research works orbit. They constitute basic knowledge, a common language, taught in all the textbooks and known to all (macro) economists; they are part of their toolbox for analysing the world. Mainstream macroeconomics is not limited to the positive affirmation of these five neutralities. On the contrary, searching for validity conditions or demonstrating violations of those neutralities based on sound frameworks has proven to be extremely fruitful in developing macroeconomics in terms of theory, application and teaching. These five neutralities are rarely upheld as absolute, insurmountable truths. There are no schools as such that define themselves by their defence of one or more of these neutralities. As the yardstick of any macroeconomic proposition (Does it respect the neutralities? If not, for what [good] reason?), they form the basis of a synthesis between the New Classicists and the New Keynesians, through the sharing of a methodology and an epistemological requirement that we might caricature by the expression 'the search for the microeconomic foundations of macroeconomics'. Axel Leijonhufvud (2009) gives a savoury description of this 'brackish' compromise between what Robert E. Hall called freshwater and saltwater economists.

Olivier Blanchard, in an article that was remarkable for its unfortunate collision with the Great Recession (Blanchard, 2009), announced that 'the state of macro is good', since the previously conflicting branches of the Keynesian reform and the neoclassical counter-reform now share a common base that enriches both of them and remedies their main defects: dominant empiricism versus axiomatic rigour; unworkable abstraction versus pragmatism and realism.

In his critique of macroeconomics, Akerlof argues that the five neutralities are misleading illusions. He calls for a rethinking of the foundations of macroeconomics, based on a radically different postulate about the behaviour of individuals. Instead of a rationality based on the 'maximization of a function subject to the relevant constraints', he proposes to start with a concept of social norms. Before returning to this proposition, we must examine the state of modern macroeconomics in more detail.

What Method for Economics?

The macroeconomic methodology revealed in the five neutralities deserves closer attention. Modern macroeconomics is characterized by a search for the microeconomic foundations of macroeconomics, and it follows a very specific path. This search for microeconomic foundations follows a hypothetico-deductive approach, more closely related to mathematics than to the experimental or observational sciences. It involves starting with an axiomatic system and deducing conclusions from it, by means of models. Lucas (1988) gives a very simple illustration of this. From a given definition of rationality (maximizing a function on the strength of the information available), accepting a certain simplification of the problem (few markets, few or only one agent) and paying particular attention to intertemporal choices (which, according to Krugman, 2000, was the most important 'advance' in macroeconomics during the decades following the 1970s), one builds a metaphor of reality that sheds light on the way the world functions.

The five neutralities are constructed from ingredients of this kind. This common base allows them to strengthen and complete each other. These ingredients are: a representative agent with an infinite life span, who prefers the present to the future (or, to put it another way, who prefers the welfare of his generation to that of following generations), whose rationality is expressed in the maximization of a particular function – namely utility – in a well-defined universe where information is perfect and uncertainty is reduced to low levels. These hypotheses are not intended to be realistic. They are meant to be relaxed, discussed and amended. Their interest lies in the fact that it is (relatively) easy to deduce the neutralities from them as results.

In this economic approach using abstract models ('toy models'), empirical validation cannot be performed following a well-defined formal procedure (*à la* Popper[5]), not only because the subject (the world, the economy) is not closed and cannot therefore (for practical and ethical reasons, according to Lucas) be subjected to experimentation, but also because the model and the conclusions of the reflection cannot produce predictions that can subsequently be confirmed or refuted. A more flexible approach is needed based on stylized facts (prices are sticky in the short run, the inflation–unemployment curve is unstable, prices on the capital markets do not contain any information that makes it possible to outperform the market) that the model must at least partly reproduce. The use of sophisticated econometric procedures sometimes conceals the fact that the question of the empirical validation of the initial intuition is incidental or, even worse, so over-determined that it has no real object. Larry Summers (1991) describes fairly conclusively how reality (in the sense of facts, whether measurable or not) rarely encumbers research in macroeconomics and is hardly ever a reason to abandon or modify a theory.

The building of complex applied models, of which the dynamic stochastic general equilibrium (DSGE) models (descended from the real business cycle, or RBC, models) have become the prototypes, follows this macroeconomic methodology. They illustrate the (mathematical) sophistication of macroeconomic reflection, conveying at least the complexity of the problem. They also illustrate the dramatic simplification that must be carried out to produce a macroeconomic model, sometimes at the price of having to make assumptions that are so strong as to be absurd, at least from an 'applied' point of view. For example, the hypothesis of the representative agent, the reductiveness of which was criticized masterfully by Alan Kirman (1992), is almost obligatory. When it is relaxed, it is often only very minimally, without actually answering the profound criticisms of this hypothesis: no motives for exchange, no asymmetry of information, no strategic behaviour, no use of institutions as instruments of interpersonal coordination, a view of welfare questions simplified to the point of uselessness, to name but a few. Consequently, introducing a smidgeon of heterogeneity into DSGE models in the form of liquidity-constrained households does nothing to approach the complexity of the problem and is in fact no more than an amendment to the (extreme) hypothesis of absolute rationality and perfect information imposed on the usual sole representative agent.

Nevertheless, the empirical validation of these terribly imperfect models provides a perfect illustration of the empirical methodology of macroeconomics. The constraint imposed on the macroeconomic model is that it must be founded both on deep parameters, which are supposed to answer the Lucas critique (because they are not affected by measures of economic policy), and at the same time on elements of *ad hoc* calibration. By reproducing a number of stylized facts (the covariance between consumption and GDP, the ratio of variances between investment and GDP), or by identifying the deep parameters on historical data (like the parameters of preference for the present or for leisure, with a consumption Euler equation), the model acquires the status of an applied model. It must be understood, however, as the modellers acknowledge and as Summers (1991) explained, that all the stylized facts – judged to be sufficient for empirical validation – form a tiny group compared with all the possibilities that the constrained but prolific imagination of the macroeconomist can produce. The empirical stage is not, therefore, a stage of validation through which one might be led to reject a model as being insufficient, but a minor step of choosing the most realistic out of a set of models, although even the most realistic model is not really realistic. Robert Solow (2010) has judged the standard result of DSGE methodology quite harshly: 'Does this really make sense? I do not think that the currently popular DSGE models pass the smell test' (p. 2).

Having said that, imposing a positivist criterion of validation on the macroeconomic approach, and thereby limiting oneself to refutable statements, would be misguided. Donald McCloskey (1983) showed not only that this is impossible, but also that it is not the methodology actually followed by scientists in general and economists in particular. He affirms, moreover, that this is not necessary, and that to increase knowledge, to be 'an engine for the discovery of concrete truth', in Alfred Marshall's words, the economist must produce a rational discourse, endeavouring by means of arguments and diverse and useful methods to convince his peers of the correctness of his view of things. Alternatively, according to Lars Syll (2010), one must proceed by abduction, associating probable and plausible causes with established consequences. In this sense, the DSGE models could be convincing, and they are not a misinterpretation of the elements accessible for economists to work with. In any event, if they are plausible, they can satisfy this less strict requirement of having the capacity to convince. Then the important question is whether they are plausible.

Finally, we must not underestimate the influence that the neutralities can have. They are obtained in a world that has been simplified to the extreme and idealized. The concept of rationality is debatable, but it is explicit. The preference function is very general and can accommodate a fairly wide range of representations. The concept of the representative individual is particularly restrictive and reduces the analysis to a sort of 'Robinsonade', but this does allow for the question of intertemporal choice to be addressed. By idealizing reality, the economic reasoning of the new macroeconomics diminishes its capacity to explain that reality. On the other hand, it acquires normative force. The five neutralities described above thus take on something of the appearance of commandments. If markets are perfect (in other words, if market imperfections are reduced to the minimum), then they will ensure the optimum outcome. If they are not perfect, then the equilibrium reached will not be the best possible one. If the economic agents were sufficiently attentive to their descendants and acted without regret, then they would be indifferent to the public debt. This classic statement of Ricardian equivalence can be turned around to make a life principle: 'Love your children in such a way that the debt you leave them is not a burden' (Timbeau, 2011). Here, the power of persuasion called for by McCloskey becomes a moral force.

The Successes of Modern Macroeconomics

One of the strengths of the core of mainstream macroeconomics is that it has achieved undeniable, concrete successes. Apart from dismantling the Keynesian legacy, which was one of the driving forces behind this project – if not the objective (at least for some economists, led by Friedman) – three important movements of modern society can be associated with the developments of mainstream macroeconomics. Whether these movements were triggered and/or justified by the reflections and contributions of a few economists or whether these intellectual 'discoveries' were simply the abstract expression of trends that were happening anyway is a moot point. Since Keynes, economists have unquestionably played an important role in the choices of society and in the conduct of public affairs. It is not unreasonable to imagine that they have exerted some influence here.

These three major movements are the fight against inflation, globalization (and the deregulation it entails) and the definition of structural public policies, intended to promote the strongest possible growth (in the private sector). All three movements have involved radical institutional changes, from the widespread introduction of independent central banks to the free circulation of capital (following the demise of the Bretton Woods system, which it may even have helped to bring about), from the deregulation of labour, goods or capital markets to the financialization of economies (in the sense that household savings, including retirement savings, are almost entirely intermediated by financial institutions).

The success of these three major movements can be summed up by the Great Moderation (after the title of a speech given by Ben Bernanke in 2004). The radical changes that took place in developed countries, the intense fight against inflation initiated by Paul Volcker at the head of the Federal Reserve at the end of the 1970s, financial and labour market deregulation, the ubiquitous and widely respected injunction to reduce the size of the public sector, led to a period that appeared blessed. The Great Moderation was a period of high world growth and low inflation, first in the developed countries and then in the developing countries, character-ized by a much lower variability of economic activity and inflation than in previous periods (Blanchard and Simon, 2001). Strong growth in the emerging countries, especially China, led to a reduction in global inequali-ties (Milanovic, 2006), although inequalities within countries increased considerably, particularly in the developed countries.

These economic successes have two links to the new classical macroeco-nomics. Of course, societies evolve in a complex way, and it is sometimes futile to look for the motives or causes. We should not overestimate the strength of ideas, and the power that a theory may exert over society is far from certain. Nevertheless, the new macroeconomics has marked the post-Bretton Woods era first by changing attitudes and practices towards inflation. At the end of the 1960s, Edmund Phelps and Milton Friedman announced the death of the Phillips curve, stressing the importance of expectations. At the end of the 1970s, the implementation of anti-inflation policies, banking on a temporary impact on unemployment and economic activity, was crowned with success. Coordination with fiscal policy was essential (the expansionary fiscal policy of the Reagan years responding to the Fed's tight monetary policy), thus departing from the purity of the concept of natural unemployment, or at any rate displaying some doubt about the capacity of an economy to return rapidly to the natural rate. But this success established the credentials of the theorists and brought about the domination of mainstream macroeconomists in central banks that continues to this day.

The second great success of the new classical macroeconomics has been its influence over the major economic institutions. The macroeconomic theorists recommended that central banks should be independent; this recommendation has been widely followed, to say the least. The increased flexibility of labour markets, and secondarily that of the markets for goods and services, was largely promoted by different international organizations and assumed an important place among the political preoccupations of the developed countries. Admittedly, governments watered down the extreme recommendations of certain economists by introducing 'flexicurity' rather than absolute flexibility of the labour market, but here again, the macroeconomic debate had a perceptible influence on society's choices by suggesting that the benefit to be gained from greater competition largely outweighed the costs imposed on part of the population.

In the same spirit, financial deregulation found strong theoretical justifications in the field of economics. Nevertheless, these visible successes must not be allowed to overshadow two facts. First, the recipes are old, and if macroeconomics appears to have renewed the arguments, methods, tools or concepts, it is striking to note that their application in the form of policies or institutional design bears a strong resemblance to the classical view of society. One may agree with Blanchard that a new synthesis has taken place, but when it comes to making recommendations, the discourse becomes extremely simplified. Second, these recommendations have also experienced failure on a large scale. From Latin America to the transition of the former Soviet bloc, modern macroeconomics has been less triumphant.

Transcending the Pure Orthodoxy: the Strength of the New Synthesis

Faced not only with real successes – although perhaps too hastily attributed – but also with major failures, the strength of the mainstream has been its ability to transcend itself. The new synthesis between the New Classicists and the New Keynesians allows for the production of something other than the old recipes, because it has made it possible to incorporate into the dominant model variations that are significant enough to change the nature of the message.

These variations that the new synthesis has made possible are numerous, and drawing up a global list is a difficult and arbitrary exercise. But we can describe some of the more noteworthy avenues.

1. The microeconomic foundations of price and wage rigidity. These elements form an important link between Keynesian short term and classical long term. Such foundations make it possible to bring into the temple of macroeconomics lines of reasoning deemed to be ad hoc or based solely on observation (prices are rigid, as one can observe). But it also makes it possible to change economists' attitude towards rigidities. When they are simply observed, one can always suggest

they be reduced. And this was indeed a standard argument drawn from the old synthesis (*à la* Samuelson): admittedly, prices are sticky, which gives the economy Keynesian properties (that is, positive multipliers), but if they were not (or less) sticky, then the economy would return to equilibrium more quickly, and we would all be better off as a result. By laying the foundations for price rigidity, one is describing a more complex world in which the concept of optimum is less naive and frictions are caused by decentralized behaviour. One example of such foundations is the job search model of Peter Diamond, Dale Mortensen and Christopher Pissarides (Diamond, 1982).

2. Information asymmetries and costs. By importing into macroeconomics situations addressed in microeconomics or industrial economics, the aim is to arrive at paradoxical conclusions compared with the general equilibrium model under perfect information and with complete markets. The main idea is that the asymmetry of information or the acquisition of information leads to a much richer discussion about the nature of rationality. Instead of reducing rational behaviour to the constrained maximization of a function under the assumption that all the arguments of the function are known, the idea is to keep a simple (or simplistic) view of rationality (constrained maximization of a function) and to investigate the conditions and the means by which one knows (or does not know) the different information necessary to the optimization programme. The idea is not new, but some authors have explored it in greater depth. The works of Joseph Stiglitz and Bruce Greenwald (2003) or Roman Frydman and Michael Goldberg (2007) are examples of successful attempts to incorporate these questions into recent macroeconomic issues.

3. Externalities. The question of externalities is not new in economics, and it is inextricably linked to the works of Arthur Pigou and Alfred Marshall. The challenge is to incorporate into macroeconomic modelling the consequences of the coordination failure induced by externalities. Externalities should no longer be considered as a market imperfection, moving us away from the ideal world of the efficient market, but as the main ingredient of a globalized and crowded world.

THE CRISIS: WHY MODERN MACROECONOMICS HAS NOTHING TO SAY

The era of the Great Moderation was not free of crises. Robert Boyer (2008) and Paul Krugman (2009a) recall the sequence of crises from Mexico to the Asian crisis of 2008, or the Argentinean crisis of 2002. For a long time, Charles Kindleberger (1996) has also been drawing attention to the recurrence of financial crises and their impact on economies. And it is probable, according to Hyman Minsky's intuition (1986), that an apparent stability in the developed countries – in other words those countries at the heart of financial activity – led economists to imagine that the system was invincible. By pushing it ever further, we sowed the seeds of the crisis.

Minsky's intuition was perceptive. There had been early warning signs of the crisis, from the stock market crash of 1987 to the bursting of the Internet bubble. Success in overcoming each of these incidents fuelled an illusory sense of confidence. The triumph of the new macroeconomics was just one more symptom of this self-deception. Those incidents should have sufficed to call into question the world view brought to us by economic theory. But we need to take this argument further. Calling for a new economic paradigm cannot be justified solely by the fact that we are dissatisfied with the current one. After all, dissatisfaction is simply the corollary of the work that remains to be done and the fact that the world is complex. It does not entail that the foundations of this macroeconomics are shaky and inevitably lead one to make mistakes about the state of the world, the policies that should be applied or the institutions that should be set up. Many economists have expressed their dissatisfaction with the state of macroeconomics. In a long article in *The New York Times Magazine*, Krugman (2009b) condemns modern macroeconomics, lost in research dead ends and incapable of answering the questions of our time. James K. Galbraith (2009) makes Krugman's critique his own, but takes it further: there were elements present in the heterodoxy that indicated the possibility of a crisis. There were arguments that had been rejected solely on the grounds that they were not 'methodologically' correct, in other words, they did not follow the canons of the new synthesis.

This is not a failure of modern economic research in general, but specifically the failure of the new synthesis. The university system ensured the hegemony of this synthesis through the combined effects of selection and publications. Other authors, from Joseph Stiglitz (2009) to Axel Leijonhufvud (2009), along with Daron Acemoglu (2009) and Charles Wyplosz (2009), have expressed their dissatisfaction, both in relation to the public putting economists on trial and the inability of macroeconomics to deal with the crisis.

At this stage, although the feeling of dissatisfaction predominates, few paths have been charted for the foundation of a macroeconomic approach capable of addressing the crisis. What is needed to understand the instabilities of capitalism? Do we need a new framework, a paradigm shift?

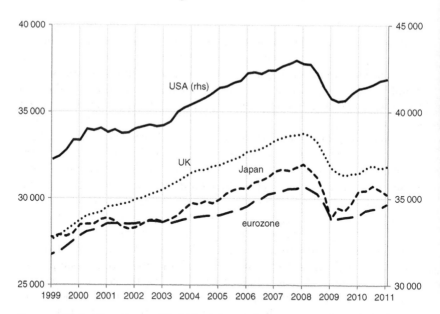

Sources: National accounting, World Bank for purchasing power parity (PPP). The GDP is divided by the total population of each zone and expressed in 2005 dollar values and PPP (based on World Bank indices for 2005). The lines for 2010 and 2011 are based on OFCE forecasts, October 2010.

Figure 1.1   GDP per capita in the USA, UK, Japan and eurozone

Can we find the necessary ingredients and research paths in the present synthesis (for example, by including the financial sector in theoretical and applied models, as is often suggested)?

The problems are considerable, presenting us with a daunting task. Let us start by recalling some 'stylized' facts about the state of the world economy in crisis and some diagrams that explain them.

Some Facts: Growth and Wealth

The developed countries have entered a recession incommensurable with anything that has been observed in these countries since the Second World War. Figure 1.1 presents the gross domestic product (GDP) per capita of four large developed economic zones since 1999.

Figure 1.1 illustrates a number of key points.

1.   The crisis is simultaneous and of similar scale in all the core countries of global capitalism. It is impossible to identify the starting point of

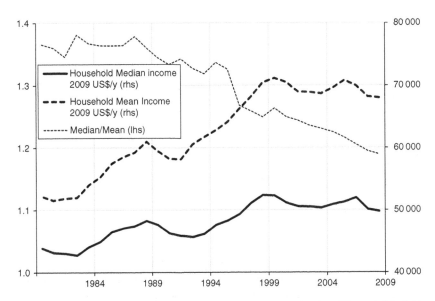

Note: Household income data differ from the national accounting data (Figure 1.1) in field and concept. National accounting income is broader and includes many additional elements.

Source: US Census Bureau, Current population survey, November 2010. Annual Social and Economic Supplements.

Figure 1.2 Median and mean income in the United States

the crisis on the basis of information. There is no epicentre that might have been affected earlier and more strongly by the crisis.

2. The crisis is of a very large scale. Since the Second World War, the periods when GDP per capita (the mean level of wealth per inhabitant) has fallen have always been short lived and, above all, rapidly cancelled by a return to better circumstances.[6] If we look at medians rather than means, we obtain the same results (Figure 1.2). Compared with the bursting of the Internet bubble, the current crisis is profound. The bursting of the Internet bubble resulted in stagnation of the GDP per capita in the United States and Europe, not in a decrease like the one we are witnessing today.

3. Reasoning in terms of means, as we have to with aggregate GDP, we lose sight of the fact that the crisis is not a homogeneous phenomenon. Previous recessions have always been accompanied by an increase in inequalities.[7] The present crisis, through its violence, is provoking divergent trajectories between individuals who remain relatively unaffected (their company survives, their patrimony has

Table 1.1   Unemployment and economic activity in the crisis of 2008

Variation between 2010q2 and 2008q1	FRA	GER	ITA	JPN	USA	UK	SPA
GDP/habitant (in %)	−3.5	−2.3	−7.1	−4.5	−3.2	−5.8	−6.0
GDP (in %)	−2.2	−2.7	−5.6	−4.3	−1.1	−4.5	−4.6
Unemployment	+2.1	−0.6 (+1.3)*	+2.2	+1.4	+4.9	+2.6	+10.8

Note: *Unemployment figure including, for Germany, partial unemployment.

Source: National statistics institutes (INSEE of France, Dstatis of Germany, Istat of Italy, and so on); calculations by the author.

not depreciated, their job is safe) and others who are caught up in spirals that amplify the initial shock (loss of job, sale of real estate or financial capital at the most unfavourable moment, and so on). Table 1.1 presents the variations in unemployment, an indicator that reveals some of the heterogeneity.

Figure 1.3 shows an aspect of the crisis that is complementary to the one we have observed for flows – the impact on stocks. The concept used here is US household wealth. Because of the way the accounts of US wealth are calculated, this concept has the advantage of summarizing the loss of wealth incurred by economic agents. The calculation involves consolidating the variations in assets and liabilities in the accounts of US households. Ultimately, along with government and foreign investors, households are the owners of variations in assets in the US economy.

Figure 1.3 gives us an idea of the magnitude of the impact that the crisis has had on wealth. Adding together financial and real estate wealth net of debt, we can see that the crisis has caused US households to lose the equivalent of 150 per cent of their income. This order of magnitude is similar to the loss of wealth that occurred when the Internet bubble burst, but it is also similar to the gain in financial wealth caused by the formation of that bubble or to the gain in wealth produced during the period before the crisis[8] (nevertheless, the post-2007 crisis appears to be more serious, and the next one may well be worse). In the space of just a few years, the average US household saw their wealth magically increase by the equivalent of one and a half year's income. This allowed them, for example, to stop saving for their retirement, since the returns on capital already saved were sufficient to maintain their standard of living. When

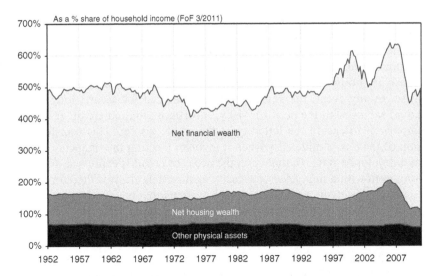

Source: Flow of Funds, Federal reserve statistical release, March 2011; calculations by the author.

Figure 1.3   US household wealth

the capital suddenly depreciated, on the other hand, they suffered a similar loss, leaving many households in a troublesome situation.

It is impossible to establish a detailed diagnosis of the impact of the inflation of wealth on the different fractiles of wealth or income. Nevertheless, and especially for the crisis of 2008, the fact that both real estate and financial wealth are affected suggests that the impact is not concentrated on the wealthiest. The financialization of modern developed economies has resulted in practically every household owning some form of wealth. Thus, home ownership rates are high, particularly when one only considers adult populations engaged in active and family life. It is facilitated by broad access to credit. Second, pension savings systems have become important in the developed countries, accumulating assets of the order of 100 per cent in the United States or the United Kingdom, to name but two. In this respect, France is very atypical, with very weak development of pension funds, which protected it from the sharp depreciation of assets experienced during the crisis.

Radical Uncertainty, Positive Feedback Loops, Instability

These elements illustrate the tremendous tension generated by the use of financial markets. On one side, households make savings equal to several times their annual income,[9] and these savings are entrusted to the financial system. On the other side, the financial system, from the banks to the pension funds by way of every imaginable type of intermediary, uses these savings to generate a return by lending them to those who need credit. These are households, governments, local authorities and private enterprise. In any event, the aim is to match the need for secure, long-term, liquid saving with the need for risky, short-term, illiquid credit. It is also important to ensure the liquidity of the whole system. This transformation of the risk is quite easy when it involves meeting the financing needs of a developed state. In that case, the need for credit is expressed over the long term with a high level of security against default. It is therefore easy to match this credit need with a need for saving that has similar characteristics. Ensuring liquidity is also easy, as long as a secondary market exists for trading in the public debt bonds, which is the case for large states or for bonds issued in euros.

The difficulty of the operation is comparable when it comes to financing the credit needs of households. These mainly concern the purchase of real estate and therefore have similar characteristics to household saving: fairly high security and long-term horizons.[10]

The transformation of risk is intrinsically more delicate for the private sector, however. The attention that has been focused on sub-prime lending as the factor that triggered the Great Recession sometimes overshadows the consequences of a sudden, sharp fall in productive assets. And yet the transformation of long-term, risk-averse savings into the financing of risky activity is problematic. If the markets are efficient, then the volatility in the value of productive assets comes from the fact that the activities involved are risky, but the absence of bias in the aggregate value of productive assets allows one to reduce the risk to zero by using the law of large numbers. This is what the capital asset pricing model (CAPM) and the Black–Scholes formula do: diversifying to create a risk-free asset, however abstract. But this is where the illusion comes into play, since there is no guarantee that there is not a general bias in the value of assets. In fact, the data have indicated the exact opposite since the end of the 1990s. The value of the assets owned by US households is known to the nearest 150 per cent of income!

Faced with such aggregate uncertainty, which is persistent enough over time to allow the formation of bubbles, no financial instrument can satisfy the need for transformation. The financial system or the households are then exposed to the failure of valuation, to that discounted value of future returns that the financial markets cannot predict.

The financialization of economies has consisted in the transfer of more and more operations of transformation of savings from isolated, specialized institutions towards a general model of market finance. So it was that housing finance moved from a closed circuit (households borrowing from the housing savings of households, collected by paragovernmental institutions) towards an open circuit (the securitization of mortgages), and intermediation by banks was pushed out by direct or structured circuits (such as private equity). At the same time, contributory pension schemes were 'complemented' by funded pension plans. In fact, this involved substitution rather than topping-up.

In this trend, ever greater masses of capital are moving about, heightening the general risk and becoming ever more dependent on an accurate valuation of the productive assets. At the same time, investors have been becoming more diversified. Instead of experienced investors financing risky productive activities with a high level of direct involvement, a whole category of investors has emerged whose sole concern is not to have any concerns, prepared to turn a blind eye to the management of their pension savings so long as they are promised a modest but secure return.

National compromises may impose a ratchet effect on this system. By promoting funded pension plans (which appeared, during a felicitous period, to give particularly good returns), and thereby avoiding the potential difficulties of trying to balance their contributory pension schemes, governments guaranteed the promise made to savers. That promise was that their savings would be worth something in a few decades and that in the meantime, they would give real positive returns. To achieve that, it is not enough for capital markets to produce fair value; they must produce constant growth in value. And for that reason, governments prefer the formation of bubbles to any other solution.

This is quite a terrible trap. In the name of market efficiency, on the grounds that the returns obtained were better than those of contributory systems, the developed world has nurtured a financial sector that is incapable of keeping its promises, quite simply because those promises have no meaning. When disaster strikes, the only solution is to keep the house of cards standing as long as possible, whatever the cost. The bubble suits everyone; uncertainty hides the fact that the promises are untenable; the positive feedback loops interact and generate instability on a macroeconomic scale. When, in addition, learned economists lend their moral and intellectual support to the edifice, one would have to be crazy to refuse this dream.

Debt Deflation: 'Fisher's Nightmare'

The entry into recession manifests itself in a fall in economic activity and in the value of assets and a rise in unemployment. Unsurprisingly, this

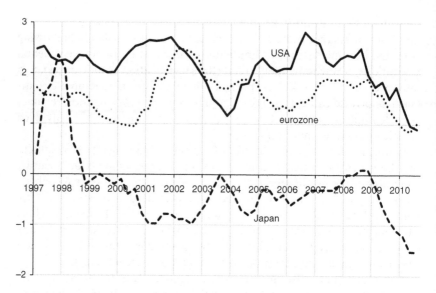

Source: National statistical institutes (INSEE of France, Dstatis of Germany, Istat of Italy, and so on). Quarterly price indices excluding volatile products (energy and food) in annual growth rhythm.

Figure 1.4　Underlying inflation for the large developed countries

causes a slowdown in inflation. Unfortunately, the rise in oil and food prices has masked this evolution in the price indices.[11] The underlying indices, presented in Figure 1.4, are unequivocal.

In all the economic zones considered here, the entry into recession has been accompanied by a reduction in underlying inflation of about half of 1 per cent per year. At that rate, the United States and the eurozone would enter deflation in 2012 while Japan would sink once again. The fact that deflation can appear despite the expansionist monetary policy being pursued (low interest rates and 'unconventional' policies) suggests that the system is caught in a liquidity trap, where this expansionist monetary policy is no longer effective. In the 1930s, it was called 'pushing on a string'. Krugman (1998) gives a more modern definition of the liquidity trap: it is a situation where the real short-term interest rate necessary to stimulate the economy would have to be negative. And yet expectations of inflation (or rather, of deflation) make it impossible to expect a negative real rate. The only solution is to increase expectations of inflation. In a situation of creeping deflation, this is indeed very much like pushing on a string.

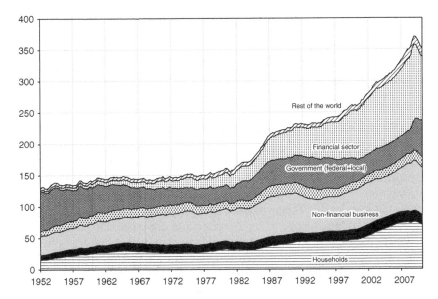

Source: Flow of Funds, Federal reserve statistical release, September 2010, calculations by the author.

Figure 1.5   *Components of US debt as a percentage of GDP*

Entering deflation would have disastrous consequences. This is the process of debt deflation described by Irving Fisher (1933). One notable difference from the 1930s is the level of financial debts that agents have accumulated. Figure 1.5 shows the components of US debt as a percentage of GDP. The figures for the other developed economic zones are similar.

For debts at fixed nominal rates of interest, deflation produces an increase in the real rate. For debts at variable rates, it has no impact. It is hard to know the exact proportions of fixed- and variable-rate debts, but we do know that a large quantity (almost all) are practically fixed rate. The rise in the cost of debts will force agents to massively reduce their debts. This process will exacerbate the recession and fuel deflation. When the rhythm of deflation falls below -2 per cent per year, real rates are at a minimum of 2 per cent. With each step deeper into deflation, real rates increase.

The process of deflation can accelerate if defaults occur rather than agents being prompted to pay back their debts as fast as possible. In a highly financialized system, the expectation of default can lead to an immediate hike in risk premiums, thereby producing the default. In this case, expectations are self-fulfilling and the economic system becomes more unstable. The Greek crisis provides a good illustration of these instabilities.

Fisher considered debt deflation to be the driving force behind the Great Depression. The state of the developed world's debts in deflation is 'Fisher's nightmare'.

CONCLUSION: A PARADIGM SHIFT?

The crisis represents a profound violation of the world view structured by the five neutralities. How can one determine a permanent income in such an event? How can one imagine that companies go through the crisis independently of their balance sheet structure? How can one believe in Ricardian equivalence when governments are embarking on massive stimulus packages? How can one uphold the existence of 'natural' or equilibrium unemployment, supposed to be an attractor of economic dynamics when unemployment is persistently above 10 per cent in the developed countries? And how can one maintain the hypothesis of market efficiency when the hegemony of markets over the organization of the globalized economy has led to unprecedented disaster?

It becomes impossible to defend these neutralities in the face of such overwhelming facts. The crisis has shown us two things: uncertainty is radical and the heterogeneity of agents plays a central role. These two elements interact, and one cannot analyse the economy without taking into consideration the nature of expectations.

It is not that economic agents are irrational, it is the definition of rationality habitually used in modern macroeconomics that completely misconstrues the universe in which we live and move. If there was no uncertainty about the future, we could all form the same expectation, corresponding *a priori* to the aggregate result *a posteriori*. Because the future is irreducible and no market can diminish that uncertainty, expectations are heterogeneous and imperfect. This heterogeneity comes on top of that of the agents and of the information they possess or are capable of acquiring.

In a universe of uncertainty and heterogeneity, institutions play a role in reducing uncertainty; they are islands of stability. They provide a form of coordination between isolated and lost economic agents. Institutions are a means to reacting to new or uncontrollable situations. They are a means of reducing the radical uncertainty that we face. They are also endogenous to the economic process, conceived and accepted with a precise objective, as a solution to a problem.

Modern macroeconomics appears to disregard all that, often on the grounds of one sole argument: moral hazard. If architects relied on the presence of fire fighters, then they might well design towers that are less safe. When individuals are certain that someone will intervene to save them in the event of disaster, they no longer run the risk of being punished for their mistakes and they behave recklessly and irresponsibly. Ensuring that everyone is responsible for their actions is commendable, but there exists a level of disaster where that consideration becomes secondary. That is all the more so since it is perfectly possible to punish those responsible *after* the firemen have done their work (although this is easier said than done, as we have seen in the crisis).

Neither methodological individualism nor the concept of rationality should be abandoned. On the other hand, as Akerlof insists, it is urgent that rationality be defined in a way that is both convincing and enlightening about how economies function, instead of continuing to entertain a misleading conception.

It would be presumptuous to call for a paradigm shift. And yet current lines of research in macroeconomics, as represented by the new synthesis, are deeply challenged by the natural experiment of the crisis. While awaiting a better explanation of how economies work, we can only express our dissatisfaction.

NOTES

1. I would like to thank the organizers of the conference held by the Cournot Centre on 2–3 December 2010, especially Therrese Goodlett and Lucia Scharpf, Robert Solow and Jean-Philippe Touffut, and the other participants, in particular Robert Boyer, Jean-Bernard Chatelain, Giovanni Dosi, Bernard Gazier, Robert Gordon and Xavier Ragot. Their remarks were invaluable to me in writing this text. Thanks also to friends Philippe Daulouède, Guillaume Daudin and Joël Maurice for re-reading the text, whose remaining shortcomings are entirely mine.
2. Here, the term 'long run' is deliberately vague. It means that inevitably, after a certain time, unemployment will have no influence on inflation. The trade-off between inflation and unemployment is therefore an illusion, or the result of temporary frictions or imperfections. In a reasonable world, that will not last very long, and the long run may be no more than a few months.
3. It is difficult to see unemployment as a product of nature. Unemployment presupposes a non-autarkic, wage-earning society. The qualification 'natural' unemployment is therefore questionable. Beyond the semantic detail, it is interesting to note that it was through natural unemployment and the concept of equilibrium unemployment that 'structural' reasoning was developed, bringing into play institutions such as unemployment insurance, employee bargaining power and the market power of employers or employees. This idea appeared to be very useful, since the cyclical (macroeconomic) and the structural only meet orthogonally, without having an effect on each other.
4. 'Mainstream' should be understood as descriptive and non-normative. The mainstream approach is rich and varied, founded on a common base (of which the five neutralities constitute a matrix) from which it has developed along many different paths, with methodological additions that are sometimes far removed from the core.
5. In other words, making propositions (predicates) that can be refuted and then

conducting reproducible, controlled experiments to test those predicates. As long as no experiment refutes the proposition, it is considered acceptable (that is to say, true in the naive sense of the word). Macroeconomics is characterized by statements that are generally not refutable.

6. This point is not visible in Figure 1.1. Long-run analyses show that the post-war period was one of strong and stable growth, compared, for example, with the nineteenth century or, obviously, the first half of the twentieth century.

7. One can even suppose that these inequalities are random and in no way related to a form of efficiency (in the sense of John Rawls, 1971) that might give them some legitimacy.

8. In changes in wealth, one can distinguish between those resulting from savings flows (net of the consumption of fixed capital) and those resulting from price variations. Unsurprisingly, a huge proportion of the recent evolution of wealth is due to price changes.

9. To ensure a relatively constant standard of living, it is necessary to save approximately 7 times one's annual income (based on 40 years' working, 20 years' retirement, 2 per cent of real return, retirement income equal to 80 per cent of net income, from savings or social security contributions). On average, in the United States, real estate wealth is equivalent to 2 to 3 times annual end-of-career income, and financial wealth around 1 to 2 times annual income. The remainder is made up by contributory pension schemes.

10. Sub-prime lending is a striking exception to this general rule. Aside from sub-prime lending, and as long as we restrict ourselves to stable populations with well identified incomes, without counting on capital gains to ensure the solvency of the whole system, mortgage lending is a risk-free activity, subject to hazards that are well measured and well controlled.

11. It could be argued that the rise in oil and food prices is the symptom of a situation of scarcity and is in itself a factor of inflation. In that case, it would be better to look at the complete indices. Price rises due to scarcity do not necessarily turn into inflation, however, and may simply cause a change (albeit substantial) in relative prices. The underlying indices filter out these components. If these indices rise, they are the symptom of a general rise in prices, in a spiral of prices, costs and wages. The scarcity of certain products may be the triggering factor. It has been shown that the underlying indices are better predictors of trends over a few quarters than price indices. This tends to confirm that scarcity is not a sufficient condition for inflation.

REFERENCES

Acemoglu, Daron (2009), 'The crisis of 2008: structural lessons for and from economics', *CEPR Policy Insight*, **28**, available at: http://www.cepr.org/pubs/policyinsights/PolicyInsight28.pdf, accessed 24 August 2011.

Akerlof, George (2007), 'The missing motivation in macroeconomics', *American Economic Review*, **97**(1), 5–36.

Barro, Robert (1974), 'Are government bonds net wealth?', *The Journal of Political Economy*, **82**(6), 1095–117.

Bernanke, Ben S. (2004), 'The great moderation', remarks by Governor Ben S. Bernanke at the meetings of the Eastern Economic Association, Washington, DC, 20 February, available at: http://www.federalreserve.gov/boarddocs/speeches/2004/20040220/default.htm, accessed 24 August 2011.

Blanchard, Olivier (2009), 'The state of macro', *Annual Review of Economics*, **1**(1), January, 209–28.

Blanchard, Olivier and John Simon (2001), 'The long and large decline in US output volatility', *Brookings Papers on Economic Activity*, **32**(1), 135–74, available at: http://www.brookings.edu/~/media/Files/Programs/ES/BPEA/2001_1_bpea_papers/2001a_bpea_blanchard.pdf, accessed 24 August 2011.

Boyer, Robert (2008), 'History repeating for economists: an anticipated financial crisis', Cournot Centre *Prisme* Series, no. 13, available at: http://www.centre-cournot.org/index.php/2008/11/26/history-repeating-for-economists-an-anticipated-financial-crisis, accessed 24 August 2011.

Diamond, Peter (1982), 'Demand management in search equilibrium', *Journal of Political Economy*, **90**, 881–94.

Fama, Eugene F. (1970), 'Efficient capital markets: a review of theory and empirical work', *Journal of Finance*, **25**(2), July, 383–417.

Fisher, Irving (1933), 'The debt-deflation theory of great depressions', *Econometrica: Journal of the Econometric Society*, **1**(4), 337–57.

Frydman, Roman and Michael D. Goldberg (2007), *Imperfect Knowledge Economics*, Princeton, NJ: Princeton University Press.

Galbraith, James K. (2009), 'Who are these economists, anyway?', *Thought and Action*, Fall, pp. 85–97.

Kindleberger, Charles (1996), *Manias, Panics, and Crashes: A History of Financial Crises*, 3rd edn, 1st edn published in 1978, New York: Basic Books.

Kirman, Alan P. (1992), 'Whom or what does the representative individual represent?', *Journal of Economic Perspectives*, **6**(2), Spring, 117–36, available at: http://www.jstor.org/stable/2138411, accessed 16 June 2011.

Krugman, Paul (1998), 'It's baaack: Japan's slump and the return of the liquidity trap', *Brookings Papers on Economic Activity*, 1998(2), 137–205.

Krugman, Paul (2000), 'How complicated does the model have to be?', *Oxford Review of Economic Policy*, **16**(4), December, 33–42.

Krugman, Paul (2009a), *The Return of Depression Economics*, New York: W.W. Norton.

Krugman, Paul (2009b), 'How did economists get it so wrong?', *New York Times Magazine*, available at: http://www.nytimes.com/2009/09/06/magazine/06Economic-t.html, accessed 24 August 2011.

Leijonhufvud, Axel (2009), 'Macroeconomics and the crisis: a personal appraisal', *CEPR Policy Insight*, 41, available at: http://www.cepr.org/pubs/policyinsights/PolicyInsight41.pdf, accessed 24 August 2011.

Lucas, Robert E. (1988), 'What economists do', *Journal of Applied Economics*, Universidad del CEMA, 0, pp. 1–4, May.

Lucas, Robert and Thomas Sargent (1978), 'After Keynesian macroeconomics', in Federal Reserve Bank of Boston, *After the Phillips Curve: Persistence of High Inflation and High Unemployment*, proceedings of conference held in June 1978, The Federal Reserve Bank of Boston Conference Series, no. 19, pp. 49–72.

McCloskey, Donald N. (1983), 'The rhetoric of economics', *Journal of Economic Literature*, **21**(2), 481–517.

Milanovic, Branko (2006), 'Global income inequality', *World Economics*, **7**(1), 131–57, available at: http://www.nupi.no/layout/set/print/content/download/3901/57934/version/5/file/GlobalIncomeInequality.pdf, accessed 21 June 2011.

Minsky, Hyman P. (1986), *Stabilizing an Unstable Economy*, New Haven, CT, and London: Yale University Press.

Modigliani, Franco and Merton Miller (1958), 'The cost of capital, corporation finance and the theory of investment', *American Economic Review*, **48**(3), 261–97.

Rawls, John (1971), *Theory of Justice*, Cambridge, MA: Belknap Press of Harvard University Press.

Solow, Robert (2010), 'Building a science of economics for the real world', prepared statement for the US House Committee on Science and Technology Subcommittee on Investigations and Oversight, 20 July.

Stiglitz, Joseph E. (2009), 'The current economic crisis and lessons for economic theory', *Eastern Economic Journal*, **35**(3), 281–96.

Stiglitz, Joseph E. and Bruce Greenwald (2003), *Toward a New Paradigm in Monetary Economics*, Cambridge, UK: Cambridge University Press.

Summers, Lawrence H. (1991), 'The scientific illusion in empirical macroeconomics', *Scandinavian Journal of Economics*, **93**(2), 129–48, available at: http://www.jstor.org/stable/3440321, accessed 21 June 2011.

Syll, Lars P. (2010), 'What is (wrong with) economic theory', *Real World Economics Review*, no. 54, August, pp. 23–57.

Timbeau, Xavier (2011), 'Solidarité intergénérationnelle et dette publique', *Revue de l'OFCE*, **116**(1), 191–212.

Wyplosz, Charles (2009), 'Macroeconomics after the crisis. Dealing with the Tobin Curse', Walter Adolf Jöhr Lecture 2009, *Contributions to Economics*, no. 10, June, Institute of Economics, University of St Gallen.

2. Model comparison and robustness: a proposal for policy analysis after the financial crisis[1]

Volker Wieland

INTRODUCTION

In the aftermath of the financial crisis, the state of macroeconomic modelling and the use of macroeconomic models in policy analysis have come under heavy criticism. Media and other commentators have criticized macroeconomists for failing to predict the Great Recession of 2008–09, or at least for failing to provide adequate warning of the risk of such a recession. Practitioners have attributed this failure to academic and central bank researchers' love of a particular modelling paradigm. They blame so-called dynamic stochastic general equilibrium (DSGE) models for misdirecting the attention of policy makers. Indeed, even some well-known academics-cum-bloggers have published scathing commentaries on the current state of macroeconomic modelling. On 3 March 2009, Willem Buiter wrote on the *Financial Times* blog,[2] 'the typical graduate macroeconomics and monetary economics training received at Anglo-American universities during the past 30 years or so, may have set back by decades serious investigations of aggregate economic behaviour and economic policy-relevant understanding'. This view was echoed by Nobel Laureate Paul Krugman on 11 June 2009 in the weekly *Economist*, 'Most work in macroeconomics in the past 30 years has been useless at best and harmful at worst'.

Against this background, this chapter aims to develop a more constructive proposal for how to use macroeconomic modelling – whether state-of-the-art or 1970s vintage – in practical policy design. It is written in the vein of the 1992 call for a pluralistic and rigorous economics by leading economists. The undersigned – among them Nobel Laureates Paul Samuelson and Franco Modigliani – were concerned with 'the threat to economic science posed by intellectual monopoly' and pleaded for 'a new spirit of pluralism in economics, involving critical conversation and tolerant communication between different approaches.'[3] It is in that spirit that I propose a systematic comparative approach to macroeconomic modelling with the objective of identifying policy recommendations that are robust to model uncertainty.[4] This approach is open to a wide variety of modelling paradigms.

Scientific rigour demands a level playing field on which models can compete. Rather than using rhetoric to dismiss competing approaches, emphasis should be placed on empirical benchmarks that need to be satisfied by the models in order to stay in the race. For example, macroeconomic models used for monetary policy could be required to be estimated to fit the empirical dynamics of key time series, such as output, inflation and nominal interest rates. Models should be able to provide answers to policy makers' typical questions, such as what is the effect of an unanticipated increase (or decrease) in the central bank's operating target for the money market rate, or of an unanticipated temporary increase (or decrease) in government spending or transfers? Another common concern is the degree of output, inflation and interest rate volatility and persistence predicted by the models under different policy rules. New modelling approaches may offer more sophisticated explanations of the sources of the Great Recession of 2008–09 and carry the promise of improved forecasting performance. This promise should be put to a test rather than presumed. Estimated models could be compared along their relative real-time forecasting performance, in particular during periods of great change, such as recessions and recoveries. An example of such a model competition is given by Volker Wieland and Maik Wolters (2010).

Macroeconomic data, however, are unlikely to provide sufficient testing grounds for selecting a single, preferred model for policy purposes. Instead, policy recommendations should be made robust to model uncertainty. In particular, the robustness of policy prescriptions can be improved by introducing them in multiple, competing models and comparing performance across models according to established target criteria. Policy makers continue to require models and are aware of the need for robustness. In November 2010, the European Central Bank President expressed these needs very clearly:

> We need macroeconomic and financial models to discipline and structure our judgemental analysis. How should such models evolve? The key lesson I would draw from our experience is the danger of relying on a single tool, methodology or paradigm. Policymakers need to have input from various theoretical perspectives and from a range of empirical approaches. Open debate and a diversity of views must be cultivated – admittedly not always an easy task in an institution such as a central bank. We do not need to throw out our DSGE

and asset-pricing models: rather we need to develop complementary tools to improve the robustness of our overall framework.[5]

Macroeconomic model comparison projects have already helped produce some very influential insights for practical policy making. For example, John B. Taylor (1993a) credits the comparison project organized by the Brookings Institution and summarized in Ralph Bryant et al. (1993) as the crucial testing ground for what later became known as the Taylor rule for monetary policy. More recently, the International Monetary Fund (IMF) organized a large-scale model comparison exercise in order to evaluate the likely consequences of temporary fiscal stimulus measures (see Coenen et al., 2012). Such model comparisons have been, nevertheless, infrequent and costly, because they require the input of many teams of researchers and multiple meetings to obtain a limited set of comparative findings.

To remedy this situation, Volker Wieland et al. (2009) have implemented a new approach to model comparison that enables individual researchers to conduct such comparisons easily, frequently, at low cost and on a large scale. This methodology comes with a model archive that includes many well-known empirically estimated models of business-cycle dynamics. These models can be used to evaluate the performance of macroeconomic stabilization policies. A computational platform that allows straightforward comparisons of models' implications using MATLAB and DYNARE[6] software is available online to download.[7] Researchers can easily include new models in the database and compare the effects of novel extensions to established benchmarks.

Our proposal is to use this comparative approach systematically in order to organize a pluralistic, yet rigorous and productive communication between competing modelling paradigms in macroeconomics. So far, the model database contains small-, medium- and large-scale macroeconomic models of different vintages and methodological traditions. The first release of November 2010 covers 38 models, including many state-of-the-art New-Keynesian DSGE models, but also earlier vintage New-Keynesian models with rational expectations and nominal rigidities, as well as some models that offer a more traditional Keynesian-style perspective on macroeconomic fluctuations with largely backward-looking dynamics. The model database and the computational platform for model comparison provide a level playing field that is open to new entrants. Going forward, we propose to cover as many competing modelling paradigms as possible, so as to compare models' empirical implications in a systematic fashion, and to search for policy prescriptions that are robust along relevant dimensions of model uncertainty.

The next section briefly describes the comparison methodology and gives an overview of the models available in the database. It also outlines a list of competing modelling paradigms that promise improvements in our understanding of macroeconomic dynamics. In future work, they should be compared to those approaches that have received the most attention in recent years. The third section gives an example of a demanding test of comparative model performance, namely the real-time forecasting evaluation of a range of models relative to those of experts in the last five US recessions, conducted by Wieland and Wolters (2010). The next section reviews findings from recent comparative studies regarding the impact of fiscal stimulus packages and reports estimates of the impact of government transfers in selected models. The final section concludes.

MODEL COMPARISON

The six older comparison projects reported in Bryant et al. (1988), Bryant et al. (1989), Klein (1991), Bryant et al. (1993), Taylor (1999), Hughes-Hallett and Wallis (2004), as well as the recent IMF exercise by Coenen et al. (2012) have all involved multiple teams of researchers, each team working only with one or a small subset of available models. The approach by Wieland et al. (2009), on the other hand, is meant to provide users easy access to the complete set of models considered in a comparison exercise. Furthermore, users should find it fairly straightforward to integrate their own models. To this end, Wieland et al. (2009) present a formal exposition of their comparative methodology. Taylor and Wieland (2012) use the model database to compare three well-known models of the US economy and analyse the robustness of simple monetary policy rules.

A general class of non-linear dynamic stochastic macroeconomic models is augmented with a space of common comparable variables, parameters and shocks. Augmenting models in this manner is a necessary precondition for a systematic comparison of particular model characteristics. Given a space of common variables and parameters, one can define common policy rules as model input and produce comparable objects as model output. These objects are also defined in terms of common variables, parameters and shocks. Examples for such objects are impulse response functions, autocorrelation functions and unconditional distributions of key macroeconomic aggregates.

The space of common variables, parameters and policy rules comprises only a subset of each model's variables, parameters and equations. Most model-specific equations remain unchanged. Only the model-specific policy rules are replaced with common policy rules that express policy variables as functions of common variables and parameters. Nevertheless, a new set of definitional equations needs to be added to each model. These definitional equations define the common variables in terms of model-specific variables. Once each model is augmented with the appropriate definitional equations and the common policy rules, it is ready for comparative exercises. For a formal exposition of the procedure for integrating new models, see Wieland et al. (2009). Several examples are carried out step-by-step in that paper. A detailed documentation of the augmented model files is also provided.

A Model Database

In the following, I give a brief overview of the model archive that is available with the comparison software. This database includes many well-known, empirically-estimated macroeconomic models that may be used for quantitative analysis of monetary and fiscal stabilization policies. It contains estimated and calibrated models of the US economy and the euro area. There are also a number of small open-economy models of countries such as Canada, Chile and Brazil. Finally, it also includes several multi-country models that cover industrialized economies. The models, made available in the first release as of November 2010, are listed in Table 2.1.

Most models could be classified as New Keynesian, because they incorporate rational expectations, imperfect competition and wage or price rigidities. A subset of the models could be characterized as monetary business cycle models where all behavioural equations are derived in a completely consistent manner from the optimization problems of representative households and firms. Many authors use the term 'dynamic stochastic general equilibrium' (DSGE) model to refer to this particular class of model. Thus, the database offers interesting opportunities for comparing policy implications of this class of model to a broader set of empirically estimated, dynamic, stochastic, economy-wide macro models.

While most of the models assume that market participants form rational, forward-looking expectations, we have also included some models that assume little or no forward-looking behaviour.[8] Comparative analysis of these classes of models will be useful to evaluate recently voiced criticisms that the newer models have been rendered invalid by the global financial crisis.

The models are grouped into five categories in Table 2.1. The first category includes small, calibrated versions of the basic New-Keynesian DSGE model. These models concentrate on explaining output, inflation and interest-rate dynamics. Some of them are calibrated to US data. The model taken from Clarida et al. (2002) is a two-country version of this type of model.

The second category covers estimated models of the US economy. It includes small models of output, inflation and interest-rate dynamics, such as Fuhrer and Moore (1995) and Rudebusch and Svensson (1999). Other models are of medium scale, such as Orphanides and Wieland (1998) or the well-known models of Christiano, Eichenbaum and Evans (2005) and Smets and Wouters (2007), which fully incorporate recent advances in terms of microeconomic foundations. The database includes the version of the Christiano–Eichenbaum–Evans model estimated by Altig et al. (2005), because this version contains other economic shocks in addition to the monetary policy shock studied by Christiano et al. (2005).[9] We have also included an additional version of the Altig et al. (2005) model used in Taylor and Wieland (2012) that omits the cost channel of monetary policy.[10] The largest model of the US economy in the database is the Federal Reserve's FRB–US model of Reifschneider et al. (1999). We have included a linearized version of this model with rational expectations that was previously used in Levin et al. (2003), as well as two more recent versions from 2008, one with rational expectations and one with adaptive expectations based on a reduced form vector-autoregression (VAR). Federal Reserve economists Rochelle Edge, Michael Kilcy and Jean-Philippe Laforte (2010) have developed a new two-sector DSGE model of the US economy that is also included in the database; a version of this model is estimated in Wieland and Wolters (2010).

In addition, there are a number of smaller estimated models of the US economy that offer new insights into the role of financial frictions in economic fluctuations. Ioan Carabenciov et al. (2008), for example, augment a simple backward-looking model with a measure of financial linkages and frictions. Ferre De Graeve (2008) and Ian Christensen and Ali Dib (2008) introduce constraints on firms' financing following Ben Bernanke et al. (1999) in a fully-fledged estimated DSGE model of the US economy. These models provide an endogenous account of firms' external finance premium over the business cycle. Matteo Iacoviello (2005) includes the housing sector in a DSGE model. The model of N. Gregory Mankiw and Ricardo Reis (2007) deviates from the assumption of rational expectations and allows for rational inattention. This mechanism introduces a role for outdated expectations (or informational frictions) in business-cycle dynamics. All these extensions of the standard DSGE framework were accomplished before the financial crisis and could potentially be helpful in rendering DSGE models more useful in explaining developments during the crisis.

The third category in Table 2.1 covers estimated models of the euro-area

Table 2.1   Models currently available in the database (November 2010)

1.	SMALL CALIBRATED MODELS	
1.1	NK RW97	Rotemberg and Woodford (1997)
1.2	NK LWW03	Levin et al. (2003)
1.3	NK CGG99	Clarida et al. (1999)
1.4	NK CGG02	Clarida et al. (2002)
1.5	NK MCN99cr	McCallum and Nelson (1999), (Calvo–Rotemberg model)
1.6	NK IR04	Ireland (2004)
1.7	NK BGG99	Bernanke et al. (1999)
1.8	NK GM05	Gali and Monacelli (2005)
2.	ESTIMATED US MODELS	
2.1	US FM95	Fuhrer and Moore (1995)
2.2	US OW98	Orphanides and Wieland (1998) equivalent to MSR model in Levin et al. (2003)
2.3	US FRB03	Federal Reserve Board model linearized as in Levin et al. (2003)
2.4	US FRB08	2008 linearized version of Federal Reserve Board model
2.5	US FRB08mx	2008 linearized version of FRB model (mixed expectations)
2.6	US SW07	Smets and Wouters (2007)
2.7	US ACELm	Altig et al. (2005) (monetary policy shock)
	US ACELt	Altig et al. (2005) (technology shocks)
	US ACELswm	No cost channel as in Taylor and Wieland (2012) (mon. pol. shock)
	US ACELswt	No cost channel as in Taylor and Wieland (2012) (tech. shocks)
2.8	US NFED08	Based on Edge et al. (2007), version used for estimation in Wieland and Wolters (2010)
2.9	US RS99	Rudebusch and Svensson (1999)
2.10	US OR03	Orphanides (2003)
2.11	US PM08	IMF projection model US, Carabenciov et al. (2008)
2.12	US PM08fl	IMF projection model US (financial linkages), Carabenciov et al. (2008)
2.13	US DG08	DeGraeve (2008)
2.14	US CD08	Christensen and Dib (2008)
2.15	US IAC05	Iacoviello (2005)
2.16	US MR07	Mankiw and Reis (2007)
3.	ESTIMATED EURO AREA MODELS	
3.1	EA CW05ta	Coenen and Wieland (2005) (Taylor-staggered contracts)
3.2	EA CW05fm	Coenen and Wieland (2005) (Fuhrer–Moore staggered contracts)
3.3	EA AWM05	ECB's area-wide model linearized as in Dieppe et al. (2005)
3.4	EA SW03	Smets and Wouters (2003)
3.5	EA SR07	Sveriges Riksbank euro area model of Adolfson et al. (2007)

Table 2.1   (continued)

3.6	EA QUEST3	QUEST III, model by DG-ECFIN EC, Ratto et al. (2009)
4.	**ESTIMATED/CALIBRATED MULTI-COUNTRY MODELS**	
4.1	G7 TAY93	Taylor (1993b) model of G7 economies
4.2	G3 CW03	Coenen and Wieland (2002) model of USA, Euro area and Japan
4.3	EACZ GEM03	Laxton and Pesenti (2003) model calibrated to Euro area and Czech Republic
4.4	G2 SIGMA08	Federal Reserve's SIGMA model from Erceg et al. (2008) calibrated to the US economy and a symmetric twin
4.5	EAUS NAWM08	Coenen et al. (2008), New Area Wide model of Euro area and USA
5.	**ESTIMATED MODELS OF SMALL OPEN ECONOMIES**	
5.1	CL MS07	Medina and Soto (2007), model of the Chilean economy
5.2	CA ToTEM10	ToTEM model of Canada, based on Murchison and Rennison (2006), 2010 vintage
5.3	BRA SAMBA08	Gouvea et al. (2008), model of the Brazilian economy

economy. Four of those models have been used in a recent study of robust monetary policy design for the euro area by Keith Kuester and Volker Wieland (2010): the medium-scale model of Smets and Wouters (2003), two small models by Coenen and Wieland (2005) that differ by the type of staggered contracts that induce inflation rigidity, and a linearized version of the Area-Wide Model that was used at the European Central Bank (ECB) for forecasting purposes. The latter was recently replaced by a new DSGE model. In addition, we have included an estimated DSGE model of the euro area recently developed at the Sveriges Riksbank (Adolfson et al., 2007), and at the European Commission (Ratto et al., 2009). The latter model was developed with a particular focus on the analysis of euro-area fiscal policy.

The fourth category includes estimated and calibrated models of two or more economies. Currently, the largest model in the database is the estimated model of the G7 economies of Taylor (1993b). The estimated model of Coenen and Wieland (2002) with rational expectations and price rigidities aims to explain inflation, output and interest-rate dynamics and spillover effects between the United States, the euro area and Japan. The model of Laxton and Pesenti (2003) is a two-country model with extensive microeconomic foundations calibrated to the economies of the euro area and the Czech Republic. The Federal Reserve's SIGMA model is similarly rich in microeconomic foundations. The parameters in the two-country version of this model from Erceg et al. (2008) are calibrated to the US economy and a symmetric twin. Finally, there is a two-country calibrated version of the ECB's new area-wide DSGE model as presented by Coenen et al. (2008). This model also covers the US economy.

The fifth category of models covers small open-economy DSGE models of Canada, Chile and Brazil. In addition to openness to trade and capital flows, these models also consider particular economic features of the respective countries, such as the important role that a natural resources sector might play in the economy.

In sum, the current breadth of model coverage allows for a variety of interesting comparison exercises, for example, between earlier vintage and more recent Keynesian-style models of business-cycle dynamics for a given country; cross-country comparisons between the United States, the euro area and some small open economies; or comparisons between standard New-Keynesian DSGE models and DSGE models that also include some financial or informational frictions.

A Proposal for Extending the Coverage of Competing Modelling Paradigms

In the aftermath of the financial crisis, the DSGE modelling approach has come under heavy criticism. Many critics have argued that models of this type that were in use prior to the crisis did not incorporate realistic treatments of banking, and therefore failed to account for the macroeconomic risks resulting from a fragile financial sector. Other critics have suggested that the crucial flaw of the DSGE approach is of a more fundamental nature. Many of them question the central assumption of homogeneous, rational expectations. They point out that in practice, economic agents are imperfectly informed, they are engaged in a learning process, and they often disagree about likely future developments. Others go further, calling into question the basic microeconomic assumption of rational optimizing behaviour by households and firms.

Policy makers are keen to have modelling frameworks at their disposal that address these criticisms. Their interest in the matter is well exemplified by the ECB President (November 2003–11), who requested the following steps:

> we need to better integrate the crucial role played by the financial system into our macroeconomic models, ... we may need to consider a richer characterisation of expectation formation, ... We need to deal better with heterogeneity across agents and the interaction among those heterogeneous agents, [and] we need to entertain alternative motivations for economic choices.[11]

The following paragraphs highlight some recent studies that explore these different directions.

Financial sector risks

Proponents of the DSGE approach have been hard at work to provide more explicit modelling of financial intermediation and risks by extending the standard DSGE framework. As a minimum, such models should include a financial sector where banks are exposed to risk and where the functioning of the banking sector affects the real economy. Recent contributions along these lines include Goodfriend and McCallum (2007), Gertler et al. (2007), De Fiore et al. (2009), DeWalque et al. (2010), Christiano et al. (2010), Gerali et al. (2010), Angeloni and Faia (2010), Meh and Moran (2010), Nolan and Thoenissen (2009), Dib (2010), Gertler and Karadi (2009) and Gertler and Kiyotaki (2010).

All these contributions examine the interaction of financial risk, business cycle dynamics and monetary policy. They differ in how banking and financial intermediation are modelled, and in the focus of the particular policy application. Some of them investigate the implications of banking and financial intermediation on business cycle fluctuations in a fully-fledged DSGE model. From the perspective of the modellers, an important question to be investigated in the future is whether such extensions offer a satisfactory explanation of the financial crisis. One would hope that such an explanation would reveal not only the sources that caused the crisis in the form of particular economic shocks, but also the propagation mechanisms that would help modellers to predict the development of such a crisis in the future.

Learning and diverse beliefs

Households and firms in complex, modern DSGE models are assumed to have access to forecasts that are equivalent to the expectation calculated under complete knowledge about the structural features of the model economy. Households and firms are typically assumed to share homogeneous expectations regarding future developments of key macroeconomic variables. Expectations play a crucial role in determining the dynamics of these models and the policy recommendations derived from them. Expectations, of course, also appear to play a very important role in actual real-world markets and economies. Thus, the debate among modellers should not be about the importance of expectations in macroeconomics, but rather about the sensitivity of the business cycle and policy implications derived under the homogeneous rational expectations assumption to alternative specifications of market participants' beliefs.

A number of different approaches to modelling less-than-fully-rational expectations and belief diversity have been proposed in the economic literature. A first step away from rational expectation is adaptive learning. It implies that market participants re-estimate simple reduced-form models of the variables to be forecasted and update the parameter estimates of these forecasting models once they obtain new data. An example of such a learning process is recursive least squares. Adaptive learning has been discussed in macroeconomics for more than two decades.[12] The expectations obtained from adaptive learning, however, are typically homogeneous across market participants in these models. Some examples of recent investigations of the implications of adaptive learning for macroeconomic dynamics as well as monetary and fiscal policy are Orphanides and Williams (2006), Slobodyan and Wouters (2008) and Wieland (2009). Nevertheless, medium- to large-scale DSGE models used at central banks and other policy institutions are typically simulated under rational expectations.

It would be of interest to conduct a systematic comparison of DSGE models with rational expectations versus DSGE models with adaptive learning in order to evaluate whether adaptive learning plays an important role in interpreting the period leading up to the global financial crisis or the reaction of market participants during the crisis. Furthermore, if adaptive learning better characterizes real-world market participants' process of expectations formation, models with adaptive learning might also perform better in forecasting exercises.

Expectation heterogeneity, however, has so far been largely ignored in structural macroeconomic models used for policy analysis. While empirical studies have documented a substantial degree of heterogeneity of professional forecasts,[13] theoretical research has emphasized that expectational heterogeneity itself can be an important propagation mechanism for economic fluctuations and a driving force for asset price dynamics. Theories of heterogeneous expectations and endogenous fluctuations have been advanced, for example, by Kurz (1994a, 1994b, 1996, 1997a,1997b, 2009), Brock and Hommes (1998), Kurz et al. (2005), Chiarella et al. (2007), Branch and McGough (2011), Branch and Evans (2011), and De Grauwe (2011).

Since belief diversity can cause economic volatility, macroeconomic policy analysis cannot ignore the diversity of expectations among households, firms and policy makers themselves. While in homogeneous models such volatility would be attributed to other shock processes, models with heterogeneous expectations offer a possibility to disentangle which fraction of economic volatility can be attributed to heterogeneous expectations and which fraction is explained by other economic shocks. Some of the above-mentioned studies explore the impact of diverse beliefs in small

New-Keynesian models. It would be of great interest to introduce such models into the macroeconomic model database and to conduct a systematic comparison of models with homogeneous and heterogeneous beliefs. Possibly, variations in the diversity of beliefs – the degree of optimism and pessimism among market participants – may have played an important role in the asset price boom before the crisis, and its subsequent collapse. If these variations in diversity act as a propagation mechanism and were themselves to some extent predictable, then models with diverse beliefs might stand a chance to deliver a better forecasting performance before such recessions than standard DSGE models.

Deviations from strictly optimizing behaviour
In the last two decades, several significant strands of literature have developed that investigate fundamental deviations from strictly optimizing behaviour by economic agents and consider alternative motivations for economic choices and decisions. Behavioural economics brings lessons from psychology to bear on the analysis of economic decision making. Contributions to this strand of the literature have argued that empirical failures of the classical paradigm of fully rational behaviour may be resolved by introducing particular psychological motivations for economic behaviour (see Diamond and Vartiaincn, 2007; Akerlof and Shiller, 2010). With regard to policy analysis with structural macroeconomic models, an important question is which behavioural macroeconomic models are best suited to be considered as competitors of standard DSGE models, or of the new DSGE models with detailed banking sector and financial frictions. Sometimes behavioural approaches are mentioned in support for more traditional Keynesian-style models with backward-looking dynamics. The richness of the behavioural economics approach would suggest, however, that a new line of structural macroeconomic models should emerge from this literature.

Another large body of literature is known under the term 'agent-based modelling' and crosses the borders between engineering, physics and economics.[14] Agent-based modelling is the computational study of economic processes modelled as dynamic systems of interacting agents. Here, 'agent' refers broadly to a bundle of data and behavioural methods representing an entity that constitutes part of a computationally constructed world. Instead of the fully optimizing rational decision makers in standard DSGE models, these agents can range from active data-gathering decision makers with sophisticated learning capabilities to passive world features with no cognitive function. Researchers have built computational 'laboratories' with thousands or even millions of such agents. These laboratories have been used to investigate whether agent-based modelling can replicate some empirical regularities in financial, goods and labour markets, as well as other areas of economics. Another aim is to test certain government regulations and policies in terms of the simulation outcomes they would generate in such models. A recent contribution that describes a model of the euro area economy is Deissenberg et al. (2008). With regard to policy analysis with structural macroeconomic models, an important question is how agent-based models can be used to deliver answers to the type of questions policy makers typically ask of DSGE models. For example, what are the models' predictions for growth and inflation over the coming year? What would be the effect of an increase in the central bank's interest rate or of an unexpected increase in fiscal transfers, such as a tax rebate? A comparison of agent-based and DSGE models with regard to such questions would be tremendously useful for practical macroeconomic policy analysis.

A RECENT MODEL COMPARISON: FORECASTING US RECESSIONS

In general, macroeconomic models used for policy analysis in a particular economy ought to be empirically estimated or calibrated to fit macroeconomic time series of that economy. A more demanding test, however, would be to evaluate the real-time forecasting performance of such models. Recently, Wieland and Wolters (2010) conducted such a forecasting exercise with six different models of the US economy. They investigated the accuracy and heterogeneity of output growth and inflation forecasts during the current and the four preceding NBER[15]-dated US recessions. Model forecasts were compared to professional forecasts from the Federal Reserve's Greenbook and the Survey of Professional Forecasters (SPF).[16] Importantly, the model parameters and model forecasts were derived from historical data vintages so as to ensure comparability to historical forecasts by professionals. The comparison was conducted for successive quarter-by-quarter forecasts up to four quarters into the future. Arguably, the periods around recessions and recoveries posed the greatest challenge for economic forecasters.

Wieland and Wolters (2010) ('WW' hereafter) considered six macroeconomic models: three small-scale New-Keynesian models that differ in terms of structural assumptions, a non-structural Bayesian value at risk (VAR) model, and two medium-scale New-Keynesian DSGE models of the type currently used by leading central banks. Two of the small-scale models were variants of the New-Keynesian models 1.1 and 1.2 in Table 2.1, estimated with US data. They were estimated by Marco Del Negro and Frank Schorfheide (2004) and Wieland and Wolters (2010), respectively, and are denoted by the acronyms NK-DS and NK-WW. The third small-scale model was a variant of model 2.1 in Table 2.1, developed by Fuhrer (1997). It is denoted by NK-Fu while the VAR model is referred to as BVAR-WW. The three small-scale, New-Keynesian models and the Bayesian VAR were estimated to fit three macroeconomic time series: real gross domestic product (GDP) growth, inflation measured by the GDP deflator, and the federal funds rate.

The first medium-scale model is the well-known DSGE model estimated by Frank Smets and Rafael Wouters (2007) (model 2.6 in Table 2.1), which itself is a version of the DSGE model developed in Christiano et al. (2005). It is referred to as the CEE-SW model in the forecasting exercise. It is estimated with seven variables, including consumption, investment, wages and hours worked. The largest model in the forecasting exercise is a version of the Federal Reserve's new DSGE model estimated by Edge et al. (2007) (model 2.8 in Table 2.1). It is denoted by FRB-EDO in the forecast evaluation. This model accounts for the breakdown in durables versus non-durables and services consumption, residential versus business investment, and the related deflators. It is estimated on 11 macroeconomic data series.

Forecasting the 2008–09 Recession: Models Versus Experts

To render model-based forecasts comparable to historical SPF and Greenbook forecasts, Wieland and Wolters (WW) have put them on a similar footing in terms of the data vintage used for parameter estimation and initial conditions. Thus, WW have created a large, real-time data set that contains all the historical quarterly vintages of the 11 time series used in the largest model. For every quarter, they re-estimate all the model parameters on the basis of the data vintage that was available at that exact point in time. Using this parameterization, they compute an estimate of the current state of the economy – the so-called *nowcast* – and forecast for one to four quarters into the future. Then, they assess the forecasting precision relative to the revised data that became available during the subsequent quarters for the dates to which the forecasts apply.

The model-based forecasts only use quarterly data vintages, where the most recent data entries concern the quarter preceding the quarter in which the forecast was made. In practice, however, there are many data series that are available on a monthly, weekly or daily frequency that can be used to improve current-quarter estimates of GDP. Examples are industrial production, sales, unemployment, money, opinion surveys, interest rates and other financial prices. These data can be used to improve nowcasts; the Federal Reserve staff and many professional forecasters make use of them. Methods for using higher frequency data systematically in combination with quarterly structural macroeconomic models in conjunctural analysis are available (see Giannone et al., 2009). To illustrate the impact of the timeliness of the nowcast on model-based forecasts, WW compare model forecasts initiated with both types of nowcasts.

The four panels in Figure 2.1 replicate the individual model forecasts from WW for the 2008–09 recession that are initialized with the mean SPF nowcast. Each panel displays model forecasts relative to the mean SPF forecast (dash-dotted line) and the actual data (solid line) that have become available so far. In addition, I have included a measure of the central tendency of SPF forecasts for comparative purposes. It is indicated by the dashed lines labelled 'SPFlow' and 'SPFhigh'. This measure of the central tendency is computed in the same manner as the Federal Reserve computes central tendencies of Federal Open Market Committee (FOMC) forecasts, that is by omitting the three greatest outliers on the high and the low side. The top left panel shows forecasts made in the third quarter of 2008. The top right panel then reports forecasts from the fourth quarter of 2008, and the two lower panels from the first two quarters of 2009.

As shown in the top left panel, professional forecasters, on average, failed to foresee the downturn as late as in the third quarter of 2008. The central tendency of professional forecasts, however, anticipated somewhat less growth than the model forecasts. The mean SPF forecast indicates a slowdown in the fourth quarter followed by a return to higher growth in the first quarter of 2009. The model-based forecasts based on the data vintage of the third quarter of 2008 do not perform any better.

Following the Lehman debacle, professional forecasters drastically revised their assessments of the current situation downwards, and continued to do so in the first quarter of 2009. Interestingly, from 2009:Q1 onwards, the model-based forecasts perform well in predicting the recovery of the US economy. From that point onwards, several of the models deliver predictions that are very similar to the mean SPF forecast, and match up with the subsequent data releases surprisingly well. The 2009:Q1 forecasts for the second and third quarter of 2009 – implied by the CEE-SW and NK-WW models – already look fairly accurate relative to the subsequent data releases. The central tendency of SPF forecasts indicates a somewhat more pessimistic outlook regarding the speed of recovery than the models. The above-mentioned two models, however, came closer to the actual data for the following quarters.

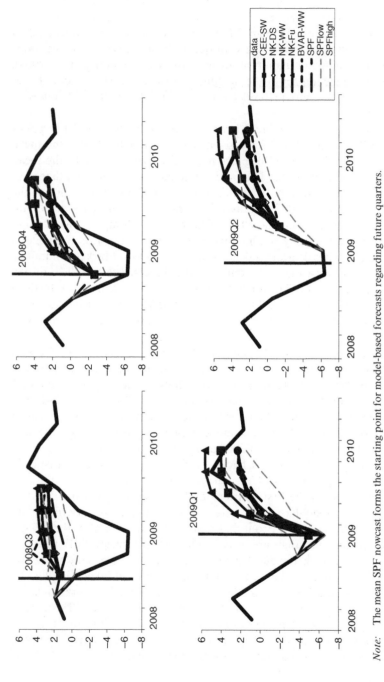

Note: The mean SPF nowcast forms the starting point for model-based forecasts regarding future quarters.

Figure 2.1 Real output growth forecasts during the 2007–09 recession

The Relative Accuracy of Model-based and Expert Forecasts

For the purpose of a systematic evaluation of forecast accuracy, WW compute the root mean squared errors (RMSE) of the nowcast and forecasts from one to four quarters ahead for each model during the five recessions. The typical recession sample covers the period from four quarters prior to the trough, determined by the NBER Business Cycle Dating Committee, to four quarters after the trough.[17] The Greenbook nowcast is used as the initial condition for the model-based forecasts, except in the latest recession where the mean SPF nowcast is applied. Models are re-estimated every quarter, and forecasts are computed for horizons of one-to-four quarters into the future. Table 2.2 reports the associated root mean squared errors of output growth and inflation forecasts for the different recession episodes from WW. It compares the accuracy of the individual model forecasts to the mean model forecast (the average of the six models), the mean SPF forecast and the Greenbook forecast.

Model forecasts perform differently. There is no single model that dominates the others in all recessions. The CEE-SW model performs best in the 1980–81 recession. It even beats the Greenbook forecast in this recession, though the Greenbook forecast is unusually far off the mark in this period compared to later ones. The NK-DS and CEE-SW models perform best among the model forecasts in the 1981–82 recession, while the Greenbook forecast performs best overall in this case. In the 1990–92 period, the FRB-EDO model and the Bayesian VAR deliver the best predictions among the models. For the short horizon, the mean SPF forecast is best, but the Greenbook dominates the other forecasts over three to four quarters. In the period around the 2001 recession, the NK-Fu model and the CEE-SW model dominate the others over a horizon of three to four quarters. In the 2008–09 period, so far, the NK-DS and NK-WW models appear to perform best among the models. Of course, as shown in Figure 2.1, it is only during the recovery phase that the models appear to have some predictive power. WW, however, obtain very similar findings for the four preceding recessions.

Interestingly, the mean model forecast outperforms the Greenbook forecast in the 1980 and 2001 recessions. The mean model forecast also compares well with the mean SPF forecast in the 1981–82 and 2001 recessions. The Greenbook forecasts still perform best in the 1981–82 and 1990–91 recessions, while the mean SPF forecast appears to be the most accurate in the ongoing recession, for which no Greenbook data and forecasts are publicly available.

The forecast comparison gives no cause for much shoulder-slapping among modellers or professional forecasters. Both tend to miss the

What's right with macroeconomics?

Table 2.2   *RMSEs of output growth forecasts initialized with expert nowcasts*

Sample/ Horizon	NK-DS	NK-WW	CEE-SW	FRB-EDO	NK-Fu	BVAR-WW	Mean	GB	SPF
1980:1–1981:3									
0	5.05	5.05	5.05	5.05	5.05	5.05	5.05	5.05	–
1	8.14	8.13	6.33	6.06	7.18	6.69	5.83	6.65	–
2	6.34	6.36	4.80	5.60	6.48	6.48	4.83	5.54	–
3	5.50	5.74	5.20	5.37	6.49	7.74	5.20	6.11	–
4	5.56	5.75	4.23	4.24	4.12	5.50	4.05	5.32	–
1981:4–1983:4									
0	2.42	2.42	2.42	2.42	2.42	2.42	2.42	2.42	2.14
1	4.28	4.50	3.74	3.27	3.80	3.23	3.54	3.58	3.88
2	3.99	4.05	4.22	4.09	3.98	4.09	3.86	3.93	4.11
3	4.14	4.23	4.05	4.52	4.64	4.87	4.25	3.91	4.41
4	4.08	4.11	4.07	4.67	4.73	4.89	4.28	3.84	4.02
1990:1–1992:1									
0	1.27	1.27	1.27	1.27	1.27	1.27	1.27	1.27	1.12
1	2.64	2.87	3.22	1.70	3.11	2.00	2.47	2.09	1.45
2	2.95	3.04	3.80	1.92	3.68	2.28	2.82	2.34	2.06
3	3.08	3.13	3.78	2.42	3.67	2.55	2.94	2.31	2.54
4	2.71	2.76	3.65	2.16	3.48	2.29	2.69	2.18	2.37
2000:4–2002:4									
0	2.28	2.28	2.28	2.28	2.28	2.28	2.28	2.28	2.22
1	2.17	2.15	2.31	2.84	2.06	2.48	2.23	2.20	2.30
2	2.09	2.10	2.11	2.61	2.35	1.98	2.11	2.34	2.21
3	2.74	2.72	2.68	2.98	2.51	2.66	2.65	2.76	2.65
4	2.25	2.26	2.08	2.40	2.24	2.30	2.19	2.18	2.13
2007:4–2009:3									
0	1.94	1.94	1.94	–	1.94	1.94	1.94	–	1.94
1	3.74	3.90	4.24	–	4.54	4.85	4.21	–	3.30
2	4.52	4.62	4.94	–	5.48	5.10	4.89	–	4.11
3	5.05	5.11	5.39	–	5.83	5.27	5.32	–	4.80
4	5.50	5.52	5.86	–	6.07	5.57	5.70	–	5.39

onset of recessions. This is not only true for the 2008–09 recession, but also for the four preceding ones. Thus, there is no reason for expert forecasters, who tend to rely more often on traditional Keynesian-style models with backward-looking dynamics, to point fingers at DSGE modellers for supposedly having too much influence on central banks. Experts and models exhibit some predictive power during the recovery phase. They predict a return to mean, and the speed of return predicted seems to be reasonably accurate once the recovery has actually started. Some encouragement for modelling efforts, however, can be drawn from the finding that mean model forecasts perform well at horizons of three to four quarters and sometimes dominate Greenbook or mean SPF forecasts.

Given these findings, it does not seem to be appropriate to utterly dismiss state-of-the-art New-Keynesian DSGE models in favour of those Keynesian-style models that only use theory from more than 30 years ago, as suggested by the Buiter and Krugman commentaries cited in the introduction of the chapter. Nevertheless, it appears urgent to investigate whether any of the innovations discussed above – such as more thorough modelling of the financial sector, the inclusion of learning and diverse beliefs, or behavioural and agent-based modelling – can deliver on the promise of improved forecasting power.

INVESTIGATING POLICY ROBUSTNESS

Model competitions in terms of empirical fit or predictive power will certainly help narrow down the field of models relevant for policy analysis. The preceding forecasting exercise suggests, however, that such competitions are not likely to deliver a unique preferred model for policy purposes. As recognized by policy makers such as the former ECB President, multiple models need to be used as tools for making policy recommendations robust to model uncertainty. There exist recent examples. Several model comparison studies have been conducted to investigate the likely consequences of temporary fiscal stimulus.

Importantly, in January 2009, Christina Romer, then Chair of the US President's Council of Economic Advisers, and Jared Bernstein, former Chief Economist of the Office of the Vice-President, used macroeconomic models in a report on the likely impact of a large-scale stimulus package proposed by the Obama Administration. Soon after, the US Congress approved 787 billion US dollars in additional spending, transfers and tax reductions with the 2009 American Recovery and Reinvestment Act (ARRA). The ARRA extended over five years, with much of the additional spending occurring in the first two years. Many other economies around the world also announced fiscal stimulus measures. In Europe, the EU initiated the European Economic Recovery Plan (EERP), while national governments announced their own fiscal stimuli. Among them, the German government launched two *Konjunkturpakete* in a row. The European stimulus packages were to be concentrated on 2009 and 2010 only.

Recent Comparative Evaluations of Fiscal Stimulus

The literature on fiscal stimulus has expanded very quickly. Here, I only focus on a few contributions that used multiple structural macroeconomic models to evaluate the likely impact of such measures, with an eye towards robustness to model uncertainty. Romer and Bernstein (2009), for example, provide numerical estimates of the impact of an increase in government spending and government transfers, respectively, on GDP and employment by averaging over models of the Federal Reserve and private-sector business consultancies. They estimate that an increase in government purchases of 1 per cent of GDP would induce an increase in real GDP of 1.6 per cent.[18] Thus, one or more of the models they use exhibit a textbook Keynesian multiplier effect.

The textbook multiplier follows from the national accounts' spending identity when combined with the Keynesian consumption function. An increase in government spending boosts aggregate spending, and thereby aggregate output and after-tax household income. Consumption is assumed to increase with current after-tax income. Consequently, a debt-financed increase in government spending boosts total spending (and therefore total GDP) more than one for one. Details of the individual model simulations behind this average effect have not been made available for the Romer–Bernstein study; however, the authors clarify that interest rates were assumed to remain constant for five years in the model simulations. On that basis, they project that a package similar in magnitude to the eventual ARRA legislation would boost US GDP by 3.6 per cent.

Shortly after the ARRA had passed the House and Senate, John F. Cogan et al. (2009) (later published as Cogan et al., 2010) evaluated its likely impact on US GDP using empirically estimated New-Keynesian models, such as the models of Taylor (1993b) and Smets and Wouters (2007), that is model 4.1 G7-TAY93 and 2.6 US-SW07 in Table 2.1. In these models, government purchases multipliers are typically smaller than one. They exhibit significant crowding-out of private consumption and private investment following an increase in government purchases. Consumption declines because forward-looking households expect increased government debt to be paid off at a later stage with higher taxes. This negative wealth effect induces additional saving and reduced consumption earlier on. Private investment declines because increased government debt puts upward pressure on interest rates. The expectation of higher interest rates and lower wealth in the future, in turn reduces private investment already in the near term. As a consequence, estimates of the GDP effects of ARRA legislation obtained with the model of Smets and Wouters (2007) are only one-sixth as large as those of Romer and Bernstein (2009).

While the original Smets–Wouters model only contains forward-looking 'permanent-income' consumers, Cogan et al. (2010) also estimated a variant of this model that includes households whose consumption is determined by their current after-tax income, as prescribed by the Keynesian consumption function. The empirically estimated share of these 'rule-of-thumb' households is 26.5 per cent. At this scale, the presence of rule-of-thumb consumers only has a small impact on the multiplier of the ARRA government purchases. It remains well below one in this model. In addition, Cogan et al. (2010) investigate the interaction of monetary and fiscal policy when monetary policy is constrained at the zero-interest-rate floor. If the central bank's desired policy rate is negative – and thus below the actual rate of zero – it will not respond to an increase in GDP by raising the policy rate as in normal times. Consequently, the crowding-out effect of an increase in government purchases would be lessened. Cogan et al. (2010) consider simulations with one and two years of constant interest rates, as well as simulations where the time spent at the zero lower bound is endogenous and projected from the trough of the recession in the first quarter of 2009 onwards. Though the GDP impact of ARRA purchases increases, it remains far below the Romer–Bernstein estimate of 3.6 per cent by the end of 2010.

The euro area stimulus measures were summarized and evaluated in Cwik and Wieland (2011)[19] using five different structural models of the euro area economy based on Fagan et al. (2005), Smets and Wouters (2003), Ratto et al. (2009), Laxton and Pesenti (2003) and Taylor (1993b), respectively, models 3.3 EA-AWM05, 3.4 EA-SW03, 3.6 EA-QUEST3, 4.3 EACZ-GEM03 and 4.1 G7 TAY93 from Table 2.1. The ECB's Area-Wide model described in Fagan et al. (2005) largely ignores forward-looking motives for private decision-making and provides a traditional Keynesian perspective. The other four models are of the New-Keynesian variety with forward-looking households and firms. Smets and Wouters' (2003) model is a euro area version of the medium-sized DSGE model of Christiano et al. (2005). The EA-QUEST3 model is an estimated DSGE model developed for fiscal policy analysis at the European Commission by Ratto et al. (2009). This model also accounts for rule-of-thumb consumers. Their share is estimated at 35 per cent, not too far from the estimate obtained with US data by Cogan et al. (2010). The EACZ-GEM03 model is a calibrated, two-country DSGE model of the euro area and Czech Republic developed by IMF researchers. Together with Taylor's multi-country model, it can account for the possible diversion of fiscal stimulus towards import demand.

Cwik and Wieland (2011) confirm the differential assessment of traditional Keynesian and New-Keynesian models concerning the size of the government purchases multiplier emphasized by Cogan et al. (2010) relative to Romer and Bernstein (2009). In their baseline scenario, the New-Keynesian models of the euro area provide no support for a traditional Keynesian multiplier effect of government purchases. Crowding-out of consumption, investment and net exports dominates. The ECB's area-wide model, however, supports a strong impact of government spending on GDP that is substantially greater than one for one. The boom is nevertheless followed by a bust. Thus, the cumulative effect of government on private spending eventually also turns negative in that model. More importantly, models with backward-looking dynamics may not be as well suited for the analysis of major policy measures as the New-Keynesian models that account for the interaction of policy announcements and private-sector expectations.

Overall, the euro area stimulus package was much smaller in magnitude than the US package, and more concentrated on 2009 and 2010. The findings in Cwik and Wieland (2011) suggest that such a shorter and sharper increase in government spending induces less crowding-out than the ARRA package, which includes significant additional spending from 2011 onwards. Cwik and Wieland (2011) also discuss some factors that may have played a role in the recession of 2008–09: namely implementation lags, the zero-interest-rate floor and the share of rule-of-thumb consumers. Time lags arise because of the steps needed to move from a timely announcement to the actual implementation of government spending plans. Such implementation lags lead to more crowding-out and may even cause an initial contraction. If interest rates are anticipated to remain constant due to zero-bound effects for two years, that represents the complete period of fiscal stimulus. Cwik and Wieland document a small crowding-in effect in some of the DSGE models. For the multiplier to be greater than one, however, it is important that the two-year constant rate window is already anticipated as of the first quarter of 2009.

A number of studies have used other structural macroeconomic models to assess the impact of different fiscal policy tools. Typically they focus on a single model. An interesting extension of the EU-Quest model by Werner Roeger and Jan in't Veld (2009) includes a third type of household that is credit constrained. Their benchmark calibration apparently has 40 per cent liquidity-constrained households and another 20 per cent credit-constrained households, which would be too high relative to the survey evidence available regarding the share of such households during the financial crisis. The IMF's new preferred model for fiscal policy analysis – the so-called GIMF model – has been used by Charles Freedman et al. (2010) to analyse the consequences of different fiscal measures. An innovative element of this model is that it features overlapping generations of households with finite horizons. As shown by Taylor (2010b), the effects of longer-lasting or permanent fiscal stimuli in the GIMF are very close to the effects reported by Cogan et al. (2010) for New-Keynesian DSGE models. A short-term government spending shock in GIMF has a multiplier of unity under normal circumstances. Unfortunately, the GIMF model is calibrated and not estimated with state-of-the-art methods to fit US or euro-area data. It would be very useful to see how it fares in estimation relative to the estimated models I have used.

Recently, a very commendable model comparison study was carried out by 17 researchers from the IMF, the Organisation for Economic Co-operation and Development (OECD), the ECB, the Federal Reserve and the European Commission in Coenen et al. (2012). It covers seven structural models used at policy institutions, including GIMF, the modified version of EU-Quest with additional constrained households, the Fed's SIGMA and FRB-US models, the OECD Fiscal Model, the Bank of Canada-GEM model and the ECB's New Area-Wide Model. For comparative purposes, they also consider the Smets–Wouters model and the version with rule-of-thumb consumer estimated by Cogan et al. (2010) (CCTW). They simulate the near-permanent fiscal expansion as well as the ARRA spending plan investigated by CCTW. In both cases, the outcomes under the CCTW model fall well inside the range of outcomes obtained with the other seven policy models. Thus, they corroborate the robustness of the evaluation of the likely impact of ARRA spending by CCTW. Coenen et al. emphasize, however, that a counterfactual one-off increase in spending restricted to two years of anticipated, constant interest rates would have delivered greater stimulative effects, also in the CCTW model. Such a shorter stimulus is closer to the euro area stimulus evaluated by Cwik and Wieland (2011). Coenen et al. (2012) neglect, however, the possibility of implementation lags investigated by Cwik and Wieland (2011). Furthermore, several of their models assume shares of 40 to 50 per cent of rule-of-thumb households, which are much higher than the 26.5 per cent share estimated by CCTW. I will address the question of whether such a higher share is more likely or not in the recent recession a little farther down.

Further comparison of the findings in CCTW and Cwik and Wieland with those by Coenen et al. (2012) would be very useful. Unfortunately, however, Coenen et al. (2012) use a traditional model comparison approach whereby separate teams of researchers conduct a specific set of experiments, each team in their own model, and report outcomes. It would be very useful if the policy institutions represented by these research teams would choose to create a platform for model comparison as in Wieland et al. (2009), or add their models to this new model database.

Such a platform would also render their model simulations directly replicable and transparent to researchers outside those teams and institutions. Replicability is a basic scientific standard that ensures that correct comparisons can be made and policy recommendations properly scrutinized. Software for replicating the Coenen et al. (2012) model simulations has been made available on the *American Economic Journal: Macroeconomics* website. Unfortunately, it is based on TROLL, a software tool that is not easily available for individual researchers outside central banks.

Government Purchases Versus Government Transfers

The preceding review of the literature focused primarily on the likely size of the government purchases multiplier. Recently, however, doubts have surfaced as to whether the 2009 ARRA legislation in the United States did achieve the announced increase in government consumption and infrastructure investment – that is, the announced multiplicand. Using new data from the Bureau of Economic Analysis (BEA) and considering developments at the federal, state and local levels, Cogan and Taylor (2010) find that the government purchases multiplicand through the second quarter of 2010 is only 2 per cent of the total spending announced by the ARRA. This increase in purchases occurred mainly at the federal level, while state and local governments used the substantial grants they received under the ARRA to reduce borrowing and increase transfer payments rather than purchases.

The Cogan and Taylor (2010) finding seems to explain why the contribution of government spending to GDP growth in the national accounts has remained rather flat. As shown in the left panel of Figure 2.2, non-defence spending (dashed line) varied little over the recession and recovery from 2008 to 2010. There is no strong upward spike in its contribution to GDP growth visible in 2009 or 2010. Interestingly, the contribution of government spending to GDP growth in the euro area also remained fairly flat throughout the recession and recovery as is apparent from the right panel of Figure 2.2 (dashed line). It seems difficult to make a case for a crucial role of government spending in stimulating growth based on the inspection of this graph. It would be very useful if the European Commission and national euro area governments would similarly publish information on the actual spending pattern in relation to the announced measures. This information is crucial for making appropriate ex-post evaluations of their effectiveness.

In light of these findings, assessments of the impact of the government stimulus packages in 2009 in the USA and euro area should perhaps focus more on the likely effect of government transfers on GDP growth. Romer

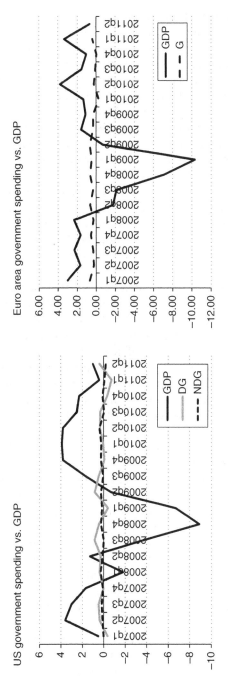

Notes: GDP: GDP growth; NDG: non-defence spending contribution to GDP growth; DG: defence spending contribution; G: government spending contribution to growth.

Sources: BEA (US Bureau of Economic Analysis) and ECB (European Central Bank).

Figure 2.2 Government spending contributions to GDP growth: 2007–10

and Bernstein (2009) estimated, based on their models, that additional permanent government transfers and tax cuts planned by the US administration would increase GDP by 2010 by one for one.[20] Given, of course, that the overall amount of the ARRA was limited, the announced changes in transfers and taxes were primarily temporary in nature. The effect of such temporary measures depends crucially on the importance of different motives for consumer behaviour. Traditional Keynesian-style models may predict a positive impact of temporary transfers on GDP, because consumption is modelled as a function of current after-tax income. Forward-looking, permanent-income consumers would instead see through the temporary increase and expect little or no boost to permanent income, because future tax increases may be needed to pay off the government debt incurred. Thus, their consumption would not change at all. For this reason, the DSGE models of Smets and Wouters (2003 and 2007), as well as the new DSGE model of Fed researchers Edge et al. (2010), predict that a temporary increase in government transfers, tax cuts or tax rebates have no effect on GDP.

As discussed earlier, some of the empirically-estimated New-Keynesian DSGE models allow for the presence of rule-of-thumb consumers. In Cogan et al. (2010), the estimated share is 26.5 per cent, similar to other estimates available in the literature. In order to illustrate the impact of government transfers and tax cuts, I simulated an increase in government transfers in that model of 1 per cent of GDP for the duration of one year (solid black line in Figure 2.3). Figure 2.3 also shows that GDP (dotted line) then increases by about 30 basis points for a year in the CCTW model. In this simulation, interest rates are set according to Taylor's rule. I have also considered interest-rate accommodation for one or two years due to zero bound effects. The resulting increase in the GDP effect of transfers is rather small, however.

For comparison, I also include a simulation of the same temporary increase in government transfers in the calibrated two-country version of the ECB's New-Area-Wide model taken from Coenen et al. (2008). An estimated, single-economy, euro-area version of this model has recently replaced the AWM model in ECB policy analysis. This estimated model is also used in the Coenen et al. (2012) study. In the calibrated two-country model, the share of rule-of-thumb agents is set at 25 per cent. Transfers, however, are assumed to be unevenly distributed, in per-capita terms, over the two types of households. The rule-of-thumb households are favoured at a ratio of 3 to 1. As indicated by the dashed line in Figure 2.3, the impact on GDP of a 1 per cent increase in transfers is similar, though slightly smaller, than the estimate obtained with the model of Cogan et al. (2010).

In sum, this exercise suggests that the effects of the temporary increase

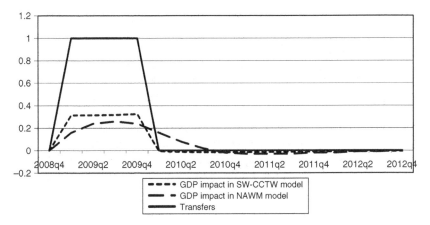

Notes: SW-CCTW: DSGE model with rule-of-thumb households estimated in Cogan et al. (2010) with US data; NAWM: calibrated two-country version of ECB's New-Area-Wide model taken from Coenen et al. (2008); transfers: temporary increase of transfers in the US economy.

Figure 2.3   The GDP impact of a temporary increase in government transfers of 1 per cent of GDP

in government transfers and tax cuts implied by the ARRA may be significantly smaller than expected by Romer and Bernstein. The two models I have considered suggest an effect between zero and 30 basis points on GDP per 1 per cent of GDP increase in transfers. A possible concern is that the share of rule-of-thumb households increased during the course of the financial crisis. The argument goes as follows. A standard justification for hard-wiring rule-of-thumb households in macro models is to capture borrowing constraints. Households that desire to borrow but are credit constrained would increase consumption along with increases in current disposable income. The number of such households might then have increased during the financial crisis, because banks were more reluctant to extend credit. Alternatively, it is also possible that the share of consumers who wanted to borrow declined during the recession. In particular, households that expect a lasting reduction in life-time income, because of less promising job opportunities, asset losses, sustained unemployment, or higher taxes, may decide to save more. In this manner, some of those households that were borrowing-constrained before may now want to save rather than spend any additional income they might receive from the government.

The tax rebate offered by the Bush administration in spring 2008 and similar tax rebates or credits by the Obama administration offered in the context of the ARRA in spring 2009 were the focus of a recent survey by Claudia Sahm et al. (2010) that may shed some light on the direction of this effect. They write that 25 per cent of households reported that the one-time economic stimulus payment in 2008 led them mostly to increase their spending. In 2009, 13 per cent of households reported that they had mostly spent the extra pay from the lower withholding. This finding, taken together with the above model-based analysis, may help to explain the behaviour of aggregate consumption and income. As pointed out by Taylor (2009 and 2010a), the rebate payments are directly apparent as upward spikes in aggregate disposable income in May and June 2008 and 2009, while aggregate consumption growth in those periods is relatively smooth and flat.

CONCLUSION

In this chapter, I have presented a proposal for a comparative approach to macroeconomic policy analysis that is open to competing modelling paradigms. I have reviewed recent work on building a macroeconomic model archive and platform that make it much easier to conduct extensive model comparisons. In addition, I have pointed towards a range of competing modelling approaches that should be the focus of a systematic model comparison exercise in the future.

To illustrate the use of empirical benchmarks in a model competition, I have reviewed findings from a recent model comparison by Wieland and Wolters (2010) in terms of forecasting performance during US recessions and recoveries. This comparison has indicated that models and experts tend to miss the onset of recessions. Both models and experts have some forecasting power during recoveries. Interestingly, several of the state-of-the-art models performed better than many experts over a horizon of three to four quarters. Thus, there is no reason for forecasting professionals using time series methods or traditional Keynesian-style models to dismiss modern DSGE models.

Model comparison can be a very valuable tool for increasing the robustness of policy recommendations. To illustrate what is meant by policy robustness, I have reviewed recent findings regarding the effectiveness of temporary fiscal stimulus measures from a range of models and studies. I found that a range of model comparisons suggests a significantly smaller impact of the government spending planned under the American Recovery and Reinvestment of 2009 as initially projected by Administration economists in Romer and Bernstein (2009). From these findings I conclude that arguments in favour of fiscal stimulus that are based on the supposed multiplicative effect of government purchases should be viewed with substantial scepticism. Furthermore, given the uncertainty about the appropriate macroeconomic model of the economy, policy analysis needs to take into account a range of models, including New-Keynesian DSGE models rather than relying only on more traditional Keynesian-style models as in Romer and Bernstein (2009).

NOTES

1. I acknowledge funding support from European Community grant MONFISPOL under grant agreement SSH-CT-2009-225149. Excellent research assistance was provided by Elena Afanasyeva, Matthias Burgert and Sebastian Schmidt. Helpful comments by Robert Boyer and the participants of the Cournot Centre's conference, 'What's Right with Macroeconomics?', held 2–3 December 2010 in Paris, were greatly appreciated. The usual disclaimer applies.
2. 'The unfortunate uselessness of most "state of the art" academic monetary economics': http://blogs.ft.com/maverecon/2009/03/the-unfortunate-uselessness-of-most-state-of-the-art-academic-monetary-economics/#axzz1SqddzN1g.
3. See the advertisement section of the *American Economic Review* – AEA Papers and Proceedings, May 1992.
4. See Taylor and Wieland (2012) and Wieland et al. (2009) for an implementation of this model comparison approach.
5. See Jean-Claude Trichet, 'Reflections on the nature of monetary policy non-standard measures and finance theory', speech given at the ECB Central Banking Conference in Frankfurt on 18 November 2010.
6. See Juillard (1996).
7. See http://www.macromodelbase.com.
8. For example, the models of Rudebusch and Svensson (1999) and Orphanides (2003) are essentially structural VAR models with some restrictions on the coefficients. The ECB's Area-Wide Model is a medium-sized structural model with a relatively limited role for forward-looking behaviour compared to the other structural rational expectations models in the database.
9. Because of complications in programming the informational timing assumptions regarding expectations in this model in DYNARE, two versions are included: one for simulating the consequences of a monetary policy shock, and the other for simulating the consequences of the other economic shocks in the model.
10. This version was created in Taylor and Wieland (2012) to evaluate the effect of this assumption in comparing the Altig et al. (2005) model with the model of Smets and Wouters (2007), which features no such cost channel.
11. See Jean-Claude Trichet, 'Reflections on the nature of monetary policy non-standard measures and finance theory', speech given at the ECB Central Banking Conference in Frankfurt on 18 November 2010.
12. A well-known textbook that provides a comprehensive framework for adaptive learning is Evans and Honjapohja (2001).
13. See Kurz et al. (2003); Kurz et al. (2005); Giordani and Söderlind (2003); Capistran and Timmermann (2009); and Wieland and Wolters (2010).
14. For a recent survey of agent-based models in economics, see Tesfatsion and Judd (2006).
15. National Bureau of Economic Research.
16. The SPF is conducted quarterly and contains responses from 30 to 50 professional forecasters. It was initiated in 1968 by the American Statistical Association and the NBER

and has been administered by the Federal Reserve Board of Philadelphia since 1990. The Greenbook is not a survey. It contains a single forecast produced by the staff of the Board of Governors of the Federal Reserve System in Washington DC, which becomes publicly available within a five-year lag.

17. Exceptions are the 1980 and 2008–09 recessions. In the first case, they start only two quarters prior to the trough because of data availability. In the second case, the trough is not yet determined. They start in 2007Q4 (peak) and end in 2009Q3.

18. See Romer and Bernstein (2009), Appendix 1, p. 12. This paper was written during the transition period in early January 2009 before Romer was sworn in as Chair of the Council of Economic Advisers.

19. See also the earlier working paper version, Cwik and Wieland (2009).

20. See Appendix 1 of Romer and Bernstein (2009): multipliers for different types of spending.

REFERENCES

Adolfson, M., S. Lasen, J. Lind and M. Villani (2007), 'Bayesian estimation of an open economy DSGE model with incomplete pass-through', *Journal of International Economics*, **72**, 481–511.

Akerlof, G. and R.J. Shiller (eds) (2010), *Animal Spirits: How Human Psychology Drives the Economy, and Why it Matters for Global Capitalism*, Princeton, NJ: Princeton University Press.

Altig, D.E., L.J. Christiano, M. Eichenbaum and J. Lind (2005), 'Firm-specific capital, nominal rigidities and the business cycle', CEPR Discussion Papers 4858.

Angeloni, I. and E. Faia (2010), 'Capital regulation and monetary policy with fragile banks', manuscript, University of Frankfurt.

Bernanke, B., M. Gertler and S. Gilchrist (1999), 'The financial accelerator in a quantitative business cycle framework', in J.B. Taylor and M. Woodford (eds), *Handbook of Macroeconomics Volume 1C*, Amsterdam: Elsevier Science, North-Holland.

Branch, W.A. and G.W. Evans (2011), 'Monetary policy with heterogeneous expectations', *Economic Theory*, **47**(2–3), 365–93.

Branch, W.A. and B. McGough (2011), 'Business cycle amplification with heterogeneous expectations', *Economic Theory*, **47**(2–3), 395–421.

Brock, W. and C. Hommes (1998), 'Heterogeneous beliefs and routes to chaos in a simple asset pricing model', *Journal of Economic Dynamics and Control*, **22**, 1235–74.

Bryant, R., P. Hooper and C. Mann (eds) (1993), *Evaluating Policy Regimes: New Research in Empirical Macroeconomics*, Washington, DC: The Brookings Institution.

Bryant, R., D. Currie, J. Frenkel, P. Masson and R. Portes (eds) (1989), *Macroeconomic Policies in an Interdependent World*, Washington, DC: The Brookings Institution.

Bryant, R., D.W. Henderson, G. Holtham, P. Hooper and S.A. Symansky (eds) (1988), *Empirical Macroeconomics for Interdependent Economies*, Washington, DC: The Brookings Institution.

Capistran, C. and A. Timmermann (2009), 'Disagreement and biases in inflation expectations', *Journal of Money, Credit and Banking*, **41**, 365–96.

Carabenciov, I., I. Ermolaev, C. Freedman, M. Juillard, O. Kamenik,

D. Korshunov and D. Laxton (2008), 'A small quarterly projection model of the US economy', IMF Working Paper 08/278.

Chiarella, C., R. Dieci and X-Z. He (2007), 'Heterogeneous expectations and speculative behaviour in a dynamic multi-asset framework', *Journal of Economic Behavior and Organization*, **62**, 408–27.

Christensen, I. and A. Dib (2008), 'The financial accelerator in an estimated New Keynesian model', *Review of Economic Dynamics*, **11**, 155–78.

Christiano, L., M. Eichenbaum and C.L. Evans (2005), 'Nominal rigidities and the dynamic effects of a shock to monetary policy', *Journal of Political Economy*, **113**(1), 1–45.

Christiano, L., R. Motto and M. Rostagno (2010), 'Financial factors in economic fluctuations', ECB Working Paper 1192.

Clarida, R., J. Gal and M. Gertler (1999), 'The science of monetary policy: a New Keynesian perspective', *Journal of Economic Literature*, **37**(4), 1661–707.

Clarida, R., J. Gal and M. Gertler (2002), 'A simple framework for international monetary policy analysis', *Journal of Monetary Economics*, **49**, 879–904.

Coenen, G. and V. Wieland (2002), 'Inflation dynamics and international linkages: a model of the United States, the euro area and Japan', ECB Working Paper Series 181.

Coenen, G. and V. Wieland (2005), 'A small estimated euro area model with rational expectations and nominal rigidities', *European Economic Review*, **49**, 1081–104.

Coenen, G., P. McAdam and R. Straub (2008), 'Tax reform and labour-market performance in the euro area: a simulation-based analysis using the new area-wide model', *Journal of Economic Dynamics & Control*, **32**(8), 2543–83.

Coenen, G., C.J. Erceg, C. Freedman, D. Furceri, M. Kumhof, R. Lalonde, D. Laxton, J. Lind, A. Mourougane, D. Muir, S. Mursula, C. de Resende, J. Roberts, W. Roeger, S. Snudden, M. Trabandt and J. in't Veld (2012), 'Effects of fiscal stimulus in structural models', *American Economic Journal: Macroeconomics*, **4**(1), 22–68.

Cogan, J.F. and J.B. Taylor (2010), 'What the government purchases multiplier actually multiplied in the 2009 stimulus package', NBER Working Paper 16505.

Cogan, J.F., T. Cwik, J.B. Taylor and V. Wieland (2009), 'New Keynesian versus old Keynesian government spending multipliers', NBER Working Paper Series 14782.

Cogan, J.F., T. Cwik, J.B. Taylor and V. Wieland (2010), 'New Keynesian versus old Keynesian government spending multipliers', *Journal of Economic Dynamics and Control*, **34**, 281–95.

Cwik, T. and V. Wieland (2009), 'Keynesian government spending multipliers and spillovers in the euro area', CEPR Discussion Paper 7389.

Cwik, T. and V. Wieland (2011), 'Keynesian government spending multipliers and spillovers in the euro area', *Economic Policy*, **26**, 493–549.

De Fiore, F., P. Teles and O. Tristani (2009), 'Monetary policy and the financing of firms', ECB Working Paper 1123.

De Graeve, F. (2008), 'The external finance premium and the macroeconomy: US post-WWII evidence', *Journal of Economic Dynamics and Control*, **32**, 3415–440.

De Grauwe, P. (2011), 'Animal spirits and monetary policy', *Economic Theory*, **47**(2–3), 423–57.

Deissenberg, C., H. Dawid and S. van der Hoog (2008), 'Eurace: a massively parallel agent-based model of the European economy', *Applied Mathematics and Computation*, **204**, 541–52.

Del Negro, M. and F. Schorfheide (2004), 'Priors from general equilibrium models for VARs', *International Economic Review*, **45**(2), 643–73.

DeWalque, G., O. Pierrard and A. Rouabah (2010), 'Financial (in)stability, supervision and liquidity injections: a dynamic general equilibrium approach', *Economic Journal*, Royal Economic Society, **120**(549), 1234–61.

Diamond, P. and H. Vartiainen (eds) (2007), *Behavioral Economics and its Applications*, Princeton, NJ: Princeton University Press.

Dib, A. (2010), 'Banks, credit market frictions, and business cycles', Bank of Canada, Working Paper 2010-24, available at: http://www.banquedu-canada.ca/2010/10/publication/recherches/document-travail-2010-24/ (accessed September 2011).

Dieppe, A., K. Kuester and P. McAdam (2005), 'Optimal monetary policy rules for the euro area: an analysis using the area wide model', *Journal of Common Market Studies*, **43**(3), 507–37.

Edge, R.M., M.T. Kiley and J-P. Laforte (2007), 'Documentation of the research and statistics division's estimated DSGE model of the US economy: 2006 version', Finance and Economics Discussion Series 07-53, Board of Governors of the Federal Reserve System.

Edge, R.M., M.T. Kiley and J-P. Laforte (2010), 'A comparison of forecast performance between Federal Reserve staff forecasts, simple reduced form models, and a DSGE model', *Journal of Applied Econometrics*, **25**(4), 720–54.

Erceg, C.J., L. Guerrieri and C. Gust (2008), 'Trade adjustment and the composition of trade', *Journal of Economic Dynamics & Control*, **32**, 2622–50.

Evans, G. and S. Honjapohja (2001), *Learning and Expectations in Macroeconomics*, Princeton, NJ: Princeton University Press.

Fagan, G., J. Henry and R. Mestre (2005), 'An area-wide model for the euro area', *Economic Modelling*, **22**, 39–59.

Freedman, C., M. Kumhof, D. Laxton, D. Muir and S. Mursula (2010), 'Global effects of fiscal stimulus during the crisis', *Journal of Monetary Economics*, **57**, 506–26.

Fuhrer, J.C. (1997), 'Inflation/output variance trade-offs and optimal monetary policy', *Journal of Money, Credit and Banking*, **29**(2), 214–34.

Fuhrer, J.C. and G. Moore (1995), 'Inflation persistence', *The Quarterly Journal of Economics*, **110**(1), 127–59.

Gali, J. and T. Monacelli (2005), 'Optimal monetary and fiscal policy in a currency union', NBER Working Paper 11815, National Bureau of Economic Research.

Gerali, A., S. Neri, L. Sessa and F. Signoretti (2010), 'Credit and banking in a DSGE model of the euro area', *Journal of Money, Credit and Banking*, **42**(6), supplement.

Gertler, M. and P. Karadi (2009), 'A model of unconventional monetary policy', mimeo.

Gertler, M. and N. Kiyotaki (2010), 'Financial intermediation and credit policy in business cycle analysis', in B.M. Friedman and M. Woodford (eds), *Handbook of Monetary Economics*, Vol. 3, Elsevier, pp. 547–99.

Gertler, M., S. Gilchrist and F. Natalucci (2007), 'External constraints on monetary policy and the financial accelerator', *Journal of Money, Credit and Banking*, **39**(2–3), 295–330.

Giannone, D., F. Monti and L. Reichlin (2009), 'Incorporating conjunctural analysis in structural models', in V. Wieland (ed.), *The Science and Practice of Monetary Policy Today*, Berlin: Springer Science, pp. 41–57.

Giordani, P. and P. Söderlind (2003), 'Inflation forecast uncertainty', *European Economic Review*, **47**, 1037–59.

Goodfriend, M. and B.T. McCallum (2007), 'Banking and interest rates in monetary policy analysis: a quantitative exploration', *Journal of Monetary Economics*, **54**(5), 1480–507.

Gouvea, S., A. Minella, R. Santos and N. Souza-Sobrinho (2008), 'Samba: stochastic analytical model with a Bayesian approach', manuscript.

Hughes-Hallett, A. and K.F. Wallis (eds) (2004), 'EMU macroeconomic model comparison exercise for the Euroconference 7–8 June 2002', *Economic Modelling*, **21**(5).

Iacoviello, M. (2005), 'House prices, borrowing constraints, and monetary policy in the business cycle', *The American Economic Review*, **95**(3), 739–64.

Ireland, P. (2004), 'Technology shocks in the New Keynesian model', *The Review of Economics and Statistics*, **86**(4), 923–36.

Juillard, M. (1996), 'Dynare: a program for the resolution and simulation of dynamic models with forward variables through the use of a relaxation algorithm', CEPREMAP Working Paper 9602.

Klein, L. (ed.) (1991), *Comparative Performance of US Econometric Models*, Oxford: Oxford University Press.

Krugman, Paul (2009), 'Paul Krugman's London lectures. Dismal science. The Nobel laureate speaks on the crisis in the economy and in economics', *The Economist*, 11 June.

Kuester, K. and V. Wieland (2010), 'Insurance policies for monetary policy in the euro area', *Journal of the European Economic Association*, **8**, 872–912.

Kurz, M. (1994a), 'On rational belief equilibria', *Economic Theory*, **4**, 859–76.

Kurz, M. (1994b), 'On the structure and diversity of rational beliefs', *Economic Theory*, **4**, 877–900.

Kurz, M. (1996), 'Rational beliefs and endogenous uncertainty: an introduction', *Economic Theory*, **8**, 383–97.

Kurz, M. (1997a), 'Endogenous economic fluctuations and rational beliefs: a general perspective', in M. Kurz (ed.), *Endogenous Economic Fluctuations: Studies in the Theory of Rational Beliefs*, Springer Series in Economic Theory (6), Berlin, Heidelberg and New York: Springer Verlag.

Kurz, M. (ed.) (1997b), *Endogenous Economic Fluctuations: Studies in the Theory of Rational Beliefs*, Springer Series in Economic Theory (6), Berlin, Heidelberg and New York: Springer Verlag.

Kurz, M. (2009), 'Rational diverse beliefs and market volatility', in T. Hens and K. Schenk-Hoppe (eds), *Handbook of Financial Markets: Dynamics and Evolution*, Amsterdam: North Holland.

Kurz, M., H. Jin and M. Motolese (2003), *Knowledge, Information and Expectations in Modern Macroeconomics: Essays in Honor of Edmund S. Phelps*, Chapter 10: 'Endogenous fluctuations and the role of monetary policy', Princeton, NJ: Princeton University Press, pp. 188–227.

Kurz, M., H. Jin and M. Motolese (2005), 'The role of expectations in economic fluctuations and the efficacy of monetary policy', *Journal of Economic Dynamics & Control*, **29**, 2017–65.

Laxton, D. and P. Pesenti (2003), 'Monetary rule for small, open, emerging economies', *Journal of Monetary Economics*, **50**, 1109–46.

Levin, A., V. Wieland and J.C. Williams (2003), 'The performance of forecast-based monetary policy rules under model uncertainty', *The American Economic Review*, **93**(3), 622–45.

Mankiw, N.G. and R. Reis (2007), 'Sticky information in general equilibrium', *Journal of the European Economic Association*, **5**(2–3), 603–13.

McCallum, B. and E. Nelson (1999), 'Performance of operational policy rules in an estimated semi-classical structural model', in J.B. Taylor (ed.), *Monetary Policy Rules*, Chicago, IL: University of Chicago Press.

Medina, J.P. and C. Soto (2007), 'The Chilean business cycles through the lens of a stochastic general equilibrium model', Central Bank of Chile Working Paper 457.

Meh, C.A. and K. Moran (2010), 'The role of bank capital in the propagation of shocks', *Journal of Economic Dynamics and Control*, **34**(3), 555–76.

Murchison, S. and A. Rennison (2006), 'ToTEM: The Bank of Canada's new quarterly projection model', Bank of Canada Technical Report 97.

Nolan, C. and C. Thoenissen (2009), 'Financial shocks and the US business cycle', *Journal of Monetary Economics*, **56**, 596–604.

Orphanides, A. (2003), 'The quest for prosperity without inflation', *Journal of Monetary Economics*, **50**, 633–63.

Orphanides, A. and V. Wieland (1998), 'Price stability and monetary policy effectiveness when nominal interest rates are bounded at zero', Finance and Economics Discussion Series 98–35, Board of Governors of the Federal Reserve System.

Orphanides, A. and J.C. Williams (2006), 'Monetary policy under imperfect knowledge', *Journal of the European Economic Association*, **4**, 366–75.

Ratto, M., W. Roeger and J. in 't Veld (2009), 'QUEST III: An estimated open-economy DSGE model of the euro area with fiscal and monetary policy', *Economic Modelling*, **26**(1), 222–33.

Reifschneider, D., R. Tetlow and J.C. Williams (1999), 'Aggregate disturbances, monetary policy and the macroeconomy: the FRB/US perspective', *Federal Reserve Bulletin*, **85**(1), 1–19.

Roeger, W. and J. in 't Veld (2009), 'Fiscal policy with credit constrained households', Economic Papers 357, Brussels: European Commission.

Romer, C. and J. Bernstein (2009), 'The job impact of the American Recovery and Reinvestment Plan', unpublished paper, 8 January.

Rotemberg, J.J. and M. Woodford (1997), 'An optimization-based econometric framework for the evaluation of monetary policy', *NBER Macroeconomics Annual*, **12**, 297–346.

Rudebusch, G.D. and L.E.O. Svensson (1999), 'Policy rules for inflation targeting', in J.B. Taylor (ed.), *Monetary Policy Rules*, Chicago, IL: University of Chicago Press.

Sahm, C., M. Shapiro and J. Slemrod (2010), 'Check in the mail or more in the paycheck: does the effectiveness of fiscal stimulus depend on how it is delivered?', NBER Working Paper 16246.

Slobodyan, S. and R. Wouters (2008), 'Estimating a medium-scale DSGE model with expectations based on small forecasting models', mimeo.

Smets, F. and R. Wouters (2003), 'An estimated dynamic stochastic general equilibrium model of the euro area', *Journal of the European Economic Association*, **1**(5), 1123–75

Smets, F. and R. Wouters (2007), 'Shocks and frictions in US business cycles: a Bayesian DSGE approach', *The American Economic Review*, **97**(3), 586–606.

Taylor, J.B. (1993a), 'Discretion versus policy rules in practice', *Carnegie-Rochester Conference Series on Public Policy*, **39**, 195–214.

Taylor, J.B. (1993b), *Macroeconomic Policy in a World Economy*, New York: W.W. Norton.

Taylor, J.B. (1999), *Monetary Policy Rules*, Chicago, IL: University of Chicago Press.

Taylor, J.B. (2009), 'The lack of an empirical rationale for a revival of discretionary fiscal policy', *American Economic Review, Papers and Proceedings*, **99**(2), 550–55.

Taylor, J.B. (2010a), 'Getting back on track: policy lessons from the financial crisis', *Federal Reserve Bank of St Louis Review*, **92**, 165–76.

Taylor, J.B. (2010b), 'Comment on "global effects of fiscal stimulus during the crisis"', *Journal of Monetary Economics*, **57**, 527–30.

Taylor, J.B. and V. Wieland (2012), 'Surprising comparative properties of monetary models: results from a new data base', *The Review of Economics and Statistics*, **94**(3), 800–816.

Tesfatsion, L. and K.L. Judd (eds) (2006), *Handbook of Computational Economics, Volume 2: Agent-Based Computational Economics*, Amsterdam: North Holland.

Wieland, V. (2009), 'Learning, endogenous indexation and disinflation in the New-Keynesian model', in C. Walsh and K. Schmidt-Hebbel (eds), *Monetary Policy under Uncertainty and Learning*, Santiago: Central Bank of Chile.

Wieland, V. and M. Wolters (2010), 'The diversity of forecasts from macro-economic models of the US economy', *Economic Theory*, **47**, 247–92.

Wieland, V., T. Cwik, G.J. Müller, S. Schmidt and M. Wolters (2009), 'A new comparative approach to macroeconomic modelling and policy analysis', manuscript, Center for Financial Studies, Frankfurt.

3. The 'hoc' of international macroeconomics after the crisis[1]

Giancarlo Corsetti

INTRODUCTION

Robert Solow once said that we economists should be concerned not about our models being 'ad hoc', but about the 'hoc' our models are 'ad'. By no means should this observation be interpreted as an expression of sympathy for conceptual and analytical short-cuts to difficult theoretical problems, obviously misrepresenting the view of a Nobel laureate in economics. Rather, it is an incisive, healthy reminder that, despite our efforts to develop models with good theoretical foundations, the end product will always include some elements or areas that simply mirror our ignorance. By focusing on the appropriate 'hoc', however, theory and models may help us to approximate the root of the problem at hand – from a policy perspective, the root of the market failures that may motivate government interventions and define the relevant trade-offs for policy design.

There are of course times in which some 'hoc' forcefully makes its way into our discipline – the global crisis and recession that began in the summer of 2007 being a case in point. In many respects, 'this time is not different'. Indeed, Carmen Reinhart and Kenneth Rogoff (2009) forcefully emphasize that contractionary crises associated with financial turmoil tend to follow similar patterns, whether they occur nationally or regionally. Yet, the impact that the global crisis will have on the economic profession is profound relative to previous crisis episodes, if anything as regards the definition of the stylized facts driving mainstream macroeconomic research. After 2008, the possibility of financial turmoil cum deep macroeconomic downturns no longer defines the emerging-market status of an economy – there is no 'South American theory' of the business cycle distinct from a North American one. The recent crisis has shattered our confidence in models of business cycles primarily shaped by the post-World-War-Two experience in industrial countries.

The goal of this chapter is to carry out a selective and admittedly biased review of emerging issues in the macroeconomics of the crisis from the vantage point of an international economist. The first part briefly discusses a few promising areas of theoretical and policy research, which recent events have put under the spotlight. These include: the transmission of shocks, intrinsically associated with a considerable rise in economic uncertainty, leading to a widespread precautionary contraction of investment and consumption plans; the role of financial channels in magnifying seemingly small real shocks, or in translating financial disturbances into real ones with far-reaching consequences for the level of economic activity; and the extent of misallocation at the root, which has emerged as a consequence of the crisis. Not surprisingly, the debate around these issues has yet again been shaped by the unresolved tension among competing views on financial instability and crises (liquidity runs versus policy/ market distortions), naturally associated with opposing policy prescriptions (guarantees versus market discipline, implying the removal/correction of policy/market failures). The same tension can arguably explain the slow pace at which analysts have been converging on a strategy to encompass financial distortions in general equilibrium models designed for policy analysis.

By means of a highly stylized model, the second part of the chapter discusses over-borrowing and (exchange rate) misalignments as general features of economies in which financial markets are incomplete. The analysis is in part motivated by the fact that recent developments in monetary theory have focused on these two implications of financial imperfections as key building blocks for welfare-based policy assessment in a global economy (see Corsetti et al., 2010a). More generally, however, it reflects the aspiration to identify a common framework in order to comprehend the different international dimensions of the crisis, ranging from global imbalances (see, for example, Caballero, 2010, and Obstfeld and Rogoff, 2010, among others), to fiscal crisis and cross-border contagion (see, for example, Bolton and Jeanne, 2011), which have so far typically been analysed as independent phenomena rather than as pieces of the same macroeconomic process.

The chapter is organized as follows. The second section identifies three questions for policy and macro modelling emphasized by the crisis. The third section discusses the fundamental issues in modelling financial frictions in policy models and draws on recent literature to develop an example that sheds light on the simple theoretical foundations of over-borrowing and (international) price misalignment. The final section concludes, spelling out implications for developing policy models.

IS MACRO MODELLING OF THE FINANCIAL TRANSMISSION MECHANISM STUCK AT A CROSSROADS?

Several crisis-related issues are likely to influence macroeconomic and policy research for some time to come.[2] To set the stage of the analysis, I will start with a discussion of some of the questions that have been forcefully raised by events since August 2007.

Three Questions

The first issue concerns the macro consequences of sharp fluctuations in uncertainty. According to most analyses, the exacerbation of the crisis in the autumn of 2008 was driven by a sudden peak in the perceived uncertainty about macroeconomic and financial developments, as well as current and future policy actions. The extent and depth of the financial crisis, which had been brewing since the virtual disappearance of the inter-bank markets in August 2007, became clear during the summer of 2008. At the time, economic news was not the only thing shattering any remaining hope that world growth would remain strong, driven by developments outside the US. Most importantly, it became obvious that the conventional policy model adopted until that point, based on liquidity provision to the financial system and occasional, limited bailouts of financial institutions, was not working well and was arguably counterproductive, as it postponed adjustment and let the root problems grow bigger. For some time, policy makers appeared unable to define a new policy framework. The 'uncertainty shock' in the autumn of 2008 was as much rooted in policy-generated distress, as it was in economic and financial hardship (on uncertainty shocks, see Bloom, 2009).

In the space of a month or two, absent the definition of a clear policy strategy to fight the crisis crescendo, private investment demand (both in infrastructure and inventories) dried up, mirrored by manufacturing production and world trade. Faced with increasing uncertainty, firms adopted strongly precautionary strategies: they cancelled existing orders and projects, took steps to reduce their wage bill, perhaps reducing hours at first, then laying off workers. The contraction of employment eventually fed a contraction in consumption demand. As households and firms drastically revised their assessment of the likelihood of the unthinkable – such as checking deposits becoming risky assets! – they embraced extremely conservative saving and financial strategies. World portfolios were strongly rebalanced in favour of assets issued by the few sovereign states with large enough fiscal shoulder relative to their financial sector, and a currency with a wide circulation.

The second issue refers to the modalities by which the transmission of financial shocks can greatly magnify arguably contained adverse developments in the credit markets, turning them, first, into a state of persistent global illiquidity, and, eventually, into generalized solvency problems of financial institutions at global levels. As is well understood, at the core of the endogenous amplification mechanism underlying the crisis was the large-scale process of securitization leading to the diffusion of assets with opaque features among highly leveraged financial intermediaries. With the dispersion of these assets across borders, many financial institutions gave the impression that sector-specific and country-specific risk was actually well diversified. The foundation of this view of course rested on ignoring the possibility that the resulting opaqueness of the portfolios held by financial intermediaries could eventually undermine mutual trust among financial market participants, turning sector- and country-specific risk into global risk.

Relative to previous episodes of sharp market adjustments (such as at the end of the 'dot.com' euphoria), a large amount of 'toxic assets' (for reasons that economics and economic historians will fully clarify at some point) remained on the balance sheets of highly leveraged financial institutions throughout the crisis. After the start of the crisis, these institutions actively engaged in buying opaque assets back from their clients, perhaps motivated by concerns about the 'house reputation', after years of marketing a wide range of these new financial products with a AAA security status. Diversification of opaque assets across financial institutions was key in generating the endogenous liquidity crisis at the systemic level. Once this materialized, it set in motion widespread deleveraging with self-reinforcing negative feedback effects on banks' balance sheets via the impact of asset sales on asset prices (see Greenlaw et al., 2008, among others).

The third and last issue concerns the extent of the misallocation of resources both as a cause and as a consequence of the crisis. Before the eruption of the crisis, relative prices across sectors and countries were arguably providing signals that were inconsistent with an efficient market allocation. The most visible examples include the sustained housing price dynamics leading to construction booms and vast accumulation of risky debt in a number of countries, as well as the large global external imbalances across regions of the world.

The effects of shocks that raise the level of uncertainty, the financial channels that amplify the transmission of shocks, and the nature and magnitude of misallocation make up essential chapters in the research agenda of macroeconomists. A few contributions already mark the potentially important progress being made in such areas: on uncertainty shocks, see for example, Gruss and Mertens (2010) and Fernández-Villaverde et al. (2011), among others. All these efforts, nonetheless, face a common challenge, consisting in defining what can explain the apparent and protracted underestimation of systemic risk by market participants before the crisis. The evidence is obviously consistent with the prediction of models of animal spirits, or non-rational market dynamics (see, for example, Shiller, 2008). Yet it is hard to ignore the role of policy in the financial turmoil. Macro and micro policy strategies contributed to the accumulation of imbalances both in the years before the eruption of the crisis and in the months between August 2007 and September 2008, when liquidity policies relied on a vastly overestimated capacity of markets to metabolize the so-called toxic assets by themselves.

Competing Views of Financial Crises

At a deeper level, our understanding of crises is made difficult by an unresolved tension among competing views of the origins of market instability – a tension which is apparent in the vast literature on currency and/or banking crises. According to one view, crises stem from the bank/ liquidity run: in the basic model, the maturity mismatch between assets and liabilities in the balance sheets of financial intermediaries (due to the costs of early liquidation of long-term assets) gives rise to the possibility of multiple equilibria, making the economy vulnerable to sudden shifts in market coordination from one equilibrium to another. According to the opposite view, crises stem from market distortions that evolve into the mispricing of risk, over-borrowing and/or generic financial imbalances. As empirical studies that attempt to discriminate between coordination-driven and fundamental crises are plagued by observational equivalence, the two opposing views are constantly developing in relation to each other.

Policy prescriptions of course define the main confrontation arena. The liquidity view emphasizes the need for instruments to rule out bad equilibria, that is, instruments that provide insurance to individuals and institutions against bad (endogenous) states of the economy. In contrast, the fundamental view emphasizes the adverse consequences of public guarantees/insurance on prices, which translate into misallocation and excessive risk-taking.

As recently argued by Martin Eichenbaum (2010), the unresolved tension between these two views may provide an explanation for the slow pace at which financial instability has been systematically incorporated into standard general equilibrium models. This is a key observation. Consider the development of dynamic stochastic general equilibrium (DSGE) models. The goal of this literature is to quantify the trade-offs that are potentially relevant for policy assessment. The DSGE macro research programme has indeed coordinated efforts around a systematic exploration of the relevance of fundamental distortions in different markets. Admittedly, before the crisis most of the effort went into understanding distortions in the goods and factor (labour) markets. Today, the pressure is on retooling the models that focus on credit markets (see, for example, the discussion in Woodford, 2010, or the syllabus of courses such as the one on 'Incorporating financial factors within macroeconomic modelling and policy analysis', taught by Mark Gertler[3]). But such a task cannot be only cosmetic – 'my model has banks in it, what about yours?' Before and after the crisis, the key question is to identify and model relevant distortions and market failures. Before the crisis, however, the unresolved tension among competing theoretical frameworks of crises has made people wary about choosing one modelling direction (liquidity runs) over the other (policy and market distortions).

How should macroeconomics proceed? Currently, it seems as if the profession is keen to follow the well-known advice of the evergreen Yogi Berra:[4] 'when you come to a fork in the road, take it'. The literature on the financial transmission channel has indeed boomed, taking conflicting directions. With the goal of understanding boom and bust cycles characterized by overborrowing and price misalignment, most general equilibrium models now encompass either credit-constrained agents, coordination failures, or both.[5] Let me reconsider briefly the former strand of the literature, if anything by virtue of the large number of contributions modelling credit constraints that have appeared during these crisis years.

In relation to the task of modelling crises with large macroeconomic effects, a specific advantage of models in which financial imperfections take the form of credit constraints is their ability to account for the amplification of fundamental shocks via 'pecuniary externalities'. In equilibrium, the constraint on firms' finance is a function of the value of the collateral they can post against loans, thus of asset prices. By altering the value of the collateral, asset price fluctuations directly translate into fluctuations in the economic activity. At a macro level, in turn, there is a key feedback effect from economic activity to asset prices: to the extent that a lower level of activity reduces asset prices, the economy's response to exogenous cyclical shocks may generate rich endogenous dynamics.[6]

In reading this literature, it is useful to keep in mind that the presence of credit constraints means that firms' investment and activity are suboptimally low. In other words, per se, these models are not obviously geared to explaining economic pathologies such as over-borrowing and excessive risk-taking.

While many authors adopt this approach to shed light on financial amplification effects during economic downturns, or the macroeconomic consequences of financial shocks, paradoxically, other authors articulate the view that, in the presence of credit constraints, bubbles and asset mispricing may actually have beneficial consequences for the economy. To the extent that inflated asset prices relax firms' credit constraints, a bubble brings investment closer to the (unconstrained) optimum level (see for example, Martin and Ventura, 2011). While analytically sharp, of course, this view is hard to square with common sense: according to main street, asset bubbles are a market pathology generating massive misallocation, not a distortion that is instrumental in bringing the economy closer to its frictionless first-best allocation (in line with the logic of the second best).

A similarly benign view of bubbles underlies analyses of global imbalances, whereas large current account deficits of the United States reflect asymmetries in the development of financial markets across regions of the world. In some of these models, the US current account imbalance is an implication of excess demand for (safe) financial assets. Under some circumstances, bubbles may raise the supply of these assets, with beneficial effects at the global level (see, for example, Caballero et al., 2008).

These considerations are by no means meant to feed scepticism on the promises of a research agenda that stresses credit constraints. On the contrary, this type of financial friction is bound to be a key ingredient for developing models where financial imperfections cause economic misallocation and instability. Suitable models, however, will need to be explicit on which types of misallocation/distortion are most relevant beyond the presence of credit constraints. An example is provided by heterogeneous sector and/or agent models, where due to the interaction of financial distortions with macro dynamics, in equilibrium, financial resources are channelled towards inefficient use (see for example, Aoki et al., 2009a, 2009b). Within these frameworks, bubbles and mispricing can amplify this mechanism, misdirecting the allocation of resources, and potentially create instability.

Even independent of credit constraints, much can be learnt from exploring the behaviour of economies where financial markets are not perfect. As a general property of economies in which financial markets are incomplete, limited risk-sharing means that the wealth effects of shocks may translate into large mispricing and global demand imbalances across individuals, regions and countries, which in turn may raise issues about the conduct of stabilization policy. In joint work with Luca Dedola and Sylvain Leduc (Corsetti et al., 2008), for instance, we reconsidered standard welfare-based models of flexible inflation targeting, precisely making the point that if markets are not complete, the policy loss function derived from first principles includes among its objective more than the output gap and inflation. Namely, it also includes a term in price misalignment, whatever its origin, and a term in demand imbalances, driven by inefficient divergences in wealth in response to cyclical disturbances.

FINANCIAL FRICTIONS, OVER-BORROWING AND ASSET PRICE (EXCHANGE RATE) MISALIGNMENT

This section characterizes misalignment and over-borrowing/over-lending in response to fundamental shocks as a general feature inherent to incomplete market economies. Drawing on joint work with Dedola and Leduc on the international business cycle and optimal policy design in an open economy (Corsetti et al., 2008; 2010a, 2010b), this chapter builds on a stylized example of a two-country model economy, intentionally abstracting from financial intermediation, credit constraints, bubbles and the like. The reason is not, of course, to deny the need for better models of the financial sector, but to underscore that market distortions with financial imperfections are pervasive even in the absence of frictions related to illiquidity and/or bubbles.

The main focus is on the economics of sustained booms in demand as a consequence of signals about future economic developments. In the model, a country can be hit by an idiosyncratic 'news shock', in the form of informative signals about the future profitability of domestic firms. For instance, new information may make agents believe that the firms operating in one country will become more profitable at some point in the future because of the ongoing adoption of innovative technologies. To expose my argument in the simplest possible way, however, the discussion below will be carried out by abstracting from the production process altogether.

The core of the analysis consists in tracing the effect of 'news shocks' depending on the structure of financial markets. In one specification of the model, residents in both countries are assumed to hold well-diversified portfolios of equities, providing perfect insurance against production risk. In a second specification, agents can only trade one non-contingent bond among each other – that is, they can only borrow from each other at the market interest rate, so that risk-sharing is not perfect. Using a standard model, the value added of this chapter consists in spelling out key comparative properties of the transmission of fundamental shocks with perfect and imperfect risk-sharing, which are usually overlooked in standard analyses.

The Model Set-up

A short description of the model is as follows. The world consists of two economies, 'Home' and 'Foreign', denoted H and F, respectively, each supplying a country-specific good. Let Y_H and Y_F denote Home and Foreign (tradable) output. The supply of these goods $\{Y_H, Y_F\}$ varies randomly. In each country, a continuum of households derives utility from consuming both goods. All prices are flexible. For simplicity, the time subscripts are omitted when all variables are contemporary (that is, they would all have a time t subscript).

The consumption basket of the Home representative consumer includes both Home and Foreign goods, according to the following constant elasticity of substation (CES) aggregator:

$$C = \left[a_H^{1/\phi} C_H^{\frac{\phi-1}{\phi}} + a_F^{1/\phi} C_F^{\frac{\phi-1}{\phi}} \right]^{\frac{\phi}{\phi-1}}, \quad \phi > 0 \tag{3.1}$$

where $C_{H,t}$ $(C_{F,t})$ is the domestic consumption of Home- (Foreign-) produced goods, a_H the share of the domestically produced good in the Home consumption expenditure, and a_F the corresponding share of imported goods, with $a_F = 1 - a_H$. $a_H > 1/2$ indexes 'Home bias' in consumption, that is, a preference by local residents for local goods. ϕ denotes the elasticity of substitution between Home and Foreign goods: the higher ϕ, the more homogeneous the goods. Analogously, in the foreign country:

$$C^* = \left[(a_H^*)^{1/\phi} (C_H^*)^{\frac{\phi-1}{\phi}} + (a_F^*)^{1/\phi} (C_F^*)^{\frac{\phi-1}{\phi}} \right]^{\frac{\phi}{\phi-1}} \tag{3.2}$$

where $C_{H,t}^*$ $(C_{F,t}^*)$ is the consumption of Home- (Foreign-) produced goods by Foreign households. Home bias in consumption is $a_F^* = 1 - a_H^* > 1/2$.

Let $P_{H,t}$ $(P_{F,t})$ denote the price of the Home (Foreign) goods in the Home currency. When starred, these prices are expressed in F- currency units. Let ε denote the nominal exchange rate, defined as units of Home currency in terms of a unit of Foreign currency. According to the conventional definition, the terms of trade (TOT) are the relative price of Foreign goods imported by the H-economy in terms of Home goods exported to the F-economy

$$TOT = \frac{P_F}{\varepsilon P_H^*} \tag{3.3}$$

In this simple model economy, the TOT coincides with the relative price of tradables.

Let P denote the price of domestic consumption in the Home economy. The welfare-based price index P is defined as the minimum expenditure needed to buy one unit of consumption good $C = 1$, given market prices. By setting up a cost minimization problem, one can easily derive the demand by H households for each good:

$$C_H = a_H\left(\frac{P_H}{P}\right)^{-\phi} C \qquad C_F = a_F\left(\frac{P_F}{P}\right)^{-\phi} C \qquad (3.4)$$

and a welfare-based consumption price index (CPI) denoted by P:

$$P = [a_H P_H^{1-\phi} + (1 - a_H) P_F^{1-\phi}]^{\frac{1}{1-\phi}} \qquad (3.5)$$

The foreign analogue, denoted P^*, is:

$$P^* = [(1 - a_F^*)(P_H^*)^{1-\phi} + a_F^*(P_F^*)^{1-\phi}]^{\frac{1}{1-\phi}} \qquad (3.6)$$

The relative price of consumption is the real exchange rate, RER.[7] Under the law of one price, the real exchange rate and the terms of trade in our economy are related to each other:

$$RER \equiv \frac{\varepsilon P^*}{P} = \left[\frac{(1 - a_F^*) P_H^{*1-\phi} + a_F^* P_F^{1-\phi}}{a_H P_H^{*1-\phi} + (1 - a_H) P_F^{1-\phi}}\right]^{\frac{1}{1-\phi}}$$

$$= \left[\frac{(1 - a_F^*) + a_F^* TOT^{1-\phi}}{a_H + (1 - a_H) TOT^{1-\phi}}\right]^{\frac{1}{1-\phi}} \qquad (3.7)$$

an expression that becomes much easier to interpret if we consider its log-linear approximation around a symmetric equilibrium:

$$\widetilde{RER} = (a_F^* + a_H - 1)\widetilde{TOT} = (2a_H - 1)\widetilde{TOT} \qquad (3.8)$$

where a tilde ($\sim$) means that variables are expressed in percentage deviations from the steady state.

Preferences are symmetrical in both economies. In the home country, the utility of the representative agent is intertemporal:

$$E_t \sum_{s=0}^{\infty} \beta^s U(C_{t+s}) = E_0 \sum_{s=0}^{\infty} \beta^s \frac{C_{t+s}^{1-\sigma} - 1}{1 - \sigma} \qquad (3.9)$$

where $1/\sigma$ is the intertemporal elasticity of substitution, and we use subscripts to indicate time. The individual flow budget constraint is:

$$B_{H,t+1} + \int q_{H,t}(s_{t+1}) B_{H,t+1}(s_{t+1}) ds_{t+1} \leq (1 + i_t) B_{H,t} + B_{H,t} + P_{H,t} Y_{H,t}$$

$$- P_{H,t} C_{H,t} - P_{F,t} C_{F,t}$$

where $B_{H,t}$ is the holdings of state-contingent claims priced at $q_{H,t}$, paying off one unit of domestic currency in the realized state of the world as of t, s_t, and i_t is the yield on a domestic nominal bond $B_{H,t}$ paid at the beginning of period t in domestic currency but known at time $t - 1$.

At the aggregate level, the resource constraint is:

$$Y_H = C_H + C_H^* \qquad Y_F^* = C_F + C_F^* \tag{3.10}$$

Holding the law of one price, total demand for good H and F can be written as:

$$Y_H = \left(\frac{P_{H,t}}{P_t}\right)^{-\phi} (a_H C_t + a_H^* RER_t^\phi C_t^*) \tag{3.11}$$

$$Y_F^* = \left(\frac{P_{F,t}}{P_t}\right)^{-\phi} (a_F C_t + RER_t^\psi a_F^* C_t^*)$$

Having defined the structure of the model, I can now delve into an analysis of allocations differing by the structure of the asset market. Specifically, I will contrast economies with complete markets with economies only trading a non-contingent bond across borders.

Roots and Consequences of Inefficient (Over) Borrowing and Lending

The market allocation in the case of complete financial markets identifies the appropriate welfare benchmark against which to define inefficient, excessive borrowing and lending. In a one-good world, if a complete set of Arrow–Debreu securities are traded across border (so that households can invest in as many assets as there are states of the world), marginal utility growth is equalized across countries in any contingency. Given that consumption baskets are not realistically identical and that PPP does not hold, one needs to account for differences in the price of consumption. By building on this basic theoretical result, David Backus and Gregor Smith (1993) combine the Euler equations for the Arrow–Debreu Home and Foreign securities to show that with perfect risk-sharing the ratio of Home-to-Foreign marginal utility of consumption is tightly linked to the real exchange rate, namely,

$$RER = \frac{U_C^*}{U_C} = \left(\frac{C}{C^*}\right)^\sigma \tag{3.12}$$

Taking a log-linear approximation of this expression, again in the neighbourhood of a symmetric equilibrium with $a_F^* = a_H$, we obtain the following key condition, characterizing perfect risk-sharing:

$$\sigma(\widetilde{C}^{fb} - \widetilde{C^*}^{fb}) = \widetilde{RER}^{fb} \tag{3.13}$$

where the superscript fb indicates that, in our simple model, prices and quantities in such allocation are 'first-best'.

Given the above condition (note that I have included no preference shocks in the analysis),[8] perfect risk-sharing implies that relative consumption and the real exchange rate be perfectly correlated. This is contrary to some popular but incorrect views, stating that perfect insurance should produce perfect correlation of consumption across individuals/countries. As apparent from the model, perfect correlation of consumption only obtains under the extreme, counterfactual assumption of purchasing power parity – whereas with identical consumption baskets ($a_H = a_F^*$), the real exchange rate is identically equal to 1, and thus invariant to shocks. In general, with the relative price of consumption changing in response to shocks, perfect risk-sharing implies that demand should be relatively high where the price of consumption is relatively low (Gravelle and Rees, 1992) – that is, in the country whose currency is relatively weak in real terms.

So, suppose that international financial markets are developed enough to ensure that agents can efficiently share production risk across borders – for example, suppose all households invest in a well-diversified portfolio of Home and Foreign equities.[9] What happens when, in reaction to a 'news shock', agents anticipate higher output in the Home country in the future? To answer that question, let us inspect the equilibrium relations between consumption and output on the one hand, and the terms of trade and output on the other, that can be derived in an economy with perfect risk-sharing. These are:

$$(\widetilde{C}^{fb} - \widetilde{C^*}^{fb}) = \frac{2a_H - 1}{[1 - (2a_H - 1)^2]\phi\sigma + (2a_H - 1)^2}(\widetilde{Y}_H^{fb} - \widetilde{Y}_F^{fb}) \tag{3.14}$$

$$\widetilde{TOT}^{fb} = \frac{\sigma}{[1 - (2a_H - 1)^2]\phi\sigma + (2a_H - 1)^2}(\widetilde{Y}_H^{fb} - \widetilde{Y}_F^{fb}) \tag{3.15}$$

Observe first that the coefficients on the right-hand side of both equations are positive. With perfect risk-sharing, Home consumption necessarily rises relative to Foreign consumption, and the Home terms of trade necessarily deteriorate in response to an increase in Home relative to Foreign output.

Most crucially, however, observe also that all the variables in the above expressions are contemporaneous. This is a key property of the complete market allocation in the above model: current relative consumption and current relative prices (both the terms of trade and the real exchange rates) do not depend at all on expectations of future output. In response to 'news shocks', there is no change in these variables. The reason is straightforward. Namely, if global portfolios are well diversified, the anticipation of future high profits in a region raises wealth everywhere in the world economy. In relative terms, there would be no demand imbalance. Minus supply reactions in the short run (the 'news' is about future, not current output), there is no need for a change in the terms of trade and the real exchange rate. The only variable that must react to the news is the interest rate, r_t, as the Euler equations in the asset markets imply that the current price of default-free bonds adjusts in anticipation of higher future consumption:

$$\frac{1}{1 + r_t} = \beta E_t \left[\frac{U_C(C_{t+1})}{U_C(C_t)} \right] \tag{3.16}$$

Intuitively, in equilibrium, the real rate must rebalance world demand towards future periods when production is expected to be more abundant – that is, the intertemporal price of consumption must change to lead households to postpone (optimally) their spending plan.

Now, let us contrast the market equilibrium with the perfect markets just analysed, with the equilibrium in economies where portfolios are *not* well diversified and markets are incomplete. To make the main point of the analysis as clear as possible, assume that preferences are logarithmic, and the pure rate of time preference is zero (that is, $\sigma = \beta = 1$). Moreover, agents can trade internationally a non-contingent bond only – that is, they can borrow and lend cross border, but cannot write insurance contracts (see also Corsetti et al., 2008). Furthermore, for notational simplicity, time is collapsed into two periods, the 'present' and the 'future', dubbed the short-run (SR) and the long-run (LR). Under these assumptions and notational convention, it can be shown that both relative consumption and the terms of trade move with both current and anticipated future output as follows:

$$(\widehat{C^{SR}} - \widehat{C^{*SR}}) = (2a_H - 1) \left[\frac{(\widehat{Y_H^{SR}} - \widehat{Y_H^{LR}}) - (\widehat{Y_F^{SR}} - \widehat{Y_F^{LR}})}{1 - 4a_H(1 - a_H)(1 - \phi)} \right]$$

$$+ \left(1 + \frac{2a_H(\phi - 1)}{2a_H - 1}\right)\frac{\widetilde{Y_H^{LR}} - \widetilde{Y_F^{LR}}}{1 - 2a_H(1 - \phi)}\Bigg]$$

$$\widetilde{TOT^{SR}} = \frac{(\widetilde{Y_H^{SR}} - \widetilde{Y_H^{LR}}) - (\widetilde{Y_F^{SR}} - \widetilde{Y_F^{LR}})}{1 - 4a_H(1 - a_H)(1 - \phi)} + \frac{\widetilde{Y_H^{LR}} - \widetilde{Y_F^{LR}}}{1 - 2a_H(1 - \phi)} \quad (3.17)$$

Current variables now respond to both current and future anticipated movements in relative output. With news shocks only, $\widetilde{Y_H^{SR}} = \widetilde{Y_F^{SR}} = 0$, the above expressions become:

$$(\widetilde{C^{SR}} - \widetilde{C^{*SE}}) = \Bigg[\frac{[2a_H - 1]}{[1 - 2a_H(1 - \phi)]}\left(1 + \frac{2a_H(\phi - 1)}{2a_H - 1}\right)$$

$$- \frac{2a_H - 1}{[1 - 4a_H(1 - a_H)(1 - \phi)]}\Bigg](\widetilde{Y_H^{LR}} - \widetilde{Y_F^{LR}})$$

$$\widetilde{TOT} = \Bigg[\frac{1}{1 - 2a_H(1 - \phi)} - \frac{1}{1 - 4a_H(1 - a_H)(1 - \phi)}\Bigg](\widetilde{Y_H^{LR}} - \widetilde{Y_F^{LR}}) \quad (3.18)$$

Only in a special case, when the trade elasticity happens to be one ($\phi = 1$), do the coefficients in front of relative output become zero in both expressions (3.18).[10] As is well known (see Cole and Obstfeld, 1991), under this restriction on the parameters' values, the allocation with and without financial markets coincide by virtue of the automatic insurance provided by terms of trade movements.[11] In general, however, and different from the case of complete markets above, news shocks will have contemporaneous effects on the market allocation and induce exchange rate volatility.

When markets are incomplete, news shocks stretch, so to speak, the dual role of the exchange rate as equilibrium price in the goods and the assets market. The exchange rate jumps upon the arrival of information about future output and moves so as to clear the goods market in response to an increase in domestic demand. Indeed, with home bias ($a_H > 1/2$), both a high trade elasticity (ϕ sufficiently above 1) or a low trade elasticity (ϕ sufficiently below 1) imply that the coefficient in front of future (Home to Foreign) relative output is positive in the relative-consumption expression (3.18), while negative in the terms of trade expression. This means that Home consumption expands, and the Home terms of trade (and real exchange rate) strengthen, in response to anticipations of a larger Home output in the future. Observe that in a low elasticity environment, the two coefficients relating relative output to relative consumption and the terms of trade can become quite large. For any given news shock, there will be much larger effects on relative demand, a larger current account, and a larger real appreciation, relative to economies characterized by a high trade elasticity.

The transmission mechanism just described is a textbook example of optimal consumption smoothing. Anticipations of output gains in the Home country necessarily translate into an asymmetric wealth shock in favour of Home residents. Since they have access to the international bonds market, Home agents are able to raise their current consumption by borrowing abroad, generating an external trade deficit. To the extent that the composition of national demand is biased towards domestic goods (which is indeed the case, especially in relatively large economies such as the US), higher demand results in higher prices, that is, real currency appreciation in the short run.

The equilibrium just described is also familiar from the vantage point of conventional models in the Mundell–Fleming tradition (see, for example, Marston, 1985). In this framework, real appreciation in response to (exogenous) demand movements is typically seen as a channel through which the domestic economy is naturally 'stabilized'. If domestic demand rises in anticipation of future income, the real appreciation is expected to counteract domestic 'over-heating' by 'crowding-out net exports'.[12]

Relative to these conventional considerations, nonetheless, the simple algebra above makes it clear that appreciation and external deficits are in fact highly inefficient. In a well-functioning market economy in which agents hold well-diversified portfolios, the country expected to produce more output (that is, with more productive firms) would not become a net importer to sustain a consumption demand boom. Over time, when output increases, if anything it will experience falling, rather than rising, product prices.

In more general model specifications with capital accumulation, of course, a trade deficit may emerge also in efficient economies in response to expectations of future gains in productivity (this would be so, for instance, in the presence of a sufficiently tight 'time-to-build' technological constraint on capital accumulation). But trade deficits in this case would be driven by the expansion of investment into efficient capital, not by inefficient movements in cross-country consumption. In other words, what is at stake is not the desirability of trade deficits/surpluses per se, but excessive borrowing and lending as an undesirable consequence of economic distortions.

It may be worth stressing, for instance, that intertemporal trade in a distorted economy provides no safeguard/insurance against the possibility that the anticipations of future output gains produced by the news shock turn out to be wrong ex post (that is, that the higher output does not materialize in the future). Let us focus again on our model economy without capital. With international borrowing and lending through trade in bonds, *wrong* expectations today create the premise for costly adjustment in the future – the Home country ends up with the cost of servicing additional foreign debt without the benefit of a higher output. In contrast, with efficient portfolio diversification ensuring perfect risk-sharing, news shocks produce no change in relative consumption in the short run, no external deficit, hence no need for costly adjustment in the future.[13] Also in this dimension, the main message is that the financial distortions of intertemporal trade may exacerbate inefficiencies.

In general, the full extent of the distortions can be assessed by solving for the constrained Pareto-efficient allocation in an economy with incomplete markets.[14] The solution will generally prescribe agents to react much less to anticipations of future output gains relative to the market allocation. Namely, the social planner will mandate agents to react only to the changes in output (now and expected in the future), which are efficient from a global perspective – not to output movements that depart from the first-best allocation (see Corsetti et al., 2010b).

RETHINKING POLICY MODELS

The model discussed in the previous section is admittedly too simple to get into the nuances of policy design. Yet the analysis conveys a key message underlying much of the recent work on stabilization policy, carried out in the framework of large macro models. The model economy characterized above, in particular, illustrates the core theoretical foundations of cross-border imbalances and misalignment in the context of micro-founded models for policy assessment, as discussed in detail in the joint work by Corsetti, Dedola and Leduc (2010a, 2010b) describing optimal monetary policy in an open economy. In addition to the output gap as defined in standard (new-Keynesian) monetary theory, a model of global stabilization naturally includes gaps in international relative prices, and a gap in international demand.

Relative price gaps identify a theory-based measure of misalignment, encompassing the real exchange rate (the relative price of consumption), the terms of trade (the relative price of imports in terms of exports), as well as differences in prices of similar products across borders (that is, failure of the law of one price). By way of example, the terms of trade gap are defined as the log-difference between the values of the terms of trade in the distorted market allocation and in the efficient (first-best) allocation:

$$TOTgap = \log\frac{TOT}{TOT^{fb}} \tag{3.19}$$

It is worth stressing that inefficiencies in international relative prices reflect more than nominal rigidities. As the stylized economy in the previous section clarifies, for flexible prices as well, the terms of trade (and the real exchange rate) are generally inefficient if markets are not perfect.

Note that the relevant misalignment captured by the relative price gap does not necessarily coincide with deviations from the 'equilibrium real exchange rate' typically studied by international organizations in relation to long-term objectives of 'external and internal balances'. Rather, the price gap is defined conceptually and analytically like the output gap, over short as well as long horizons. Like the output gap, it is difficult to estimate in practice.

By the same token, the relative demand gap provides a theory-based measure of cross-border imbalances:

$$Dgap = \log\left[RER\frac{U_C}{U_C^*}\right] = \log\left[RER\left(\frac{C}{C^*}\right)^{-\sigma}\right] \tag{3.20}$$

The so-defined gap is equal to zero when risk-sharing is perfect. A non-zero value instead points to situations in which, at the current real exchange rate, consumption in one country is inefficiently high relative to consumption in the rest of the world, which evolves into inefficient current account deficits and capital inflows, as well as into general misallocation of production at domestic and international levels.

These gaps are relevant to policy making, in the same way that output gaps and inflation are. The welfare-based objective function for the analysis of optimal policy can (and should) in fact be written as a function of all these gaps. In addition to the adverse consequences of nominal price frictions, it is natural for policy makers to confront the consequences of financial frictions (incomplete markets), causing over-borrowing, inefficient movements in international relative prices, as well as sub-optimal employment and consumption levels, relative to the efficient allocation benchmark. Given the set of the available policy instruments, stabilization policy needs to be optimized over the trade-offs among the competing objectives, meaning, closing all the welfare-relevant gaps.

Some striking results concern monetary policy. Corsetti et al. (2010a, 2010b) show that in more general versions of the incomplete market economy above (accounting for an elastic labour supply, production and sticky prices), there are reasonable parameter configurations for which monetary policy is particularly effective in preventing both mispricing (inefficient appreciation) and over-borrowing (global imbalances in demand). Specifically, under international policy coordination, monetary authorities optimally 'lean against the wind' of appreciation and external imbalances, improving the world allocation at small costs in terms of short-run domestic inflation: price stability remains the overriding objective in the medium run. Importantly, the optimal conduct of monetary policy does *not* imply unreasonable variations in interest rates. Indeed, in their calculations, the variance of the interest rate is quite contained, relative to a suboptimal regime of inflation targeting that ignores these important dimensions of the optimal monetary policy.

The degree to which monetary policy is effective as a stabilization tool varies across economies with different structures. Under some parameterizations of the model, monetary instruments are optimally geared mostly towards closing output gaps and keeping prices stable – the traditional, inward-looking objectives. But even so, there are other tools available to policy makers to address potential concerns. When monetary policy is ineffective, or to the extent that its use is deemed inappropriate relative to the task of correcting excessive borrowing and misalignments, alternative instruments may and should be considered, ranging from fiscal policy (raising issues in fiscal and monetary interactions), to regulation and supervision of financial markets.

The recent evolution in the literature on open economies provides a clear example of the ongoing shift in theory and policy analysis, catalysed by the global crisis. Before the crisis, most of the discussion was framed in models predicting a high degree of equilibrium risk-sharing, thus centring the analysis almost exclusively on the distortions due to nominal rigidities (see, for example, the discussion in Corsetti, 2008). Also in this context, misalignments in international pricing and consumption demand are possible, but these exist only as a by-product of sticky prices – for instance, with complete markets, the demand gap (3.20) is always identically equal to zero. Once nominal distortions are redressed, the economy operates near first-best. Indeed, in this context, it is easy to produce examples of the 'divine coincidence' discussed by Olivier Blanchard and Jordi Galí (2010), whereas one instrument is enough to close all the relevant gaps in the economy. Heterogeneity across borders appears to raise no specific policy issues – see, for example, the conclusions from the collection of essays in Jordi Galí and Mark Gertler (2009) on the 'International dimensions of monetary policy'. The new contributions in international economics are clearly moving away from this premise.

More contributions need to be written in this area of economics. By way of example, the analysis above assumes that asset prices – namely, the exchange rate – react to fundamentals only. Indeed, in the model, the real exchange rate moves only in reaction to new information about current and future fundamentals – it acts as a 'shock absorber'. Yet, its adjustment is inefficient because of the distortions plaguing the market economy. An important new avenue of research could provide workable frameworks where asset prices are driven by bubbles, identifying plausible conditions for these to arise, and especially clarifying the scope for addressing them via alternative policy strategies.

While the economic example used in this text draws on international economics, my own field of specialization, it should be clear that similar analytical schemes could be developed to understand income and production dynamics, accounting for sectoral or regional differences, or heterogeneity in wealth and/or participation in financial markets across agents within the same national economy, sharing the same currency. Also in these contexts, inefficient markets would, in general, be associated with demand imbalances (excessive borrowing) among heterogeneous agents and misalignments in relative prices – although exchange rate movements, in their unique function of clearing both the goods and the asset markets, would obviously be out of the picture.

NOTES

1. I thank Charles Gottlieb and Saverio Simonelli for comments.
2. On account of the crisis, there is a long list of excellent contributions. The chapter relies mostly on my own experience (working in the European Economic Advisory Group at CESifo, 2009), as well as on the contributions of Markus Brunnermeier (2009), Gary Gorton (2009), and John Taylor (2009), among others.
3. See http://www.nyu.edu/econ/user/gertlerm/gertlerboereadinglist.pdf.
4. Lawrence Peter 'Yogi' Berra (born 12 May, 1925) is not only widely regarded as one of the greatest catchers in baseball history: his legendary quotations provide an endless source of wit and wisdom in graduate schools in economics and other disciplines in the USA.
5. A very incomplete list includes Bianchi and Mendoza (2010), Brunnermeier and Sannikov (2011), Curdia and Woodford (2010), Geanakoplos (2010b) and Lorenzoni (2009), among many others.
6. In addition to the list above, see also Bianchi (2011), Christiano et al. (2009), Geanakoplos (2010a), Gertler and Kiyotaki (2010).
7. Note that if the law of one price holds in the goods markets, once converted into a common currency, the price of each good will be identical everywhere in the world economy: $P_H = \varepsilon P_H^*$, $P_F = \varepsilon P_F^*$. Then, if the Home and Foreign consumption baskets were identical, namely, if there was no Home bias in the world economy, $a_H = 1 - a_F^*$, the price of consumption would also be equalized across countries and purchasing power parity (PPP) would hold: $P = \varepsilon P^*$. In what follows, home bias will be assumed throughout the analysis.
8. With taste shocks, the strict link between the relative marginal utilities and the relative price of consumption in (3.12), implied by perfect risk-sharing, would not necessarily translate into a strict link between quantities and prices (as in (3.13)).
9. When production/output uncertainty is the most important source of risk (that is,

shocks to tastes are absent or small enough), it can be shown that the perfect risk-sharing condition above would hold approximately, even if there were not as many financial markets as states of the world. Agents in each country could nevertheless invest in a well diversified portfolio of domestic and foreign stocks, so as to share income generated by firms everywhere in the world. In other words, perfect diversification of equity would be enough to guarantee full insurance against production risk.

10. See Corsetti et al. (2010a) for a discussion of more general conditions in the log-linearized version of the model.

11. With unit elasticity, any increase in Home output is matched by a proportional fall in the international price of domestic goods, raising the purchasing power of foreign residents in line with that of domestic residents. Relative (Home to Foreign) incomes remain in fixed ratio.

12. But this reasoning downplays the first-order implications of the boost in Home private wealth and demand from favourable movements of the terms of trade in the short run – in our example, it is inherently connected to the ability of agents to borrow from abroad against future income. Indeed, the structure of traditional models fails to account for the fact that real appreciation also has a positive feedback effect on the asymmetric wealth effects from shocks, feeding external imbalances.

13. Of course, with capital accumulation, time-to-build or adjustment cost in investment may mean that investment reacts immediately to the news shock. This may also create costly adjustment over time if the anticipation of higher future productivity turns out to be wrong.

14. Specifically, this is the solution to the problem of the social planner, maximizing a weighted sum of the expected utilities of the Home and Foreign residents, subject to the same informational and institutional constraints faced by agents in the incomplete market economy.

REFERENCES

Aoki, K., G. Benigno and N. Kiyotaki (2009a), 'Adjusting to capital account liberalization', mimeo, Princeton University.

Aoki, K., G. Benigno and N. Kiyotaki (2009b), 'Capital flows and asset prices', mimeo, Princeton University.

Backus, D.K. and G.W. Smith (1993), 'Consumption and real exchange rates in dynamic economies with non-traded goods', *Journal of International Economics*, **35**, 297–316.

Bianchi, J. (2011), 'Overborrowing and systemic externalities in the business cycle', *American Economic Review*, **101**(7), 3400–426.

Bianchi, J. and E. Mendoza (2010), 'Overborrowing, financial crises and macroprudential policy', NBER Working Paper 16091.

Blanchard, O. and J. Galí (2010), 'Labor market frictions and monetary policy: a new Keynesian model with unemployment', *American Economic Journal: Macroeconomics*, **2**(2), 1–30.

Bloom, N. (2009), 'The impact of uncertainty shocks', *Econometrica*, **77**(3), 623–85.

Bolton, P. and O. Jeanne (2011), 'Sovereign default risk and bank fragility in financially integrated economies', NBER Working Paper 1689.

Brunnermeier, M. (2009), 'Deciphering the liquidity and credit crunch 2007–08', *Journal of Economic Perspectives*, **23**(1), 77–100.

Brunnermeier, M. and Y. Sannikov (2011), 'A macroeconomic model with a financial sector', mimeo, Princeton University.

Caballero, R. (2010), 'A caricature (model) of the world economy', paper prepared for the Ninth Macroeconomic Policy Research Workshop, 'Understanding financial frictions', Magyar Nemzeti Bank, Budapest.

Caballero, R., E. Farhi and P.O. Gourinchas (2008), 'Financial crash, commodity prices, and global imbalances', *Brookings Papers on Economic Activity*, Fall, pp. 1–55.

Christiano, L., R. Motto and M. Rostagno (2009), 'Financial factors in economic fluctuations', mimeo, Northwestern University.

Cole, H.L. and M. Obstfeld (1991), 'Commodity trade and international risk sharing: how much do financial markets matter?', *Journal of Monetary Economics*, **28**, 3–24.

Corsetti, G. (2008), 'New open economy macroeconomics', in Steven N. Durlauf and Lawrence E. Blume (eds), *The New Palgrave Dictionary of Economics*, 2nd edn, Basingstoke: Palgrave Macmillan.

Corsetti, G., L. Dedola and S. Leduc (2008), 'International risk sharing and the transmission of productivity shocks', *Review of Economic Studies*, **75**, 443–73.

Corsetti, G., L. Dedola and S. Leduc (2010a), 'Optimal monetary policy in open economies', in B.M. Friedman and M. Woodford (eds), *Handbook of Monetary Economics*, vol. 3, Amsterdam: Elsevier, pp. 861–933.

Corsetti, G., L. Dedola and S. Leduc (2010b), 'Demand imbalances, exchange rates misalignment and monetary policy', mimeo, Cambridge University.

Curdia, V. and M. Woodford (2010), 'Credit spreads and monetary policy', *Journal of Money Credit and Banking*, **42**(S1), 3–35.

Eichenbaum, M. (2010), 'Shortcomings in macro modeling strategies: what have we learned from the crisis?', paper presented at the Sixth ECB Central Banking Conference, 'Approaches to monetary policy revisited – lessons from the crisis', Frankfurt-am-Main, 18–19 November.

European Economic Advisory Group at CESifo (2009), 'Report on the European economy', Munich: CESifo.

Fernández-Villaverde, J., P. Guerrón-Quintana, J. Rubio-Ramírez and M. Uribe (2011), 'Risk matters: the real effects of volatility shocks', *American Economic Review*, **101**(6), 2530–61.

Galí, J. and M. Gertler (eds) (2009), *International Dimension of Monetary Policy*, London: The University of Chicago Press.

Geanakoplos, J. (2010a), 'Solving the present crisis and managing the leverage cycle', *Federal Reserve Bank of New York Economic Policy Review*, August, pp. 101–31.

Geanakoplos, J. (2010b), 'The leverage cycle', in D. Acemoglu, K. Rogoff and M. Woodford (eds), *NBER Macroeconomics Annual 2009*, vol. 24, Chicago: University of Chicago Press, pp. 1–65.

Gertler, M. and N. Kiyotaki (2010), 'Financial intermediation and credit policy in business cycle analysis', in B.M. Friedman and M. Woodford (eds), *Handbook of Monetary Economics*, vol. 3, Amsterdam: Elsevier, pp. 547–99.

Gorton, G. (2009), 'The panic of 2007', in *Maintaining Stability in a Changing Financial System*, Proceedings of the 2008 Jackson Hole Conference, Federal Reserve Bank of Kansas City.

Gravelle, H. and R. Rees (1992), *Microeconomics*, London: Longman.

Greenlaw, D., J. Hatzius, A. Kashyap and H.S. Shin (2008), 'Leveraged losses: lessons from the mortgage market meltdown', US Monetary Policy Forum Report no. 2.

Gruss, B. and K. Mertens (2010), 'Regime switching interest rates and fluctuations in emerging markets', mimeo, Cornell University.

Lorenzoni, G. (2009), 'A theory of demand shocks', *American Economic Review*, **99**(5), 2050–84.

Marston, R. (1985), 'Stabilization policies in open economies', in R.W. Jones and P.B. Kenen (eds), *Handbook of International Economics*, Amsterdam: North Holland, pp.859–916.

Martin, A. and J. Ventura (2011), 'Theoretical notes on bubbles and the current crisis', *IMF Economic Review*, **59**, 6–40.

Obstfeld, M. and K. Rogoff (2010), 'Global imbalances and the financial crisis: products of common causes', CEPR Discussion Paper 7606.

Reinhart, C. and K. Rogoff (2009), *This Time is Different: Eight Centuries of Financial Folly*, Princeton, NJ: Princeton University Press.

Shiller, R.J. (2008), *The Subprime Solution: How Today's Global Financial Crisis Happened, and What to Do About it*, Princeton, NJ: Princeton University Press.

Taylor, J. (2009), *Getting Off Track: How Government Actions and Interventions Caused, Prolonged, and Worsened the Financial Crisis*, Stanford, CA: Hoover Institution Press.

Woodford, M. (2010), 'Financial intermediation and macroeconomic analysis', *Journal of Economic Perspectives*, **24**(4), 21–44.

4. Try again, macroeconomists

Jean-Bernard Chatelain

INTRODUCTION

The world financial and economic crisis that broke out in the summer of 2007 has sparked ground-breaking thinking in the field of macroeconomics and finance. The purpose of this chapter is to assess where most macroeconomists are in relation to those ideas.

I will begin with a description of the conditions that led to a great reversal of weakly regulated international finance to strongly regulated international finance for the period 1945–73. These days the bargaining power of international banking is too strong to observe the same kind of trend. Weakly regulated international capital markets are likely to persist in the next decades. There is thus a high probability that the financial crisis will lead to very costly world recessions in terms of welfare. For that reason, macroeconomic theory must deal with weakly regulated international capital markets, which lead to a systematically erroneous valuation of assets (the efficient market hypothesis is not valid).

The second section deals with the best theoretical models that were available before the crisis began in 2007 for dealing with imperfect capital markets: the 'financial accelerator' dynamic stochastic general equilibrium (DSGE) models (Kiyotaki and Moore, 1997; Bernanke et al., 1999; Bernanke and Gertler, 2000, 2001; Iacoviello, 2005). These models considered bankruptcy costs and credit rationing for non-financial firms and, for some of them, banking firms. They assumed that debt was backed by the future valuation of collateral. They maintained the assumption, however, that the expected valuation of collateral was made according to its fundamental value. In other words, they assumed imperfect capital markets along with the efficient financial market hypothesis. I will list seven inconsistencies of these models with respect to their ability to describe the economic crisis.

The third section emphasizes that five key assumptions must be changed in order to change mainstream macroeconomics: (1) the absence of a confidence crisis or liquidity crisis with systemic bankruptcy risk; (2) the efficient financial market hypothesis where the price of an asset is always equal to its fundamental value; (3) the no-Ponzi Game condition, such that the growth rate of public and private debt must always be below a real interest rate; (4) the *linearization* around the equilibrium of the *unique* stable path leading to a *unique* long-term equilibrium, reducing the study of macroeconomic dynamics to qualitatively similar responses of macroeconomic variables to shocks; (5) the unconstrained Euler equation for households, where the growth rate of consumption depends only on the real interest rate and on the preference for smoothing consumption over time. These assumptions are compatible with the structural research programme that takes into account the Lucas critique (1976). I will then briefly sketch that the ongoing macroeconomics research may come close to our goal, but haltingly.

IT CAN HAPPEN AGAIN TOMORROW

A Great Reversal in the Regulation of International Finance?

What is expected to change in the real economy in the two decades following the crisis? Let us consider two possibilities with the following stylized facts describing two regulation regimes.

1. *Weakly regulated international finance* (regime A): international banking capital flows and offshore finance lead to widespread opacity.
   - A1. International banks that trade international assets have balance sheets that are highly uncertain (on their solvency). They may use offshore financing to hide profits (tax evasion) and losses (soft budget constraint).
   - A2. The share of assets, whose valuation is highly uncertain and never close to the fundamental value, is large.
   - A3. Incentives are there for banks to take huge risks due to the bail-out by the government of banks that are too interconnected. Banks therefore remain highly leveraged in a weakly regulated financial system.
   - A1, A2 and A3 lead to a larger probability of an expectation-driven, loss-of-confidence systemic crisis, in particular among banks, which are more aware of the risk of other banks than depositors. This could be expected to occur, say, once every three normal business cycles of eight years.

- Universal banks doing retail banking and market finance operations are likely to increase the risk of the transmission of bubbles on asset prices to the real economy through credit. Capital gains and losses on the equity market would be linked to simultaneous increases or (respectively) decreases in retail credit.
- In this context, government-owned banks able to do international finance are likely to speculate in the same way as privately owned banks, because it has become too easy to make profits and losses in the same manner as their privately owned competitors.

The benefit of this regime is a potentially better allocation of capital at the international level, along with the drawback of a higher probability of systemic risk at the world level.

2. *Strongly regulated international finance* (regime B) is an alternative regime. It implies the control of the international capital flows of large international banks, and the control of the amount of credit by large retail banks in order to limit bubbles at the national level, when this amount of credit is 'too high' or 'too low' for small and medium-sized firms or households (strong macro-prudential policy). This means that the government is highly involved in the decisions on the allocation of capital.

The drawback of the strong regulation regime B may be a misallocation of capital at the international level; its advantage is a lower probability of systemic risk at the world level.

The shift from regime A to regime B is a 'great reversal' as described by Raghuram Rajan and Luigi Zingales (2003), similar to the one that followed the Bretton Woods United Nations Monetary and Financial Conference from 1945–73, with respect to the period 1870–1940.

The Weak Bargaining Power of International Banking in 1945

Let us consider an incomplete list of the conditions under which regime B occurred after 1945, leading to a great reversal:

- immediate post-war economy with a strong government stake in the allocation of capital;
- future reconstruction plans with a strong government stake in the allocation of capital (Marshall Plan Aid), along with competition with the Soviet Union's economic system;
- capitalism in search of employment stability for wage earners, with a weaker influence of the owners of capital;

- international banking in shambles in several countries due to war and destruction;
- weak political pressure to ensure stability of exchange rates.

The Bretton Woods context occurred simultaneously with other factors that supported a great reversal in the relative bargaining power of international banking and finance:

- international capital flows decreased and were under the control of the government;
- international trade decreased widely;
- government stakes in the banking sector in the allocation of capital remained large in a number of countries (France, Japan, Germany);
- large stakes of the private banking sector were confined to national retail banking, while facing: effective direct credit control in France up to 1983, competition of nationalized financial institutions for deposits (Japanese post office), and regulatory walls against cross-state banking in the USA and against universal banking (merging retail banking with market-finance activities banking), with the Glass–Steagall Act enacted in 1933 (a law that established the Federal Deposit Insurance Corporation in the United States and introduced banking reforms).

The Bretton Woods agreements led to a large decrease in the world occurrence of financial crises for the period 1945–73, as recorded by Carmen Reinhart and Kenneth Rogoff (2009). This is a key explanation of the low frequency of world financial crises over the last 100 years. Hence, any computation of the probability of the occurrence of a world financial crisis has to deal with the relative bargaining power of international finance with respect to governments and wage earners, in particular in its ability to limit the control of international capital flows and maintain a large degree of opacity on those international capital flows.

The Strong Bargaining Power of International Banking in 2010

In 2010, the pre-conditions of the Bretton Woods era, which were already limiting the bargaining power of international banking, were obviously not met. The current economic and geopolitical framework is completely different from the immediate post-World-War-Two context of Bretton Woods in 1945. Unless, perhaps, several very large countries of the G7 default on their sovereign debt, which would leave the door open to unintended consequences, the balance of power between international finance, government and wage earners will remain in favour of international finance, with the usual international coordination problems between governments and jurisdictions playing their role.

For this reason, the G20 is currently unable to foster influential reforms limiting effectively the power of international finance. Government control of international capital flows and the aim to decrease their opacity (fighting against offshore finance) and the control of credit aggregates (which is the true objective of the euphemized macro-prudential regulation) are words that are not likely to be backed by political decisions.

Hence, international banking and finance will be in a position to maintain a non-negligible probability of a third financial and economic world crisis in the next 20 years. So it is likely to happen again, with the third global financial and economic crisis coming much sooner than 70 years down the road, and accompanied by a large output and welfare loss due to another depression for the world economy.

Furthermore, governments may need the support of bubbles in emerging markets (China and India) or on commodities, so that the market finance activities of private international banks restore the profits and the solvency of those banks much faster than through retail credit activities. As a consequence, these bubbles would allow governments to sell assets that they owned in private banks in order to support them during the liquidity crisis. This income coming back may partially limit their budget deficit and may decrease their probability of default. This could happen within three years' time, a duration that could match electoral cycles. Therefore, the support for bubbles, driven by international banking by governments, may exist as a short-term exit of sovereign default risk.

In addition, such opacity favours soft-budget constraints during crises. Imagine a bank in Ireland declaring bankruptcy at the same time as the risk premium on the sovereign debt there is high because of IMF negotiations. The ability to delay by a few months the news of the losses of the private banks by hiding them in offshore financial centres makes it possible for the government to avoid a liquidity crisis.

Because a great reversal in the regulation of international finance is not likely to happen, one business cycle over the next 30 years is likely to be driven by a world financial crisis. As a consequence, the dominant theories of business cycles (as described by DSGE models), which do not deal with world financial crises, must be revised. The overall cost of business cycles predicted by those models also needs to be revised: the costs of depressions are much higher than those of recessions. The key assumptions of these models thus need to be changed.

THE FAILURE OF DSGE MODELS WITH A FINANCIAL ACCELERATOR

The Hypothesis of the DSGE Model with a Financial Accelerator

The DSGE methodology attempts to explain aggregate business cycles. It describes gross domestic product (GDP), consumption, investment, prices, wages, employment, and interest rates, and especially the effects of monetary policy (and to a small extent, the effects of fiscal policy), on the basis of macroeconomic models derived from intertemporal utility maximization.

New-Keynesian DSGE models assume that prices are set by monopolistically competitive firms and cannot be instantaneously and costlessly adjusted. Money plays a role in the short run. The behaviour of central banks follows, for example, a Taylor rule (Smets and Wouters, 2003).

The DSGE methodology includes extensions with the 'financial accelerator' effect, which takes into account financial constraints. In this setting, households are heterogeneous: some are lenders, some are borrowers. Two key assumptions are currently used that lead to models that are relatively close in results (Kiyotaki and Moore, 1997; Bernanke et al., 1999; Bernanke and Gertler, 2000, 2001; Iacoviello, 2005).

1. The first assumption presupposes credit rationing with a collateral constraint, where debt B is limited by the collateral K, which is priced at its expected price q next period, with a cyclical maximal loan-to-value ratio m, which may depend on several characteristics Z.

$$(1 + r_t) \cdot B_t < m(Z_t) \cdot E_t(q_{t+1}) \cdot K_t$$

These characteristics Z may depend on a number of factors that have not been fully investigated up to now. For example, these variables may be related to the inter-bank liquidity market, to the liquidity provided by central banks, to imperfect competition in the banking sector, to the heterogeneity of borrowers' proportion of liquid collateral in their balance sheet, to the heterogeneity of the expectations of lenders, and so on.

The current debt/current value of the collateral is limited, with the relative capital gains growth factor over the interest rate factor,

$$\frac{B_t}{q_t K_t} < m(Z_t) \cdot \frac{1 + \dfrac{E_t(q_{t+1}) - q_t}{q_t}}{1 + r_t}$$

2. An alternative assumption states that interest rates on credit include a default premium, related to a probability of default, which increases with the debt/asset ratio, where the price of the asset may be the next-period, expected price of the asset. The probability of default matters, because there are deadweight costs in case of bankruptcy (bankruptcy costs):

$$r_t = r_0 + g\left(\frac{B_t}{\dfrac{E_t(q_{t+1})}{q_t} \cdot q_t K_t} \right)$$

The higher the current leverage, the larger the risk premium. The higher the expected growth of asset prices, the lower the risk premium.

3. Once these two equations are used, wealth accumulation, also labelled 'flow of funds' accounting equality, creates a specific dynamic relation for the financial structure (debt/assets). Typically, the models assume that new shares issues are too expensive for financially constrained firms, so that their flow of investment is financed by new debt and by internal savings.

$$q_t(K_t - K_{t-1}) = B_t - B_{t-1} + F(K_t) - (1 + r_{t-1})B_{t-1}$$

4. A final key relation is an arbitrage condition for lenders that may own some assets, and arbitrage between lending with a given return and investment in their own firm, with marginal return $G'(K)$, along with capital gains or losses on asset prices (see, for example, Kiyotaki and Moore, 1997; Miller and Stiglitz, 2010),

$$r_t = \frac{G'(K_{t,lenders}) + E_t(q_{t+1}) - q_t}{q_t}$$

When the capital gains are equal to zero, the arbitrage equation leads to the perpetual rent equation for the 'steady state' price of the asset:

$$q_t = \frac{G'(K_{t,lenders})}{r_t}$$

But the dynamic equation diverges from this steady-state price once the capital gains no longer equal zero at a given date:

$$E_t(q_{t+1}) = (1 + r_t)q_t + G'(K_{t,lenders})$$

This is an unstable dynamic equation for asset prices leading to bubbles, as soon as the price is not exactly equal to its long-term value (the net present value of all the future marginal returns discounted by the opportunity cost, which is the return on lending). This equation is at the origin of the infinite number of unstable paths, with the exception of the one that is stable for linearized systems. This is the equation that needs to be tamed by assuming that only the stable path is chosen by the economic agents. In this case, the *efficient market hypothesis* is valid: the asset price does not differ from its fundamental value at any period during the model simulations.

As such, the DSGE model with the financial accelerator assumed that capital markets were *imperfect*, with either the assumption of credit rationing or of bankruptcy costs (also labelled agency costs). They assumed, however, the *efficient market hypothesis* for the valuation of asset prices, which valued the collateral of the financial constraints.

The financial accelerator results were consistent with policy advice that is now challenged in central banks. After the Internet Stock Market Bubble (2001), the 'Jackson Hole conference' consensus that followed was that central banks should not try to stop asset price bubbles before they burst. They must accommodate them ex post to decrease their repo interest rate only once the bubble has burst. Taylor rules with asset prices have a negligible effect in DSGE models, including the financial accelerator effect. Researchers of the Bank of International Settlements, such as Claudio Borio and Philip Lowe (2002), have consistently presented opposite views. More precisely, these DSGE models augmented by the financial accelerator have presented a list of failures with respect to the crisis.

The Failures of the DSGE Models with a Financial Accelerator

Let us analyse the failures of these models at the beginning of 2011 in order to describe the current crisis.

1. The welfare cost of the crisis, related to the large GDP fall in the USA, was much larger in the contemporary crisis than expected from the model. In a DSGE model, the size of the initial shock is exogenous. Let us assume that an initial large shock occurred. The problem is that the subsequent recovery should have been much faster according to the model. A large shock on output should be followed in the next period by a (less) large rise in GDP, and then by a smoothed convergence of output returning back to its trend. The current crisis has led to a more persistent loss of output than expected from the model.

2. Because the shock was initially related to a negative shock on housing asset prices, the persistence of the recession implies that the effect of a fall in asset prices on the subsequent level of output was understated.
3. The variation of the asset prices with respect to the variation of output is much larger than predicted by the model. Moreover, the variation (or the volatility) of asset prices with respect to the consumer price index is understated. Even though output fell significantly during the depression, the variation of asset prices fell very widely. In technical terms, the slope of the unique stable path relating the variation in asset prices as a function of the variation in output is too small.
4. The variation in the asset prices with respect to the variation in output was more rapid during the crisis than during the boom. The asymmetry of the volatility of asset prices for a negative shock with respect to a positive shock is not taken into account in linearized DSGE models.
5. Because of point (3), the proportion of the variance in the asset price that is not brought by the variance in output and the variance in the consumer price index is relatively small. (Technically, this comes from the linearized relations between these variables on the unique stable path.) As a consequence, the models predict that there will be negligible changes in welfare when the Taylor rule takes into account asset prices in addition to the output gap and to the consumer price index. Hence, central banks should not take into account asset prices. This view has been revised, taking into account macro-prudential policies.
6. The central bank is relatively efficient for accommodating the negative shock according to the model with a Taylor rule that does not take into account asset prices, even in simulations including a liquidity trap. During the crisis, monetary policy turned out to be less efficient than expected. The ability of a monetary policy to accommodate the crisis has been overstated.
7. The ability of fiscal policy to accommodate the crisis has been understated due to an emphasis on the Ricardian effect.

Because the cost of the recession is much higher than expected, the ex ante benign neglect of central banks with respect to the building-up period of the bubble is now being challenged. If the ex post cost of the financial crisis is very large, it is useful to spend sizeable resources against asset price bubbles.

The DSGE models with the financial accelerator take into account bankruptcy costs. Nevertheless, liquidity problems and systemic stability of the financial systems (systemic bankruptcy due to the loss of confidence in banks and/or investors) were set outside the model. A *second equilibrium* was set aside from the model, which considered only a unique equilibrium.

This existence of a second equilibrium is another asymmetric property of the economy during crisis, with respect to the boom period.

FIVE ALTERNATIVE ASSUMPTIONS

The Structural Research Programme Compatible with the Lucas Critique

Although the DSGE models with a financial accelerator assumed imperfect capital markets, this was not sufficient to describe the mechanism of the 2007– crisis. In addition to the imperfect capital markets assumptions of the previous section, five alternative assumptions are required to explain macroeconomics during a financial crisis. For each hypothesis, I will detail whether it contradicts the structural modelling research programme. The latter tends to follow the 'Lucas critique' – the common argument against changes in fundamental hypotheses used in macroeconomic modelling.

The defence of the mainstream DSGE model continues to be based on recurrent references to the Lucas critique (1976):

> Given that the structure of an econometric model consists of optimal decision rules of economic agents, and that optimal decision rules vary systematically with changes in the structure of series relevant to the decision maker, it follows that any change in policy will systematically alter the structure of econometric models (p. 41).

Because the parameters of large-scale macroeconometric models at the time were not structural, that is, not policy invariant, they necessarily changed whenever policy (the rules of the game) changed. Policy conclusions based on those models would therefore be potentially misleading.

The 'structural research programme' followed the Lucas critique. It suggests that if we want to predict the effect of a policy experiment, we should model the 'deep parameters' (relating to preferences, technology, and resource constraints) that govern *individual* behaviour as well as government policy behaviour. We can then predict what individuals will do, *taking into account* the change in policy. In other words, the expectations, the behaviour of individual agents and of governments were not correctly specified in the macroeconometric models of the 1970s.

I highlight that the five following alternative hypotheses are not inconsistent with the 'structural research programme', built on the Lucas critique.

Hypothesis 1: A Second Equilibrium with Systemic Bankruptcy is Possible

First, the financial accelerator is a partial summarization of Irving Fisher's ideas. Ben Bernanke is one of the most eminent scholars on the subject, given his long interest in the crisis of the 1930s and his revival of Fisher's debt deflation ideas during the last 30 years. Bernanke and Mark Gertler (2000), however, proposed this misleading statement of a posteriori management of asset price bubbles by central banks, without ex ante control of asset price bubbles:

> We explore the implications of asset price volatility for the management of monetary policy. We show that it is desirable for central banks to focus on underlying inflationary pressures. Asset prices become relevant only to the extent they may signal potential inflationary or deflationary forces. Rules that directly target asset prices appear to have undesirable side effects. We base our conclusions on (i) simulation of different policy rules in a small scale macro model and (ii) a comparative analysis of recent US and Japanese monetary policy (p. 2).

A central claim for this error is that it came from a common misunderstanding of Fisher's (1933) ideas as being only related to a financial accelerator that amplifies technological and productivity shocks leading to over-investment, such as the new car industry in the 1920s, the Internet industry in the 1990s, and so on. For Gottfried Haberler (1937 [1946]) it is clear that:

> over-investment rather than over-indebtedness is the primary cause of the breakdown . . . We may thus conclude that the 'debt-factor' plays an independent role as intensifier of the depression, but can hardly be regarded as an independent cause of the breakdown. (Chapter 4, pp. 115–16)

Fisher (1933), however, also makes the frequent comparison to the 'capsizing' of a ship:

> To take another simile, such a disaster is somewhat like the 'capsizing' of a ship which, under ordinary conditions, is always near stable equilibrium but which, after being tipped beyond a certain angle, has no longer this tendency to return to equilibrium, but, instead, a tendency to depart from it. (p. 339)

Small waves make the ship oscillate around Fisher's first equilibrium, inside a 'stability corridor'. By analogy, this describes regular economic cycles, not large crises. Large waves, on the other hand, make the ship pass below a threshold angle and capsize (a second equilibrium). This is a low-level equilibrium related to 'economic instability'. Hence, Fisher's is not only a story of amplified oscillation *around a single equilibrium* (in a corridor of stability), it is also a story of bifurcation toward a second bad equilibrium ('instability') – an autarky with an overall risk of macroeconomic bankruptcy, a breakdown of the financial system and low production levels. This equilibrium may also be related to low-equilibrium bank runs as dealt with by Douglas Diamond and Philip Dybvig (1983) in the field of the microeconomics of banking. The economy may only be able to pass the downward threshold (the threshold angle for the boat) leading to the second bad equilibrium due to the over-lending amplification of over-investment. Otherwise, over-investment theories alone may lead only to minor shocks, and the economy remains in the stability corridor. Since without the financial accelerator the shift to the low equilibrium ('instability') is unlikely to occur, *over-lending is then a cause of the breakdown.*

Let us look at a graphical, dynamic model representing a possible relationship between asset prices at the current date $q(t)$ and asset prices at the next date $q(t+1)$. Starting from the equilibrium E1, if a *small negative shock* on the asset price $q(t)$ occurs, such that $q(t)$ is equal to B, then the economy will exhibit small fluctuations around the stable equilibrium E1. These fluctuations occur in a *corridor of stability*.

If, however, a *large negative shock* occurs, such that the asset price $q(t)$ is below the value of a second unstable equilibrium E2, then the asset price dynamics follow a different decreasing and diverging path towards a third equilibrium that is also stable, where the asset price is equal to zero.

Until recently, modern mainstream macroeconomics dealing with the financial accelerator very rarely considered this second equilibrium. Hyman Minsky's (1982) question, 'Can it happen again?', referring to the 1929 crisis, was answered as 'Never'. This argument was based on an under-valuation of the probability of a world financial crisis: the probability was assumed to be close to zero. It was also based on an under-valuation of the ex post cost of a world financial crisis. For example, the evaluation of the costs of a financial crisis in developed countries such as Sweden in the 1990s were two to five times less than the costs incurred by emerging economies such as Argentina. This was also backed by Lucas's (1987) small valuation of business cycles' loss of welfare for a representative agent with a constant intertemporal elasticity of substitution. In 2010, central bankers changed their views and considered the possibility of macro-prudential regulation policies.

The problem highlighted is not that bankruptcy costs were missing in the financial accelerator. What is missing is systemic bankruptcy due to expectations of a high probability of default caused by a lack of confidence.

The Lucas critique does not assume that there are never multiple

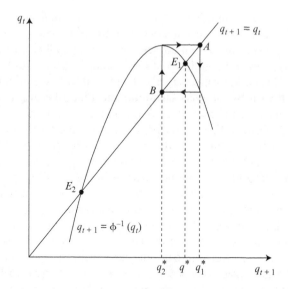

Figure 4.1   Small cycle in a stability corridor and large shock crisis

equilibria in the economy. The structural modelling research programme emphasizes the neat modelling of expectations. It is inconsistent to claim that the possibility of a liquidity crisis equilibrium, which is *ontologically expectation driven*, contradicts the 'structural research programme' following the Lucas critique.

Bank runs and banking crises are followed by governments bailing out banks or insuring deposits, with a risk of a public debt crisis, which may sometimes be followed by a rise in inflation to decrease public debt. As taxes are needed as well to bail out the banks, savers and pensioners and/or wage earners pay, along with a transfer from an older generation (facing the crisis) to a younger generation that may not face a crisis next period (Amable et al., 2002). A banking crisis may also last a long time, with continuing 'Zombie' lending to bankrupt banks and firms, such as in Japan (Caballero et al., 2006). All these events lead to large swings in income distribution due to transfers between lenders, borrowers, bankers, governments, savers and wage earners.

Hypothesis 2: Reject the Efficient Market Hypothesis that the Price of an Asset Always Reflects its Fundamental Value

The problem with the DSGE model with a financial accelerator is that the expected price of collateral is equal to its fundamental value (no over-valuation or under-valuation). There are no under-valuations fostered by fire sales. There are no liquidity crises breaking down exchanges on the financial markets. This explains the asymmetry between an under-valuation brisk fall during crises and longer periods building up to the over-valuation of assets during booms. With weakly regulated international banks, opacity implies that asset prices are never equal to their fundamental value.

Macroeconomists seem to find it difficult to reject this assumption. The opposite is true in the field of the microeconomics of banking: researchers such as Andrei Shleifer and Robert Vishny (2010) have no difficulties rejecting it when describing unstable banking.

A key consequence is that one exit option from a banking crisis is the start of a new bubble elsewhere. Describing this phenomenon is currently forbidden in the existing macroeconomic modelling. It seems that international capital surfed from the Asian Bubble to the Internet Bubble to the Housing Bubble to the next bubble: Chinese bank lending, or Chinese or Indian stock markets, or commodities. In the case of China, who knows whether asset prices are correctly valued, or whether Chinese statistics are reliable.

Rejecting the efficient financial market hypothesis is not incompatible with the structural research programme. If two groups of agents face different information on the expected value of an asset on the same date – some are correctly informed, some are not – the research programme would require a neat modelling of different resource constraints (information), preferences and technology for rational investors. It could be rational for naive investors to follow the herd when the cost of acquiring the true information is too great. In that case, the price of an asset could differ systematically from the fundamental value of that asset.

Hypothesis 3: Reject the No-Ponzi Game Condition

This condition eliminates the possibility of Ponzi schemes by stating that the growth of public or private debt has to be lower than the real interest rate charged on that debt in the infinite horizon:

$$g(B) < r_t$$

1. This assumption is used to rule out *the existence* of bubbles *prior to the infinite horizon* in macroeconomic models. This is consistent with the efficient financial market hypothesis eliminating the possibility of bubbles.
2. It implies bounded utility. Note that it is not a necessary assumption of infinite horizon optimization. An infinite objective function is a

possible solution, as in the Ramsey model (1928). If one maximizes discounted utility over time, why should one refuse infinite utility?

3. It is a key assumption to obtain Ricardian equivalence (for example, the inefficiency of budgetary policy financed by debt and followed by taxes later on) (Barro, 1974). The assumption is related to an infinite horizon government solvency. This may be different from short-run solvency, however. Imagine that we apply a similar reasoning to that in the financial accelerator: public debt is solvent based on expected taxes net of public expenditures:

$$(1 + r_t) \cdot B_t < \tau_{t+1} \cdot Y_t(1 + g_{t+1}(Y)) - G_t(1 + g_{t+1}(Y))$$

If the expected growth of output is large and if the interest rate on public bonds is low, this solvency constraint is likely to be respected. This is what bond holders may think about in the short run. They would like taxes to increase and public expenditures to fall, but would enjoy more output growth, which increases the tax base.

Imagine that that is the case for *all* future periods. Then, for all dates, the public debt is 'short-term' solvent. Imagine that at the same time, the growth rate of output is equal to the growth rate of public debt, but is larger than the real interest rate on public debt. Then, the 'infinite horizon' (no-Ponzi game) solvency constraint is not fulfilled, whereas the short-run solvency constraint is always fulfilled. In this case, the infinite horizon solvency constraint is meaningless. Utility is unbounded. In this context, one does not know whether Ricardian equivalence holds or not.

4. In the endogenous growth literature, balanced growth implies that debt grows at the same rate as output. This equation is inconsistent with growth miracles lasting more than 20 years, where the growth of output consistently exceeds the real rate of interest for several decades (Japan 1960–90; China 1990–2010) (Amable et al., 2010):

$$g(B) = g(Y) < r_t$$

If the non-efficient financial market hypothesis is consistent with the research programme following the Lucas critique, then one could reject the no-Ponzi game condition.

Hypothesis 4: Reject the Unique Stable Path Dynamics

Intertemporal optimization with a discount rate leads nearly always to saddle-path dynamics, with only one path having a stable lower dimension. All the others are unstable. A rational expectation hypothesis rules out all unstable paths by assumption. It is an additional assumption with respect to the Lucas critique. A consequence is that, for the same optimizing model, the volatility of asset prices on this path is much lower than that on the others.

The *linearization* around the equilibrium of the *unique* stable path leading to a *unique* long-term equilibrium reduces the study of macroeconomic dynamics to dampened responses of macroeconomic variables to *small* shocks.

The first point: rejecting the *unique* equilibrium goes along with accepting the 'expectation-driven' liquidity crisis alternative equilibrium. Multiple equilibria driven by expectations are consistent with the research programme.

The second point: *the unique stable path* goes along with the no-Ponzi game condition, which rules out that the economy follows temporary bubble paths for asset prices *prior* to the infinite horizon. That means that *all* agents know when an asset price is on a bubble path, and that they decide ex ante *never to be* on the unstable path. Nevertheless, let us imagine the scheme proposed, for example, by Shleifer and Vishny (2010) on rational unstable banking. A number of naive investors do not know that the asset is not correctly priced. Knowledgeable investors (banks) expect that a boom with over-priced assets will be followed by a crisis with under-priced assets. In that context, it is easy to compute the conditions for more informed rational banks to speculate.

Linearization considers only small shocks, which do not correspond to recessions. It leads to a repetitive representation of macroeconomic dynamics as dampened responses to small shocks. Along with the multiple equilibria hypothesis, *large* shocks are likely to shift the regime of the economy, and the dynamics will differ dramatically.

Hypothesis 5: Reject the Unconstrained Consumption-smoothing Euler Equation

The unconstrained Euler equation for households, where the growth of consumption is determined only as an increasing function of the rate of interest on savings, decreases with the aversion to consumption volatility:

$$g(C) = \frac{r_t - \rho}{\sigma}$$

This equation is rarely challenged in macroeconomic textbooks, yet

1. it does not match the data (Caroll, 1997);

2.   and it leads to overly small costs of cycles for the representative agent. The social cost of consumption volatility is far too small (Lucas, 1987; Gollier, 2001, p. 224). According to Lucas (1987, p. 30), 'It indicates that economic instability at the level we have experienced since the Second World War is a minor problem, even relative to historical inflation and certainly relative to the cost of modestly reduced rates of economic growth'.

The clear-cut distinction between growth and business cycle theories that does exist in macroeconomic textbooks faces an empirical problem with recessions and world financial crises. The possibility to disentangle the growth component from the cycle component from macroeconomic time series changes with respect to more regular periods. Large crises last long and affect the growth trend, not only the cyclical component: USA 1929–46, Japan 1990s–2010.

The above equation assumes very specific *resource constraints*, which are not valid with credit rationing or lack of demand on a market during a liquidity crisis. The structural research programme allows for other possibilities for defining resource constraints for households. Using the unconstrained Euler equation for describing household behaviour may lead to low values when measuring the welfare costs of recessions.

THE ONGOING MACROECONOMIC CRISIS LITERATURE

It is too early and very difficult to have a judgement on the ongoing macroeconomic literature dealing with the crisis. It is in the making, based on working papers whose content changes every three months.

The aim of such papers is to introduce banking leverage, interbank liquidity, large shocks, fire sales and systemic crisis into macroeconomics. Here are my first impressions from a limited sample.

1.   Although DSGE bashing has been very fashionable for the last three years, there is a slight inconsistency with these revolutionary declarations and the recent output supposed to renew macroeconomics. Most of the papers keep the DSGE framework. Most assume a greater amount of initial shocks than previously made in order to mimic the larger swing of the crisis in their simulations.
2.   Many papers remain very orthodox with respect to the valuation of assets based on their fundamental value (efficient market hypothesis).

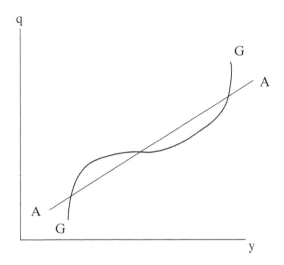

Figure 4.2   Krugman's fourth generation crisis

3. Perhaps because they are in the making, these models are often neither elegant nor parsimonious. They are packed with a large number of heavy equations, intending to model into great detail, for example, the interbank market, as well as banks and non-financial firms' wealth accumulation.
4. In contrast, there is clearly a need to offer an undergraduate-level model for explaining the crisis. A good starting point may be the Krugman (2002) 'fourth generation' crisis paper, which relates asset prices to output with simple equations.

CONCLUSION

For now, we do not know to what extent the forthcoming macroeconomic theory will take into account a weakly regulated financial sector and the rejection of the efficient capital market hypothesis. I am disturbed by the presentiment that we are on the eve of failing once again, and that key assumptions in the current way of doing mainstream macroeconomics may not be changed for a long time.

To understand the world economy with weakly regulated international finance, it is necessary to broaden the perspective beyond macroeconomic policies. To be fruitful, research will have to investigate the interplay between innovative macroeconomic policy and relevant or feasible banking and financial regulatory policy at the micro level, as well as political economy issues.

REFERENCES

Amable, B., J-B. Chatelain and O. De Bandt (2002), 'Optimal capacity in the banking sector and economic growth', *Journal of Banking and Finance*, **26**(2–3), 491–517.
Amable, B., J-B. Chatelain and K. Ralf (2010), 'Patents as collateral', *Journal of Economic Dynamics and Control*, **34**(6), 1092–104.
Barro, R.J. (1974), 'Are government bonds net wealth?', *The Journal of Political Economy*, **82**(6), 1095–117.
Bernanke, B. and M. Gertler (2000), 'Monetary policy and asset price volatility', NBER Working Paper 7559.
Bernanke, B. and M. Gertler (2001), 'Should central banks respond to movements in asset prices?', *American Economic Review*, **91**(2), 253–57.
Bernanke, B., M. Gertler and S. Gilchrist (1999), 'The financial accelerator in a quantitative business cycle framework', *Handbook of Macroeconomics*, Amsterdam: Elsevier, pp. 1341–93.
Borio, C.E.V. and P.W. Lowe (2002), 'Asset prices, financial and monetary stability: exploring the nexus', BIS Working Paper 114.
Caballero, R.J., T. Hoshi and A.K. Kashyap (2006), 'Zombie lending and depressed restructuring in Japan', NBER Working Paper 12129.
Caroll, C.D. (1997), 'Death to the log-linearized consumption Euler equation! (and very poor health to the second-order approximation)', NBER Working Paper 6298.
Diamond, D.W. and P.H. Dybvig (1983), 'Bank runs, deposit insurance and liquidity', *The Journal of Political Economy*, **91**(3), 401–19.
Fisher, I. (1933), 'The debt-deflation theory of great depressions', *Econometrica*, **1**(4), 337–57.
Gollier, C. (2001), *The Economics of Risk and Time*, Cambridge, MA: MIT Press.
Haberler, G. (1937 [1946]), *Prosperity and Depression: A Theoretical Analysis of Cyclical Movements*, 3rd edn, New York: United Nations, Lake Success.
Iacoviello, M. (2005), 'House prices, borrowing constraints, and monetary policy in the business cycle', *American Economic Review*, **95**(3), 739–64.
Kiyotaki, N. and J.H. Moore (1997), 'Credit cycles', *Journal of Political Economy*, **105**(2), 211–48.
Krugman, P. (2002), 'Crisis: the next generation?', in *Economic Policy in the International Economy: Essays in Honor of Assaf Razin*, Cambridge: Cambridge University Press, pp. 15–32.
Lucas, R.E. (1976), 'Econometric policy evaluation: a critique', *Carnegie-Rochester Conference Series on Public Policy*, **1**, 19–46.
Lucas, R.E. (1987), *Models of Business Cycles*, Oxford: Basil Blackwell.
Miller, M. and J. Stiglitz (2010), 'Leverage and asset bubbles: averting Armageddon with chapter 11', *Economic Journal*, **120**(544), 500–518.
Minsky, H.P. (1982), *Can 'it' Happen Again?: Essays on Instability and Finance*, Armonk, NY: M.E. Sharpe.
Rajan, R.G. and L. Zingales (2003), 'The great reversals: the politics of financial

development in the twentieth century', *Journal of Financial Economics*, **69**(1), 5–50.

Ramsey, F.P. (1928), 'A mathematical theory of saving', *Economic Journal*, **38**(152), 543–59.

Reinhart, C.M. and K. Rogoff (2009), *This Time is Different, Eight Centuries of Financial Folly*, Princeton, NJ: Princeton University Press.

Shleifer, A. and R. Vishny (2010), 'Unstable banking', *Journal of Financial Economics*, **97**(3), 306–18.

Smets, F. and R. Wouters (2003), 'An estimated dynamic stochastic general equilibrium model for the euro area', *Journal of the European Economic Association*, **1**(5), 1123–75.

5. Economic policies with endogenous innovation and Keynesian demand management[1]

**Giovanni Dosi, Giorgio Fagiolo,
Mauro Napoletano and Andrea Roventini**

INTRODUCTION

The global crisis has strikingly brought to the fore the importance of banking and financial markets for the dynamics of real economies. It has also revealed itself to be a 'natural experiment' for economic analysis, exposing the inadequacy of the predominant theoretical frameworks. The basic assumptions of mainstream models[2] – such as rational expectations, optimizing, representative agents, and so on – are to a large extent responsible for the failure to forecast the crisis. They also seem to be unable to propose a remedy for putting economies back on a steady growth path (Colander et al., 2008; Kirman, 2010). In fact, the crisis sets a tall challenge for alternative, evolutionary theories, linking micro behaviour and aggregate dynamics.

In this chapter, we develop an evolutionary, agent-based model to try to fill the theoretical vacuum present nowadays in macroeconomics. The model addresses three major, interrelated, questions. First, it explores the processes by which technological change affects macro variables, such as unemployment, output fluctuations and average growth rates. In addition to this 'Schumpeterian' question, we also ask how such endogenous, firm-specific changes in the supply side of the economy interact with demand conditions. This is a basic 'Keynesian' issue. Finally, we explore the possible existence of long-term effects of demand variations. Is long-term growth only driven by changes in technology, or does aggregate demand affect future dynamics? Are there multiple growth paths whose selection depends on demand and institutional conditions?

To do so, we refine and expand the model in Dosi et al. (2010),[3] which we use also as a sort of 'policy laboratory' where both business cycle and growth effects of different public policies can be evaluated under diverse institutional scenarios. In this respect, the model makes it possible to experiment with an ensemble of policies related to the supply side of the economy (for example, technology), as well as to the macro-management demand side (for example, fiscal and monetary policies).

From a historical perspective, a separation has emerged in macro-economics: growth theories have tried to explain the trends present in macro time series, whereas business cycle models have accounted for the observed fluctuations around the trend. The IS–LM interpretation of John Maynard Keynes (Hicks, 1937) and growth models rooted in the seminal work of Robert Solow (1956) are prominent examples of such a division of labour.

In the business cycle theoretical camp, different theories have been competing over time. On the one hand, 'New Classical' and 'Real Business Cycle (RBC) theories' have considered irrelevant any 'Keynesian' feature of the economy. On the other hand, New Keynesians have stressed the importance of aggregate demand shocks in economic fluctuations, often relying on nominal and real rigidities as well as on informational and behavioural frictions (see Blanchard, 2009, for an insightful overview), with just a small subset of them considering such 'imperfections' as structural, long-term characteristics of the economy (see, for example, Akerlof and Yellen, 1985; Greenwald and Stiglitz, 1993a, 1993b; Akerlof, 2002, 2007).

More recently, the New Neoclassical Synthesis between real business cycle and a major breed of New Keynesian models – rooted in the dynamic stochastic general equilibrium (DSGE) models (see Woodford, 2003; Galí and Gertler, 2007) – has added modest quantities of Keynesian elements to an otherwise supply-side model of economic fluctuations. The backbone of DSGE models is indeed a RBC model augmented with sticky prices, imperfect competition, monetary-policy (Taylor-like) rules, and any other possible types of imperfections.[4] DSGE models, however, are not suited to deal with long-run growth issues since their RBC core prevents them from exploring any Schumpeterian source of endogenous innovation.

On the opposite side, endogenous growth models (see Romer, 1990; Aghion and Howitt, 1992; Dinopoulos and Segerstrom, 1999) have a Schumpeterian core, which makes innovation and the ensuing dynamics in technology endogenous. There is no room, however, for demand-driven fluctuations in this set of models, even if some of them (for example, Aghion and Howitt, 1998; Aghion et al., 2010; Aghion and Marinescu, 2007; Aghion et al., 2008) allow for *equilibrium fluctuations* wherein Keynesian features do not have any role.

This issue is also present in evolutionary models (Nelson and Winter,

1982). They are driven indeed by a Schumpeterian engine with endogenous innovations, but they do not take sufficiently into account any demand-related forces affecting macroeconomic activity.[5]

Our model has evolutionary roots. It explicitly accounts for an endogenous technological search, heterogeneous 'boundedly rational' agents and competitive dynamics entailing some form of market selection across firms, and through that, across technologies – all fundamental building blocks of evolutionary interpretations of economic dynamics (following the seminal Nelson and Winter, 1982). Unlike most 'first generation' evolutionary models, however, it abandons any assumption of market clearing on the labour or the product markets. In line with some New Keynesian insights (see, for example Stiglitz, 1994), it tries to study the feedbacks between the factors affecting aggregate demand and those influencing technological change. This allows us to develop a unified framework where one can jointly study long-term dynamics and business cycles.

The model belongs to the growing literature on *agent-based computational economics* (ACE) (see Tesfatsion and Judd, 2006; LeBaron and Tesfatsion, 2008), and it thus allows for many heterogeneous agents who interact without any ex ante commitment to the reciprocal consistency of their actions (for example, market clearing).[6] The model thus satisfies Robert Solow's call for micro heterogeneity (Solow, 2008).

Furthermore, the model, in line with most agent-based models (ABMs), is based on a 'realistic' representation of what agents do, how they adjust, and so on. In that, it provides an explicit microfoundation of macro dynamics. At the same time, we try to describe micro behaviours as closely as possible to the available micro-empirical evidence. This is in line with George Akerlof's plea for 'behavioural microeconomics' (Akerlof, 2002). In this way, we reduce our degrees of freedom in modelling agents' behaviour. Moreover, we test the capability of the model to jointly account for a large set of stylized facts related to 'micro/meso' aggregates (for example, firm size and growth-rate distributions, productivity dispersions, firm investment patterns) together with macro-statistical properties (for example, persistent output growth, output volatility, unemployment rates, and so on).

The model portrays an artificial economy composed of capital- and consumption-good firms, workers, a bank, and the public sector. Capital-goods firms perform research and development (R&D) and produce heterogeneous machine tools. Consumption-goods firms invest in new machines and produce a homogeneous consumption good. Firms finance their production and investment choices employing internal funds as well as credit provided by the banking sector. Finally, the public sector levies taxes on firms' profits and workers' wages and pays unemployment benefits.

As every ABM, the properties of the model must be analysed via extensive computer simulations. To overcome the usual problems, shared by many ABMs, related to parameterization sensitivity,[7] we look for policy results that: (i) are robust to reasonable changes in the parameters of the model; (ii) stem from model set-ups and parameterizations wherein the output of the model is empirically validated (that is, the statistical properties of simulated microeconomic and macroeconomic data are similar to those observed in reality). We think that this is a positive feature of our study, because very often in the literature, no empirical validation constraints are imposed on policy experiment results (Fukac and Pagan, 2006; Canova, 2008; Fagiolo and Roventini, 2012). Moving to the normative side, different 'control' parameters and institutional, market, or industry set-ups can mimic different public policies, whose impact is then quantitatively assessed by employing ensuing aggregates, such as average output growth, output volatility, average unemployment, and so on.

Extensive empirical validation exercises show that the model is able to deliver self-sustaining patterns of growth characterized by the presence of endogenous business cycles. Moreover, the model is also able to replicate the most important stylized facts concerning macroeconomic dynamics (for example, cross-correlations, relative volatilities), as well as microeconomic dynamics (such as firm size distributions, firm productivity dynamics, firm investment patterns).

Our policy-simulation exercises show a strong complementarity between Schumpeterian technology policies and Keynesian fiscal policies. Both types of policies are needed to put the economy onto a long-run steady growth path. Schumpeterian policies foster economic growth, but they are not able alone to sustain long-run high economic growth patterns characterized by mild business cycle fluctuations and low unemployment. If Keynesian policies are present, Schumpeterian policies also affect the performance of the economy in the short run, contributing to the reduction in output volatility and unemployment. Moreover, Keynesian policies are the best instrument for tackling short-run problems, having a strong impact on output volatility and unemployment. We show that monetary policy can have strong effects on growth as well. In particular, high interest rates not only exacerbate volatility and unemployment rates, but also are capable of worsening the long-run growth prospects of the economy. Our results also point to a strong interplay between monetary policy and the income distribution characteristics of the economy. More specifically, on the one hand, income distributions that are more favourable to wages stabilize aggregate consumption demand and lower both volatility and unemployment. On the other hand, lower profit rates magnify the effects of changes in interest rates by increasing the dependence of firms on external financing from the bank.

The chapter is organized as follows. We first describe the model. Next, we perform empirical validation checks and present results of policy exercises. The final section concludes and discusses future extensions.

THE MODEL

The economy is composed of a machine-producing sector made of F_1 firms (denoted by the subscript i), a consumption-goods sector made of F_2 firms (denoted by the subscript j), L^s consumers/workers, a bank, and a public sector. Capital-goods firms invest in R&D and produce heterogeneous machines. Consumption-goods firms combine machine tools bought from capital-goods firms and labour in order to produce a final product for consumers. The bank provides credit to firms using firms' savings. Credit is allotted to firms on a pecking-order basis according to their net worth. Moreover, the supply and the dynamics of debt of the firms in the economy can be influenced by various policy instruments (capital requirements, mandatory reserves, interest rates). Finally, the public sector levies taxes on firms' profits and pays unemployment benefits.

The Timeline of Events

In any given time period (t), the following microeconomic decisions take place in sequential order.

1. Policy variables (for example, the central bank interest rate, the reserve requirement, the tax rate, unemployment benefits, and so on) are fixed.
2. Total credit provided by the bank to each firm is determined.
3. Machine-tool firms perform R&D to try to discover new products and more efficient production techniques and to imitate the technology and the products of their competitors. Capital-goods firms advertise their machines with consumption-goods firms.
4. Consumption-goods firms buy the machines ordered in the previous period and decide how much to produce and invest. If internal funds are not enough, firms borrow from the bank. If investment is positive, consumption-goods firms choose their supplier and send in their orders.

5. In both industries, firms hire workers according to their production plans and start producing.
6. An imperfectly competitive consumption-goods market opens. The market shares of firms evolve according to their price competitiveness.
7. Firms in both sectors compute their profits. If profits are positive, firms pay back their loans to the bank and deposit their savings.
8. Entry and exit take place. In both sectors, firms with near zero market shares and negative net worth are eschewed from their industry and replaced by new firms.
9. Machines ordered at the beginning of the period are delivered and become part of the capital stock at time $t + 1$.

At the end of each time step, aggregate variables (for example, gross domestic product [GDP], investment, employment) are computed, summing up the corresponding microeconomic variables.

The Capital-goods Industry

The technology of a capital-goods firm is (A_i^τ, B_i^τ), where the former coefficient stands for the labour productivity of the machine tool manufactured by i for the consumption-goods industry (a rough measure of producer quality), while the latter coefficient is the labour productivity of the production technique employed by firm i itself. The positive integer τ denotes the current technology vintage. Given the monetary wage w, the unit cost of production of a capital-goods firm is:

$$c_i(t) = \frac{w(t)}{B_i^\tau} \tag{5.1}$$

With a fixed mark-up ($\mu_1 > 0$) pricing rule,[8] prices (p_i) are defined as:

$$p_i(t) = (1 + \mu_1)c_i(t) \tag{5.2}$$

The unit labour cost of production in the consumption-goods sector associated with each machine of vintage τ, produced by firm i is:

$$c(A_i^\tau, t) = \frac{w(t)}{A_i^\tau}$$

Firms in the capital-goods industry 'adaptively' strive to increase their market share and profits to try to improve their technology via innovation and imitation. Both are costly processes. Firms invest in R&D a fraction of their past sales (S_i):

$$RD_i(t) = vS_i(t - 1) \qquad (5.3)$$

with $0 < v < 1$. R&D expenditures are used to hire researchers, who are paid the market wage $w(t)$.[9] Firms split their R&D efforts between innovation (IN) and imitation (IM) according to the parameter $\xi \in [0,1]$:[10]

$$IN_i(t) = \xi RD_i(t)$$

$$IM_i(t) = (1 - \xi) RD_i(t)$$

We model innovation as a two-step process. The first step determines whether or not a firm obtains an access to innovation – irrespective of whether it is ultimately a success or a failure – through a draw from a Bernoulli distribution, whose parameter $\theta_i^{in}(t)$ is given by:

$$\theta_i^{in}(t) = 1 - e^{-\zeta_1 IN_i(t)} \qquad (5.4)$$

with $0 < \zeta_1 \leq 1$. Note that according to (5.4), there are some scale-related returns to R&D investment: access to innovative discoveries is more likely if a firm puts more resources into R&D. If a firm innovates, it may draw a new machine embodying technology (A_i^{in}, B_i^{in}) according to:

$$A_i^{in}(t) = A_i(t) (1 + x_i^A(t))$$

$$B_i^{in}(t) = B_i(t) (1 + x_i^B(t))$$

where x_i^A and x_i^B are two independent draws from a Beta (α_1, β_1) distribution over the support $[\underline{x}_1, \overline{x}_1]$ with $\underline{x}_1$ belonging to the interval $[-1, 0]$ and $\overline{x}_1$ to $[0, 1]$. Note that the notional possibilities of technological advance – that is, *technological opportunities* – are captured by the support of the Beta distribution and by its shape. So, for example, with low opportunities, the largest probability density falls over 'failed' innovations – that is, potential capital goods that are 'worse' in terms of costs and performance than those already produced by the searching firm. Conversely, under a condition of rich opportunities, innovations that dominate incumbent technologies will be drawn with high probability. As we shall show below, a crucial role of 'Schumpeterian' technology policies is precisely that of influencing opportunities and micro capabilities.

Like the innovation search, imitation follows a two-step procedure.

The possibilities of accessing imitation come from sampling a Bernoulli $(\theta_i^{im}(t))$:

$$\theta_i^{im}(t) = 1 - e^{-\zeta_2 IM_i(t)} \tag{5.5}$$

with $0 < \zeta_2 \leq 1$. Firms accessing the second stage are able to copy the technology of one of their competitors (A_i^{im}, B_i^{im}). We assume that firms are more likely to imitate competitors with similar technologies, and we use Euclidean metrics to compute the technological distance between every pair of firms to weigh imitation probabilities.

All firms that draw a potential innovation or imitation have to put it on production or keep producing the incumbent generation of machines. Comparing the different technologies competing for adoption, firms choose to manufacture the machine characterized by the best trade-off between price and efficiency. More specifically, knowing that consumption-goods firms invest following a payback period routine (see below), capital-goods firms select the machine to produce according to the following rule:

$$min[p_i^h(t) + bc^h(A_i^h, t)], \quad h = \tau, in, im \tag{5.6}$$

where b is a positive payback period parameter (see equation (5.10) below). Once the type of machine is chosen, we capture the imperfect information pervading the market, assuming that each firm sends a 'brochure' with the price and the productivity of its offered machines to both its historical (HC_i) clients and to a random sample of potential new customers (NC_i), whose size is proportional to HC_i (that is, $NC_i(t) = \gamma HC_i(t)$, with $0 < \gamma < 1$).

The Consumption-goods Industry

Consumption-goods firms produce homogeneous goods using capital (that is, their stock of machines) and labour under constant returns to scale. Firms plan their production (Q_j) according to adaptive demand expectations (D_j^e):

$$D_j^e(t) = f(D_j(t - 1), D_j(t - 2), \ldots, D_j(t - h)) \tag{5.7}$$

where $D_j(t - 1)$ is the demand actually faced by firm j at time $t - 1$ (h positive integer).[11] The desired level of production (Q_j^d) depends on the expected demand as well as on the desired inventories (N_j^d) and the actual stock of inventories N_j:

$$Q_j^d(t) = D_j^e(t) + N_j^d(t) - N_j(t - 1) \qquad (5.8)$$

with $N_j^d(t) = \iota D_j^e(t), \iota \in [0, 1]$. The output of consumption-goods firms is constrained by their capital stock (K_j). If the desired capital stock (K_j^d) – computed as a function of the desired level of production – is higher than the current capital stock, firms invest (EI_j^d) in order to expand their production capacity:[12]

$$EI_j^d(t) = K_j^d(t) - K_j(t) \qquad (5.9)$$

The capital stock of each firm is obviously composed of heterogeneous vintages of machines with different productivity. We define $\Xi_j(t)$ as the set of all vintages of machine tools belonging to firm j at time t. Firms scrap machines following a payback period routine. Through that, technical change and equipment prices influence the replacement decisions of consumption-goods firms.[13] More specifically, firm j replaces machine $A_i^\tau \in \Xi_j(t)$ according to its technology obsolescence as well as the price of new machines:

$$RS_j(t) = \left\{ A_i^\tau \in \Xi_j(t) : \frac{p^*(t)}{c(A_{i,\tau}, t) - c^*(t)} \leq b \right\} \qquad (5.10)$$

where p^* and c^* are the price and unit cost of production for the new machines. Firms compute their replacement investment by summing up the number of old machine tools that satisfy equation (5.10).[14]

Consumption-goods firms choose their capital-goods supplier by comparing the price and productivity of the currently manufactured machine tools that they know of. As mentioned above (in 'The Capital-goods Industry'), the capital-goods market is systematically characterized by imperfect information. This implies that consumption-goods firms compare 'brochures' that describe the characteristics of machines only from a subset of equipment suppliers. Firms then choose the machines with the lowest price and unit cost of production (that is, $p_i(t) + bc(A_i^\tau, t)$) and send their orders to the corresponding machine manufacturer. Machine production is a time-consuming process: capital-goods firms deliver the ordered machine tools at the end of the period.[15] Gross investment of each firm (I_j) is the sum of expansion and replacement investment. By pooling the investment of all consumption-goods firms, one gets aggregate investment (I).

Consumption-goods firms have to finance their investments as well as their production, as they advance worker wages. In line with a growing number of theoretical and empirical papers (see, for example, Stiglitz and Weiss, 1992; Greenwald and Stiglitz, 1993a; Hubbard, 1998), we assume imperfect capital markets. This implies that the financial structure of firms matters (external funds are more expensive than internal ones), and firms may be credit rationed. More specifically, consumption-goods firms finance production using their stock of liquid assets (NW_j). If liquid assets do not fully cover production costs, firms borrow the remaining part from a bank, paying an interest rate r_L. The maximum amount of credit lent by the bank to firm $j(TC_j)$ is a positive function of the firm's stock of liquid assets, as well as its size proxied by its past sales (see 'The Banking Sector' below). Only firms that are not production rationed can try to fulfil their investment plans by employing their residual stock of liquid assets first, and then their residual borrowing capacity.[16]

Given their current stock of machines, consumption-goods firms compute average productivity (π_j) and unit cost of production (c_j). Prices are set by applying a variable mark-up (μ_j) on unit costs of production:

$$p_j(t) = (1 + \mu_j(t))c_j(t) \tag{5.11}$$

Mark-up variations are regulated by the evolution of firms' market shares (f_j):[17]

$$\mu_j(t) = \mu_j(t - 1)\left(1 + v\frac{f_j(t - 1) - f_j(t - 2)}{f_j(t - 2)}\right)$$

with $0 \le v \le 1$.

The consumption-goods market is also characterized by imperfect information.[18] This implies that consumers do not instantaneously switch to products made by more competitive firms. Prices, however, are clearly one of the key determinants of firms' *competitiveness* (E_j). The other component is the level of unfulfilled demand (l_j) inherited from the previous period:

$$E_j(t) = -\omega_1 p_j(t) - \omega_2 l_j(t) \tag{5.12}$$

where $\omega_{1,2}$ are positive parameters.[19] Weighting the competitiveness of each consumption-goods firm by its past market share (f_j), one can compute the *average competitiveness* of the consumption-goods sector:

$$\overline{E}(t) = \sum_{j=1}^{F_2} E_j(t)f_j(t - 1)$$

Such variables also represent a moving *selection criterion* driving, other things being equal, expansions, contractions and extinctions within the population of firms. We parsimoniously model this market set-up, letting firms' market shares evolve according to a 'quasi' replicator dynamic (for antecedents in the evolutionary camp, see Silverberg et al., 1988; Metcalfe, 1994a):

$$f_j(t) = f_j(t-1)\left(1 + \chi \frac{E_j(t) - \overline{E}(t)}{\overline{E}(t)}\right) \qquad (5.13)$$

with $\chi > 0$.[20]

The profits (Π_j) of each consumption-goods firm read:

$$\Pi_j(t) = S_j(t) - c_j(t)Q_j(t) - r_L Deb_j(t) + r_D NW_j(t-1)$$

where $S_j(t) = p_j(t)D_j(t)$ and $Deb_j(t)$ denote the stock of debt. The investment choices of each firm and its profits determine the evolution of its stock of liquid assets (NW_j):

$$NW_j(t) = NW_j(t-1) + \Pi_j(t) - cI_j(t)$$

where cI_j is the amount of internal funds employed by firm j to finance investment.

The Banking Sector

In the banking sector, there is only one commercial bank (or n commercial banks that are equal) that gathers deposits and provides credit to firms. In what follows, we first describe how total credit is determined by the bank, and how credit is allocated to each firm. We then move on to describe the organization of the credit flow in the economy and the balance sheet of the bank. Finally, we describe how profits and net worth of the bank are determined.

The maximum credit available in the economy is set by the credit multiplier. More precisely, in each period, the bank reinvests in credit the funds obtained through deposits from firms. This amount of credit returns to the bank in the form of deposits. The bank then subtracts from this amount the mandatory reserve and lends the remainder, which returns again in the form of deposits, and so on. If we let α_R be the mandatory reserve coefficient, then total deposits obtained from the above procedure, $Dep(t-1)$, are determined as:

$$Dep(t-1) = \frac{\sum_{i=1}^{N1} NW_i(t-1) + \sum_{j=1}^{N2} NW_j(t-1)}{\alpha_R}, \ 0 \le \alpha_R \le 1 \qquad (5.14)$$

where $\sum_{i=1}^{N1} NW_i(t-1)$ and $\sum_{j=1}^{N2} NW_j(t-1)$ are the total net worth of upstream and downstream firms at time $t-1$.

From the above equation, it follows that total credit available in the economy at time t, $MTC(t)$ is:

$$MTC(t) = (1 - \alpha_R) Dep(t-1) \tag{5.15}$$

Total credit is allocated to each firm in the consumption-goods sector on a pecking-order basis, according to the ratio between stock of liquid assets and sales, $\frac{NW_i(t)}{S_i(t)}$. More precisely, the bank first ranks firms on the basis of their stock of liquid assets-to-sales ratio; then it starts to satisfy the demand of the first firm in the rank, then the second one, and so on. If the total credit available is insufficient to fulfil the demand of all the firms in the pecking order list, the firms that are credit rationed go bankrupt. On the other hand, the total demand for credit can also be lower than the total supply of credit. In this case, all demands of firms in the pecking order are fulfilled, and no firm goes bankrupt. It follows that in any period the stock of loans of the bank satisfies the following constraint:

$$\sum_{j=1}^{N2} Deb_j(t) = Loan(t) \leq TC(t) \tag{5.16}$$

The profits of the bank are equal to interest rate receipts from redeemable loans and from interest on reserves held at the central bank minus interest paid on deposits. Furthermore, the bank fixes its deposit and loan rates by applying respectively a mark-down and a mark-up on the central bank rate r. For simplicity, we assume that bank reserves, $Cash(t)$, are remunerated at the same rate as deposits:

$$r_D = (1 - \psi_D)r, \quad 0 \leq \psi_D \leq 1 \tag{5.17}$$

$$r_L = (1 + \psi_L)r, \quad 0 \leq \psi_L \leq 1 \tag{5.18}$$

From the above hypotheses it follows that the expression for the bank's profits, $\pi^b(t)$ is:

$$\pi^b(t) = r_L Loan(t) - r_D Dep(t) + r_D Cash(t-1) \tag{5.19}$$

To complete the description of the banking sector, we need to determine the bank's net worth at the end of the period, $NW^b(t)$. The net worth of the bank is equal to the stock of liquid assets of the bank minus the stock of bad debt accumulated up to time t, that is, $BD(t)$. Liquid assets are given by the stock of cash accumulated up to time t, plus the profits of the period. Accordingly, the expression for the net worth of the bank reads as:

$$NW^b(t) = Cash(t) + \pi^b(t) - BD(t) = NW^b(t - 1) + \Delta Cash(t)$$

$$+ \pi^b(t) - BD(t) \qquad (5.20)$$

The bank goes bankrupt if its net worth becomes negative. Note that this allows us to appreciate the difference between liquidity and solvency risks, which has been a hot topic during the crisis. Similar to what happened in the post-2007 financial turmoil, we assume that the insolvency of the bank is solved by allowing the public sector to buy the bank's bad debt.

Schumpeterian Exit and Entry Dynamics

At the end of each period, a firm exits for two reasons: (i) competition, that is, the firm has a (quasi) zero market share; or (ii) bankruptcy, that is, the firm's net worth becomes negative and the bank is not willing to provide additional credit. If a firm fails, the bank's stock of bad debt is increased accordingly.

We keep the number of firms fixed, hence any dead firm is replaced by a new one. Furthermore, in line with the empirical literature on firm entry (Caves, 1998; Bartelsman et al., 2005), we assume that entrants are on average smaller than incumbents, with the stock of capital of new consumption-goods firms and the stock of liquid assets of entrants in both sectors being a fraction of the average of that of the incumbents.[21] Concerning the technology of entrants, new consumption-goods firms select amongst the newest vintages of machines, according to the 'brochure mechanism' described above. The process- and product-related knowledge of new capital-goods firms is drawn from a Beta distribution, whose shape and support is shifted and 'twisted' according to whether entrants enjoy an advantage or a disadvantage vis-à-vis incumbents.[22] In fact, the distribution of opportunities for entrants versus incumbents is a crucial characteristic of different sectoral *technological regimes* and plays a role somewhat akin to the distance from the technological frontier of entrants discussed in Aghion and Howitt (2007).

The Labour Market

The labour market is certainly not Walrasian: real wages do not clear the market, and involuntary unemployment as well as labour rationing are the rules rather than the exceptions. The aggregate labour demand

(L^D) is computed by summing up the labour demand of capital- and consumption-goods firms. The aggregate supply (L^S) is exogenous and inelastic. Hence, aggregate employment (L) is the minimum between L^D and L^S.

The wage rate is a function of institutional and market factors, with both indexation mechanisms on consumption prices and average productivity, on the one hand, and adjustments to unemployment rates, on the other:

$$\frac{\Delta w(t)}{w(t-1)} = g\left(\frac{\Delta cpi(t)}{cpi(t-1)}, \frac{\Delta \overline{AB}(t)}{\overline{AB}(t-1)}, \frac{\Delta U(t)}{U(t-1)}\right) \qquad (5.21)$$

where cpi is the consumer price index, $\overline{AB}$ the average labour productivity, and U the unemployment rate.[23]

Consumption, Taxes and Public Expenditures

An otherwise black-boxed public sector levies taxes on firm profits and worker wages or on profits only and pays to unemployed workers a subsidy (w^u), which is a fraction of the current market wage (that is, $w^u(t) = \varphi w(t)$, with $\varphi \in (0,1)$). In fact, taxes and subsidies are the fiscal levers that contribute to the aggregate demand management regimes.

Aggregate consumption (C) depends on the income of both employed and unemployed workers as well as on past savings:

$$C(t) = c[w(t)L^D(t) + w^u(L^S - L^D(t)) + r_D(1-c)C(t-1)] \qquad (5.22)$$

where $0 < c \leq 1$ is the marginal propensity to consume (in the present set-up $c = 1$). The model satisfies the standard national account identities: the sum of the value added of capital- and consumption-goods firms (Y) equals their aggregate production, since in our simplified economy, there are no intermediate goods; that in turn coincides with the sum of aggregate consumption, investment and change in inventories (ΔN):

$$\sum_{i=1}^{F_1} Q_i(t) + \sum_{j=1}^{F_2} Q_j(t) = Y(t) \equiv C(t) + I(t) + \Delta N(t)$$

The dynamics generated at the micro level by decisions of a multiplicity of heterogeneous, adaptive agents and by their interaction mechanisms is the explicit microfoundation of the dynamics for all aggregate variables of interest (for example, output, investment, employment, and so on).

EMPIRICAL VALIDATION

The foregoing model does not allow for analytical, closed-form solutions. This general ABM distinctive feature stems from the non-linearities present in agent decision rules and their interaction patterns. It also forces us to run computer simulations to analyse the properties of the stochastic processes governing the co-evolution of micro and macro variables.[24] In what follows, we therefore perform extensive Monte Carlo analyses to wash away cross-simulation variability. Consequently, all results below refer to averages taken from over a hundred Monte Carlo replications.[25]

Let us start from a sort of 'benchmark' set-up for which the model is empirically validated, meaning it is studied in its ability to replicate a wide spectrum of microeconomic and macroeconomic stylized facts. Initial conditions and parameters of the benchmark set-up are presented in Table 5.1. As already mentioned, the model embodies both a *Schumpeterian engine* and a *Keynesian* one. The former belongs to the generation of innovations created by an ensemble of equipment producers that expensively search for and endogenously differentiate between the technology they are able to master. The Keynesian engine has two parts: a direct one – through fiscal policies – and an indirect one – via investment decisions and workers' consumption. Hence, the benchmark model appropriately embodies all such Schumpeterian and Keynesian features.

Next, we tune, so to speak, 'up' and 'down' the key policy variables (for example, tax rates, unemployment benefits, interest rates), and we experiment with different conditions affecting the access to and exploitation of new technological opportunities (for example, the patent regime, anti-trust policies) or the distribution of income between profits and wages (mark-up rates of firms).

Let us first explore the ability of the model to reproduce the major stylized facts regarding both the properties of macroeconomic aggregates and the underlying distribution of micro characteristics (for more on both in the direct antecedents to this model, see Dosi et al., 2006, 2008).

Growth and Fluctuations

The model is able to robustly generate endogenous, self-sustained growth patterns characterized by the presence of persistent fluctuations (see Figure 5.1). At business cycle frequencies, the bandpass-filtered output (Bpf), investment and consumption series (Bpf: see, for example, Baxter and King, 1999) display the familiar 'roller-coaster' dynamics (see Figure 5.2) observed in real data (see, for example, Stock and Watson, 1999; Napoletano et al., 2006). Moreover, in tune with the empirical evidence,

Table 5.1   Benchmark parameters

Description	Symbol	Value
Number of firms in capital-goods industry	F_1	50
Number of firms in consumption-goods industry	F_2	200
R&D investment propensity	ν	0.04
R&D allocation to innovative search	ξ	0.50
Firm search capabilities parameters	ζ	0.30
Beta distribution parameters (innovation process)	(α_1, β_1)	(3, 3)
Beta distribution support (innovation process)	$[\underline{x}_1, \bar{x}_1]$	$[-0.15, 0.15]$
New-customer sample parameter	γ	0.50
Capital-goods firm mark-up rule	μ_1	0.10
Desired inventories	ι	0.10
Payback period	b	3
'Physical' scrapping age	η	20
Mark-up coefficient	ν	0.01
Competitiveness weights	$\omega_{1,2}$	1
Replicator dynamics coefficient	χ	1
Uniform distribution supports (consumption-goods entrant capital)	$[\phi_1, \phi_2]$	[0.10,0.90]
Uniform distribution supports (entrant stock of liquid assets)	$[\phi_3, \phi_4]$	[0.10,0.90]
Beta distribution parameters (capital-goods entrants technology)	(α_1, β_2)	(2, 4)
Wage setting $\Delta\overline{AB}$ weight	ψ_1	1
Wage setting Δcpi weight	ψ_2	0
Wage setting ΔU weight	ψ_3	0
Tax rate	tr	0.10
Unemployment subsidy rate	φ	0.40
Maximum debt/sales ratio	Λ	2
Interest rate	r	0.025
Bank mark-up coefficient	ψ_L	0.50
Bank mark-down coefficient	ψ_D	1

both consumption and investment appear to be procyclical variables, with the latter series being also more volatile than GDP.

The insights coming from visual inspection of time series data are confirmed by more quantitative analyses. Table 5.2 reports descriptive statistics on output, consumption and investment time series. As the table clearly shows, output, consumption and investment display strictly positive average growth rates[26] and, according to the Dickey–Fuller tests, they seem to exhibit a unit root. After detrending the series with a bandpass filter, we compute standard deviations and cross-correlations between

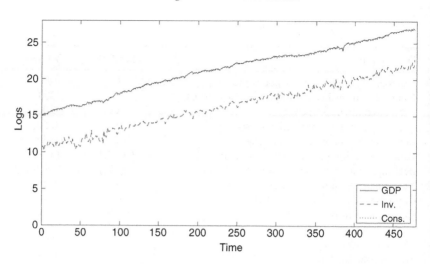

Figure 5.1   Level of output, investment and consumption (logs)

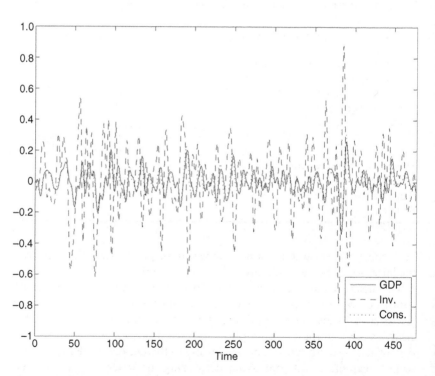

Figure 5.2   Bandpass-filtered output, investment and consumption

Table 5.2   Output, investment and consumption statistics

	Output	Consumption	Investment
Avg. growth rate	0.0254	0.0252	0.0275
	(0.0002)	(0.0002)	(0.0004)
Dickey–Fuller test (logs)	6.7714	9.4807	0.2106
	(0.0684)	(0.0957)	(0.0633)
Dickey–Fuller test (Bpf)	−6.2564*	−5.8910*	−6.8640*
	(0.0409)	(0.0447)	(0.0905)
Std. Dev. (Bpf)	0.0809	0.0679	0.4685
	(0.0007)	(0.0005)	(0.0266)
Rel. Std. Dev. (output)	1	0.8389	5.7880

Notes:
Bpf: bandpass-filtered (6,32,12) series.
Monte-Carlo simulation standard errors in parentheses.
(*): Significant at 5%.

output and the other series (see respectively Tables 5.2 and 5.3). In line with the empirical literature on business cycles (see, for example, Stock and Watson, 1999), in our model, investment is also more volatile than output, whereas consumption is less so; consumption, investment, change in inventories, and employment are procyclical; unemployment is countercyclical. Consumption and net investment are also coincident variables matching yet another empirical regularity in business cycles. Changes in inventories are instead slightly lagging.[27]

Furthermore, the model is also able to match the business-cycle properties concerning productivity, labour market, and price variables (see Table 5.3). Indeed, productivity is procyclical; prices are countercyclical and leading; inflation is procyclical and lagging; mark-ups are strongly countercyclical (for the empirics and discussion, see Stock and Watson, 1999; Rotemberg and Woodford, 1999).

The model is also in line with the major business cycle stylized facts concerning credit (see Table 5.3). Indeed, firms' total debt displays a strong procyclical character. In addition, its fluctuations are contemporaneous to output movements. The cross-correlations in Table 5.3 also shed light on the characteristics of the credit dynamics underneath business cycles in the model, which has strong 'Minskian' features (see Minsky, 1986). First, bank deposits are countercyclical and lag GDP. Moreover, bankruptcy rates are procyclical and lag GDP dynamics very closely. This behaviour is mapping the evolution of firms' financial health over the cycle. At the onset of an expansionary phase, firms' profits and cash flows improve. This pushes higher production and investment expenditures, therefore

Table 5.3 Correlation structure

Series (Bpf)	t-4	t-3	t-2	t-1	Output (Bpf) t	t+1	t+2	t+3	t+4
Output	-0.1022	0.1769	0.5478	0.8704	1	0.8704	0.5478	0.1769	-0.1022
	(0.0090)	(0.0080)	(0.0048)	(0.0014)	(0)	(0.0014)	(0.0048)	(0.0080)	(0.0090)
Consumption	-0.1206	0.0980	0.4256	0.7563	0.9527	0.9248	0.6848	0.3394	0.0250
	(0.0123)	(0.0129)	(0.0106)	(0.0062)	(0.0017)	(0.0018)	(0.0038)	(0.0058)	(0.0072)
Investment	-0.2638	-0.3123	-0.2646	-0.0864	0.1844	0.4473	0.5950	0.5757	0.4206
	(0.0102)	(0.0137)	(0.0182)	(0.0210)	(0.0206)	(0.0175)	(0.0139)	(0.0123)	(0.0129)
Net Investment	-0.0838	0.0392	0.2195	0.4010	0.5114	0.5037	0.3850	0.2105	0.0494
	(0.0122)	(0.0167)	(0.0216)	(0.0235)	(0.0211)	(0.0153)	(0.0103)	(0.0112)	(0.0138)
Ch. in investment	0.0072	0.1184	0.2349	0.2948	0.2573	0.1331	-0.0199	-0.1319	-0.1640
	(0.0081)	(0.0070)	(0.0060)	(0.0072)	(0.0090)	(0.0098)	(0.0097)	(0.0085)	(0.0067)
Employment	-0.3240	-0.1901	0.0796	0.4083	0.6692	0.7559	0.6451	0.4067	0.1555
	(0.0087)	(0.0123)	(0.0151)	(0.0160)	(0.0149)	(0.0120)	(0.0084)	(0.0069)	(0.0082)
Unempl. rate	0.3357	0.2084	-0.0596	-0.3923	-0.6607	-0.7550	-0.6489	-0.4112	-0.1583
	(0.0083)	(0.0118)	(0.0147)	(0.0158)	(0.0148)	(0.0120)	(0.0084)	(0.0070)	(0.0082)

Productivity	0.1180	0.3084	0.5316	0.7108	0.7672	0.6656	0.4378	0.1664	-0.0609
	(0.0097)	(0.0088)	(0.0092)	(0.0093)	(0.0076)	(0.0067)	(0.0097)	(0.0126)	(0.0128)
Price	0.2558	0.3181	0.2702	0.0916	-0.1645	-0.3950	-0.5067	-0.4688	-0.3249
	(0.0167)	(0.0218)	(0.0235)	(0.0216)	(0.0198)	(0.0212)	(0.0225)	(0.0210)	(0.0176)
Inflation	-0.1070	0.0841	0.3110	0.4456	0.4021	0.1966	-0.0628	-0.2478	-0.2900
	(0.0151)	(0.0135)	(0.0175)	(0.0226)	(0.0228)	(0.0188)	(0.0154)	(0.0146)	(0.0131)
Mark-up	0.2183	0.1599	0.0411	-0.0988	-0.2040	-0.2361	-0.1968	-0.1226	-0.0580
	(0.0118)	(0.0088)	(0.0128)	(0.0184)	(0.0213)	(0.0206)	(0.0174)	(0.0135)	(0.0107)
Total debt	0.1225	0.2460	0.3793	0.4848	0.5250	0.4824	0.3691	0.2203	0.0763
	(0.0249)	(0.0229)	(0.0211)	(0.0216)	(0.0238)	(0.0253)	(0.0243)	(0.0212)	(0.0173)
Bank deposits	-0.0907	-0.2375	-0.3659	-0.4322	-0.4154	-0.3264	-0.2001	-0.0760	0.0196
	(0.0215)	(0.0171)	(0.0127)	(0.0118)	(0.0144)	(0.0168)	(0.0171)	(0.0157)	(0.0138)
Bankruptcy rate	0.1077	0.2667	0.3827	0.4104	0.3424	0.2132	0.0776	-0.0202	-0.0667
	(0.0082)	(0.0120)	(0.0159)	(0.0178)	(0.0170)	(0.0144)	(0.0127)	(0.0128)	(0.0132)

Notes:
Bpf: bandpass-filtered (6,32,12) series.
Monte-Carlo simulation standard errors in parentheses.

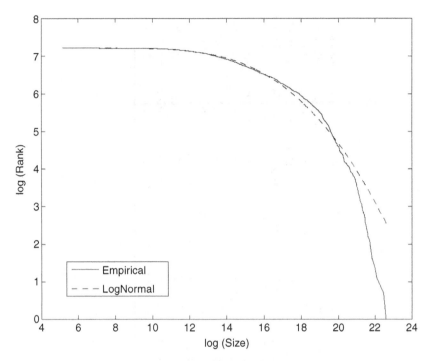

*Figure 5.3   Pooled (year-standardized) capital-goods firms' sales
distributions: log rank vs. log size plots*

inducing a rise in firms' debt. In turn, the rise in the cost of debt gradually
erodes firms' cash flows and savings, therefore leading to higher bankruptcy ratios and setting the premises for the incoming recession phase.

Distributions of Microeconomic Characteristics

Together with the ability of the model to account for a rich ensemble of
macro phenomena, how does it fare in replicating cross-sectional evidence on firms' dynamics? Let us consider the regularities concerning
firm-size and growth-rate distributions, firm-productivity dynamics, firm-
investment and firm-bankruptcy patterns generated by the model.
    Figures 5.3 and 5.4 show the rank-size plot of the pooled firm size in the
capital-goods and consumption-goods sectors. As the plots indicate quite
starkly, firm size distributions are right-skewed in both cases, and thus
in tune with empirical evidence (Dosi, 2007). In addition, this qualitative
evidence is reinforced by the analysis of firms' growth rates (not shown),
which display fat tails in both sectors.

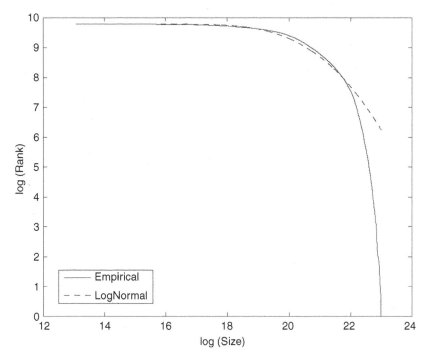

Figure 5.4   Pooled (year-standardized) consumption-goods firms' sales distributions: log rank vs. log size plots

Turning to firm productivity and investment, again in line with the empirical evidence (see the surveys in Bartelsman and Doms, 2000; Dosi, 2007), firms differ strikingly in terms of labour productivity in both sectors (see the standard deviations in labour productivity across firms plotted in Figure 5.5). Furthermore, the model is able to generate, as an emergent property, investment lumpiness (Doms and Dunne, 1998; Caballero, 1999). Indeed, in each time step, consumption-goods firms with very low investment levels coexist with firms experiencing investment spikes (see Figure 5.6, in relation to Gourio and Kashyap, 2007).

Finally, we have analysed firm bankruptcy patterns. The recent evidence on this issue (see, for example, Fujiwara, 2004; Di Guilmi et al., 2004) has pointed out that the distribution of bankruptcy rates is highly skewed to the right and fat tailed, also displaying power-law-like behaviour. This implies that business cycles are typically characterized by episodes of large bankruptcy avalanches. As the plots in Figure 5.7 clearly show, this empirical evidence is well replicated by our model.

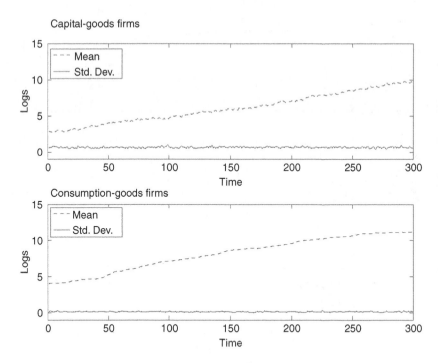

Figure 5.5   Firms' productivity moments (logs)

POLICY EXPERIMENTS: TUNING SCHUMPETERIAN AND KEYNESIAN ENGINES

The model, we have seen, is empirically robust in that it accounts, together, for a large number of empirical regularities. It certainly passes a much higher 'testing hurdle', as Robert Solow (2008) puts it, than simply reproducing 'a few of the low moments of observed time series: ratios of variances or correlation coefficients, for instance' (p. 245) as most current models content themselves with. Encouraged by that empirical performance of the model, we turn to experiments with different structural conditions (for example, concerning the nature of innovative opportunities) and policy regimes, and we study their impact on output growth rates, volatility and rates of unemployment.[28]

Alternative Innovation and Competition Regimes

Consider first the Schumpeterian side of the economy, holding the 'Keynesian engine' constant as compared with the benchmark scenario.[29]

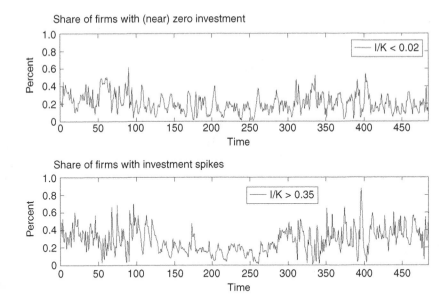

Figure 5.6   Investment lumpiness

In this framework, we first turn off endogenous technological opportunities. Note that by doing this, the model collapses onto a bare-bone, two-sector Solow (1956) model in steady state, with fixed coefficients and zero growth (absent demographic changes).

Opportunities and search capabilities
What happens if one changes the opportunities of technological innovation and the ability to search for them? Experiment 1 (Table 5.4) explores such a case. As compared to the benchmark, we shift rightward and leftward the mass of the Beta distribution governing new technological draws (that is, the parameters α_1 and β_1; see above). Note that the support of the distribution remains unchanged, so that one could informally state that the *notional* possibilities of drift in the technological frontier remain unchanged, too. The 'pool' of opportunities, however, that agents actually face gets either richer or more rarefied. We find that higher opportunities have a positive impact on the long-term rate of growth, reduce average unemployment and slightly increase GDP volatility (a mark of Schumpeterian 'gales of creative destruction'?).

Somewhat similarly, higher search capabilities approximated by the possibilities of accessing 'innovations' – whether they are failed or successful ones – (see the $\zeta_{1,2}$ parameters in equations (5.4) and (5.5)), positively

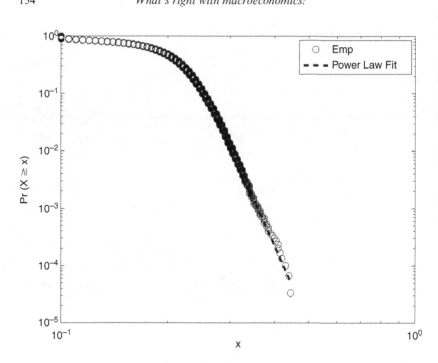

Figure 5.7   Empirical distribution of consumption-goods firms' bankruptcy rate together with power-law fit

influence the rates of growth and lower unemployment. Together, business cycle fluctuations are dampened possibly because a population of 'more competent' firms entails lower degrees of technological asymmetries across them, and, indeed, also lower degrees of 'creative destruction'. See experiment 2, Table 5.4.

Note that such a role of innovative opportunities and search capabilities is in principle equivalent to the one played by the more aggregate notions of 'human capital' (Nelson and Phelps, 1966; Benhabib and Spiegel, 1994) and 'appropriate institutions' (Acemoglu et al., 2006).[30]

Appropriability conditions

In many current models with a (neo) Schumpeterian engine, appropriability conditions play a key role via their assumptions on the forward-looking rationality of the agent(s) investing in an uncertain innovative search: the degrees of monopoly appropriation of the economic benefits of a successful search parameterize the equilibrium relation between investment in R&D and rates of innovation. In this model, we took a much

Table 5.4 Schumpeterian regime technological and industrial policy experiments

Experiment	Description	Avg. GDP Growth Rate	GDP Std. Dev. (Bpf)	Avg. Unemployment
0	benchmark scenario	0.0254 (0.0002)	0.0809 (0.0007)	0.1072 (0.0050)
1.1	low technological opportunities	0.0195 (0.0001)	0.0794 (0.0008)	0.1357 (0.0050)
1.2	high technological opportunities	0.0315 (0.0002)	0.0828 (0.0007)	0.1025 (0.0051)
2.1	low search capabilities	0.0231 (0.0002)	0.0825 (0.0008)	0.1176 (0.0059)
2.2	high search capabilities	0.0268 (0.0002)	0.0775 (0.0008)	0.1031 (0.0048)
3.1	patent (length only)	0.0242 (0.0002)	0.0761 (0.0008)	0.1132 (0.0060)
3.2	patent (breadth, too)	0.0163 (0.0001)	0.0631 (0.0007)	0.1329 (0.0067)
4.1	low entrant expected productivity	0.0183 (0.0003)	0.0798 (0.0012)	0.1402 (0.0084)
4.2	higher entrant expected productivity	0.0376 (0.0002)	0.0697 (0.0006)	0.0853 (0.0047)
5.1	weak antitrust	0.0265 (0.0002)	0.0698 (0.0006)	0.1036 (0.0043)
5.2	strong antitrust	0.0273 (0.0001)	0.0508 (0.0005)	0.0837 (0.0036)
6	Schumpeter-only, no fiscal policy	0.0110 (0.0018)	1.5511 (0.0427)	0.7855 (0.0274)

Note: Bpf: bandpass-filtered (6,32,12) series. Monte-Carlo simulations standard errors in parentheses.

135

more behavioural route and assumed a fixed propensity to invest in R&D. Granted that, how do changes in appropriability conditions affect aggregate dynamics?

We try to answer this question by mimicking the effect of a patent system. Under a 'length only' patent scenario, the innovative technology cannot be imitated for a given number of periods determined by the patent length (see experiment 3.1, Table 5.4). Such patenting possibility is *detrimental to long-run growth* and also augments the average rate of unemployment. The negative aggregate impact of the patent system is reinforced if each firm cannot innovate in some neighbourhood of the other firms' technologies – that is, in the presence of a patent breadth: see experiment 3.2, Table 5.4.[31]

Entry and competition policies
Important dimensions of distinct Schumpeterian regimes of innovation concern, first, the advantages/disadvantages that entrants face vis-à-vis incumbents and, second, the market conditions placing economic rewards and punishments on heterogeneous competitors.

The first theme cuts across the evolutionary and neo-Schumpeterian literature and is sometimes dramatized as a 'Schumpeterian Mark I' versus a 'Schumpeterian Mark II' scenario, meaning systematic innovative advantages for entrepreneurial entrants versus cumulative advantages of incumbents (see Malerba and Orsenigo, 1995; Dosi et al., 1995). In our model, technological entry barriers (or advantages) are captured by the probability distribution over the 'technological draws' of entrants. Again, we hold constant the support over which the economy (that is, every firm therein) may draw innovative advances, conditional on the technology at any time t. In this case, we do it for the sake of consistency: results apply even more so if different regimes are also allowed to entail different probability supports. Let us first tune the Beta distribution parameters α_2 and β_2 (see section on 'Schumpeterian exit and entry dynamics'). Our results are broadly in line with the evidence discussed in Aghion and Howitt (2007): *other things being equal,* the easiness of entry and the competence of entrants bear a positive impact on long-term growth, mitigate business cycle fluctuations and reduce average unemployment. See experiments 4.1 and 4.2, Table 5.4. The *ceteris paribus* condition is equally important, however: the same aggregate growth patterns can be proved to be equally guaranteed by the competent, cumulative learning of incumbents (see above the exercises on search capabilities).

What about competitive conditions? We introduce antitrust policies by forbidding capital goods firms to exceed a given market share (75 per cent in experiment 5.1 and 50 per cent in experiment 5.2, Table 5.4): the

Table 5.5   Keynesian regime fiscal policy experiments

Tax Rate	Unemployment Subsidy (in % of wages)	Avg. GDP Growth Rate	GDP Std. Dev. (Bpf)	Avg. Unemployment
0	0	0.0035	1.5865	0.8868
		(0.0012)	(0.0319)	(0.0201)
0.05	0.20	0.0254	0.1539	0.1952
		(0.0002)	(0.0025)	(0.0086)
0.10	0.40	0.0252	0.0809	0.1072
		(0.0002)	(0.0007)	(0.0050)
0.15	0.60	0.0251	0.0630	0.0846
		(0.0002)	(0.0005)	(0.0034)
0.20	0.80	0.0254	0.0584	0.0602
		(0.0002)	(0.0006)	(0.0027)
0.25	1	0.0252	0.0564	0.0551
		(0.0002)	(0.0005)	(0.0023)

Note: Bpf: bandpass-filtered (6,32,12) series. Monte-Carlo simulations standard errors in parentheses.

outcome is a lower unemployment rate, smaller business cycle fluctuations and also higher GDP growth (on this point, see also Fogel et al., 2008). Note that such a property has little to do with any static 'welfare gains' – which our model does not explicitly contemplate – but it relates rather to the multiplicity of producers, and thus of innovative search avenues, that antitrust policies safeguard.[32]

Fiscal and Monetary Policies

We now focus on the effects of Keynesian policies. More precisely, following Dosi et al. (2010), we check whether the 'Schumpeterian' dynamics embedded in the model is enough to generate sustained and steady growth, or whether instead this can be reached only if Keynesian aggregate demand policies are also well in place. Table 5.5 and Figure 5.8 present the results of the experiments.

First, simulation results show that Keynesian policies have a strong triggering effect on long-run average growth rates. If both the tax rate and unemployment subsidy are set to zero, the economy is trapped in an (almost) zero growth pattern characterized by extreme fluctuations and persistently high unemployment. Tuning up fiscal policies releases the economy from the 'bad' trajectory and puts it on the 'good' (high growth) one, which our benchmark scenario also happens to belong to (see Table 5.5 and Figure 5.8). If we further increase both the tax rate

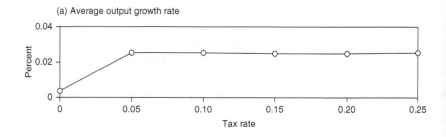

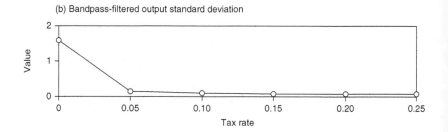

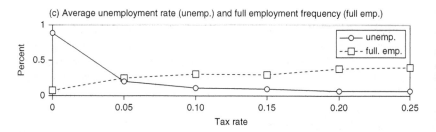

Notes: In such policy experiments, the unemployment subsidy rate (Φ) is four times the tax rate.

Figure 5.8   Fiscal policy experiments

and unemployment benefits, average output growth rates do not change in relation to the benchmark scenario, but output volatility and unemployment fall significantly, and the economy spends more time in full employment (see again Table 5.5 and Figure 5.8).[33]

The above results confirm that the Schumpeterian engine alone is not enough to guarantee steady growth in the model. Robust Keynesian policies must be well in place both to dampen output fluctuations and to sustain long-run growth.[34] This pervasive effect follows from the fact that countercyclical redistributive policies act as a parachute during recessions, sustaining consumption and, indirectly, investment on the demand side. In addition, the introduction and diffusion of new technologies in the economy rest upon sustained and stable investments in R&D and in new machines, which in turn are viable only in the presence of stable consumption demand.

Distributional aspects also play an important role in shaping the aggregate dynamics of the economy in the model. In order to further explore this insight, we conducted experiments on monetary policy under different income distribution scenarios. More specifically, we ran several Monte Carlo experiments by varying the level of the interest rate, and we repeated these experiments for high and low levels of consumption-goods firms' mark-up rate. Note that firms' mark-ups have two important effects in the model. First, they tune the distribution of productivity gains between wages and profits. In particular, higher (lower) mark-up rates imply that firms (workers) appropriate a larger share of productivity gains in the economy. Second, by tuning the level of firms' profits, mark-up rates impact the growth pace of firms' internal funds, thereby determining the degree of firms' dependence on external financing. It follows that higher (lower) levels of firms' mark-ups imply lower (higher) degrees of firms' financial dependence, and therefore lower (higher) sensitivities of firms' balance sheets to changes in interest rates.

The results of the above-described experiments are reported in Table 5.6. Let us discuss the main findings emerging from the table. First, interest rates have a significant effect on GDP volatility, unemployment and the probability of crises. Indeed, raising (lowering) the interest rate raises the levels of all three foregoing variables. Furthermore, interest rates have an important effect on the average growth rate as well. More precisely, raising interest rates has negligible effects on the average growth rate up to a threshold – increasing with the mark-up rate – above which higher levels of interest rate lock the economy into a low-growth path. This outcome is in line with the above-discussed results on fiscal policies and provides further support to the claim that active Keynesian policies (both fiscal and monetary) not only have a stabilizing effect, but also do impact on the long-run performance of the aggregate economy.

Finally, the experiments in Table 5.6 reveal other interesting features regarding the interplay between income distribution and the overall dynamics of the economy. Indeed, low mark-up rates result, *ceteris paribus*, in a sharp reduction of the levels of output volatility and average unemployment. In contrast, the effects of changes in interest rates are significantly magnified at lower mark-up rates. Two distinct mechanisms underlie these results. The first one is real and is implied by the fact that lower mark-up levels move the distribution of income in favour of wages,

Table 5.6   Effects of interest rate for different mark-up rates

Description	Avg. GDP Growth	GDP Std. Dev. (bpf)	Avg. Unempl.	Prob. of large neg. growth (< −3%)
High Mark-Up				
r=0.00001	0.0277	0.0749	0.0382	0.1618
r=0.05	0.0277	0.0739	0.0435	0.1488
r=0.1	0.0277	0.0760	0.0538	0.1431
r=0.15	0.0288	0.0777	0.0488	0.2102
r=0.2	0.0291	0.0898	0.0604	0.2799
r=0.35	0.0250	0.2056	0.1333	0.3699
r=0.4	0.0144	0.3633	0.3549	0.3878
Low Mark-Up				
r=0.00001	0.0274	0.0541	0.0191	0.1012
r=0.05	0.0281	0.0469	0.0145	0.0908
r=0.1	0.0290	0.0505	0.0180	0.1329
r=0.15	0.0298	0.0623	0.0217	0.2439
r=0.2	0.0288	0.1460	0.0586	0.3885
r=0.35	0.0099	0.4164	0.4546	0.4482
r=0.4	0.0010	0.4268	0.6346	0.4711

thus stabilizing consumption dynamics (*redistributive effect*). The second mechanism is financial and displays its effect via the higher financial dependence of firms implied by low mark-up levels (*financial dependence effect*, see above). These results also militate in favour of the conjecture (see Kaldor, 1955, and more recently Fitoussi and Saraceno, 2010) that more equal economies are also those characterized by milder fluctuations and by a lower occurrence of crises. Finally, they hint at the fact that monetary policies are much more effective in regimes characterized by low income inequality.

CONCLUDING REMARKS

In this chapter, we have studied the properties of an agent-based model that bridges Schumpeterian theories of technology-driven economic growth with Keynesian theories of demand generation.

The model is characterized by the presence of both a real and a banking sector. On the real side, the model entails the explicit account of search and investment decisions by populations of firms that are heterogeneous in the technologies they master and, possibly, in their decision rules. Aggregate macro properties emerge from the thread of interactions among economic agents, without any ex ante consistency requirements amongst their expectations and actions. In that sense, the model may be considered as an exercise in *general disequilibrium analysis*. Firms in the model endogenously generate new technologies – embodied in new types of 'machines' – via expensive and mistake-ridden search processes. Inventions then diffuse via the adoption decisions of machine users. Hence, agents generate both micro-technological shocks and micro-demand shocks, which together propagate through the economy. The linchpin between these two engines is represented by the credit provided by the banking sector. The bank employs firms' savings to finance firms' production and investment activities according to a credit multiplier rule.

A central question that we address in this chapter is whether the 'Schumpeterian engine' by itself is able to maintain the economy on a steady growth path characterized by full employment. We find that this is not the case: the endogenous innovation engine is able to do that only in the presence of a 'Keynesian' demand-generating engine, captured in the model by fiscal and monetary policies.

Our results cast serious doubts on the traditional dichotomy between variables affecting long-run growth (typically, technology-related changes) and variables impacting short-run business fluctuations (traditional demand-related variables). First, we find that technological innovations appear to exert their effects at all frequencies. Second, Keynesian demand-management policies not only contribute to reducing output volatility and unemployment rates, but, for a large set of parameterizations, they also affect long-run growth rates in so far as they contribute to 'releasing' the economy from the stagnant growth trajectory, which is indeed one of the possible emergent meta-stable states. Finally, our results indicate that bank credit and monetary policies can heavily affect business cycle dynamics by amplifying micro-level shocks. In this respect, our results point to the diverse effects of monetary policy in the presence of different income distributions between profits and wages.

In the future, we plan to further exploit the flexibility and modularity of our agent-based model to study new policy experiments under different institutional set-ups. In particular, given the post-2007 worldwide crisis, an obvious direction of development is to make an in-depth study of credit and financial markets. More specifically, we will employ the model to assess (i) how financial crises emerge; (ii) which policies (for example, monetary versus fiscal policies) are more suitable for coping with financial shocks; (iii) how the regulatory framework of the banking and the financial sectors (for example, Basel-like capital requirements) can prevent the formation of financial crises; and (iv) how the market structure of the banking sector (for example, regional versus big national banks) can amplify or dampen the effects of financial shocks. To explore the last point, we will introduce heterogeneous banks into the model, taking into account the emerging credit network structure between them and between banks and firms.

NOTES

1. Thanks to Willi Semmler, Robert Solow and Tania Treibich. Thanks also to the participants of the conference, 'What's right with macroeconomics?', organized by the Cournot Centre. All usual disclaimers apply.
2. For DSGE models, see Woodford (2003) and Galí and Gertler (2007).
3. See also Dosi et al. (2006) and Dosi et al. (2008).
4. As Blanchard (2009, p. 26) puts it, 'To caricature only slightly: a macroeconomic article today follows strict, haiku-like, rules: it starts from a general equilibrium structure, in which individuals maximize the expected present value of utility, firms maximize their value, and markets clear. Then, it introduces a twist, be it an imperfection or the closing of a particular set of markets, and works out the general equilibrium implications. It then performs a numerical simulation, based on calibration, showing that the model performs well. It ends with a welfare assessment.'
5. See, however, Dosi et al. (1994) for an exception. See also Dawid (2006) for an exhaustive survey of agent-based models of innovation and technical change.
6. For agent-based models with both Keynesian and Schumpeterian features, see Verspagen (2002), Ciarli et al. (2008), Saviotti and Pyka (2008), and the discussion in Silverberg and Verspagen (2005). See also the EURACE large-scale ABM that is aimed at capturing the main characteristics of the European economy and addressing European-policy analyses (Dawid et al., 2008).
7. See Fagiolo et al. (2007) for a discussion and the special issue on 'Agent-based models for economic policy design', *Journal of Economic Behavior and Organization*, 2008, **67**(2), edited by Herbert Dawid and Giorgio Fagiolo. More on that in the following section.
8. Survey data evidence summarized in Fabiani et al. (2006) show that European firms mostly set prices according to mark-up rules.
9. In the following, we assume all capital-producing firms to be identical in their R&D propensity. This is not too far from reality: R&D intensities are largely sector specific and associated with the sector-wide nature of innovative opportunities and modes of innovative search (see Pavitt, 1984; Dosi, 1988; and Klevorick et al., 1995).
10. Firms on the technological frontier, lacking anyone to imitate, obviously invest their entire R&D budget in the search for innovations.
11. For maximum simplicity, here we use the rule $D_j^e(t) = D_j(t - 1)$. In Dosi et al. (2006), we check the robustness of the simulation results employing more sophisticated expectation-formation rules. We found that increasing the computational capabilities of firms does not significantly change either the average growth rates or the stability of the economy. These properties still hold in the model presented here.
12. We assume that in any given period, firms' capital growth rates cannot exceed a fixed maximum threshold consistent with the maximum capital growth rates found in the empirical literature on firms' investment patterns (see, for example, Doms and Dunne, 1998).
13. This is in line with a large body of empirical analyses (see, for example, Feldstein and Foot, 1971; Eisner, 1972; Goolsbee, 1998) showing that replacement investment is typically not proportional to the capital stock.
14. Moreover, they also scrap the machines older than η periods (with η being a positive integer).

15. Among the empirical literature investigating the presence of gestation-lag effects in firms' investment expenditures, see, for example, Del Boca et al. (2008).

16. If investment plans cannot be fully realized, firms give priority to capital stock expansion, as compared to the substitution of old machines.

17. This is close to the spirit of 'customer market' models originated by the seminal work of Edmund Phelps and Sidney Winter (1970). See also Klemperer (1995) for a survey, and the exploration of some important macro implications by Bruce Greenwald and Joseph Stiglitz (2003).

18. Antecedents in the same spirit are Phelps and Winter, 1970; Klemperer, 1987; Farrel and Shapiro, 1988; see also the empirical literature on consumers' imperfect price knowledge surveyed in Rotemberg, 2008.

19. Recall that consumption-goods firms fix production according to their demand expectations, which may differ from actual demand. If the firm produces too much, the inventories pile up, whereas if its production is lower than demand plus inventories, its competitiveness is reduced accordingly.

20. Strictly speaking, a canonic replicator dynamic evolves on the unit simplex with all entities having positive shares. Equation (5.13) allows shares to become virtually negative. In that case, the firm is pronounced dead, and market shares are re-calculated accordingly. This is what we mean by a 'quasi-replicator' dynamic. Note that an advantage of such a formulation is that it determines simultaneously changes in market shares and extinction events.

21. The stock of capital of a new consumption-goods firm is obtained by multiplying the average stock of capital of the incumbents by a random draw from a Uniform distribution with support $[\phi_1, \phi_2], 0 < \phi_1, < \phi_2 \leq 1$. In the same manner, the stock of liquid assets of an entrant is computed by multiplying the average stock of liquid assets of the incumbents of the sector by a random variable distributed according to a Uniform with support $[\phi_3, \phi_4], 0 < \phi_3, < \phi_4 \leq 1$.

22. More precisely, the technology of capital-goods firms is obtained by applying a coefficient extracted from a Beta (α_2, β_2) distribution to the endogenously evolving technology frontier $(A^{max}(t), B^{max}(t))$, where $A^{max}(t)$ and $B^{max}(t)$ are the best technology available to incumbents.

23. For simplicity, we assume in the following that $\frac{\Delta w(t)}{w(t-1)} = \frac{\Delta \overline{AB}(t)}{\overline{AB}(t-1)}$. Simulation results are robust to wage dynamics involving adjustment to inflation and unemployment. For more detailed modelling of the labour market in an evolutionary/ACE framework, see, for example, Tesfatsion (2000) and Fagiolo et al. (2004).

24. Some methodological issues concerning the exploration of the properties of evolutionary/ACE models are discussed in, for example, Lane (1993); Pyka and Fagiolo (2007); Fagiolo et al. (2007); Fagiolo and Roventini (2012).

25. Preliminary exercises confirm that, for the majority of statistics under study, Monte Carlo distributions are sufficiently symmetric and unimodal to justify the use of across-run averages as meaningful synthetic indicators.

26. The average growth rate of variable X (for example, GDP) is simply defined as:

$$\overline{GR}_X = \frac{\log X(T) - \log X(0)}{T + 1},$$

where $T = 600$ is the econometric sample size. This value for T is a conservative choice, as the first iterative moments of growth statistics converge to a stable behaviour well before such a time horizon. This means that the model reaches a relatively (meta) stable behaviour soon after simulations start. Our experiment shows that choosing larger values for T does not alter the main economic implications resulting from the simulation of the model.

27. In addition, aggregate growth rates of output display fat-tailed distributions (not shown) that are well in tune with the empirical evidence (see Castaldi and Dosi, 2008; Fagiolo et al., 2008). Informally, that means that both in our model and in reality,

relatively big 'spurs of growth' and recessions occur much more frequently than might be predicted on the grounds of normally distributed shocks (see also the discussion on firm growth patterns below).

28. Interestingly, many statistical regularities concerning the structure of the economy (for example, size distributions, fatness of firms' growth rates, and so on) appear to hold across an ample parameter range, under positive technological progress, even when policies undergo the changes we study in the following section.

29. The full list of parameters under different policy scenarios is available from the authors on request.

30. In fact, given the increasing availability of micro data, one can start thinking of disaggregated empirical proxies for our variables. The issue is well beyond the scope of this chapter, however.

31. On purpose, we did not introduce any feedback between changes in IPR regimes and propensities to search.

32. The thrust of our results on policies affecting entry, competition, and variety preservation are indeed broadly in tune with the advocacy for 'evolutionary technology policies' in Metcalfe (1994b), while it runs against the so-called 'Schumpeterian hypothesis', according to which degrees of industrial concentration should be conducive to higher rates of innovation.

33. On the long-run, growth-enhancing effects of countercyclical macroeconomic policies, see the empirical evidence provided by Aghion and Marinescu (2007).

34. We also ran Monte Carlo experiments to check the robustness of Keynesian properties of the system to alternative institutional regimes governing the labour market captured by the parameters affecting the wage rate (see equation (5.21)). In particular, we allow wages to move as a (negative) function of the unemployment rate. Under these 'classical' circumstances, wages may fall during recessions, inducing price cuts, which in turn may increase output, supposedly weakening the case for Keynesian fiscal policies. These experiments suggest, however, that the dynamics of the systems are largely independent of how wages are determined. For more on that, see Dosi et al. (2010).

REFERENCES

Acemoglu, D., P. Aghion and F. Zilibotti (2006), 'Distance to frontier, selection, and economic growth', *Journal of the European Economic Association*, **4**, 37–74.

Aghion, P. and P. Howitt (1992), 'A model of growth through creative destruction', *Econometrica*, **60**, 323–51.

Aghion, P. and P. Howitt (1998), *Endogenous Growth*, Cambridge: MIT Press.

Aghion, P. and P. Howitt (2007), 'Appropriate growth policy: a unifying framework', *Journal of the European Economic Association*, **4**, 269–314.

Aghion, P. and I. Marinescu (2007), 'Cyclical budgetary policy and economic growth: what do we learn from OECD panel data?', in *NBER Macroeconomics Annual*, **22**, 251–78.

Aghion, P., G. Angeletos, A. Banerjee and K. Manova (2010), 'Volatility and growth: credit constraints and the composition of investment', *Journal of Monetary Economics*, **57**, 246–65.

Aghion, P., P. Askenazy, N. Berman, G. Cette and L. Eymard (2008), 'Credit constraints and the cyclicality of R&D investment: evidence from France', Working Paper 2008-26, Paris School of Economics.

Akerlof, G.A. (2002), 'Behavioral macroeconomics and macroeconomic behavior', *American Economic Review*, **92**, 411–33.

Akerlof, G.A. (2007), 'The missing motivation in macroeconomics', *American Economic Review*, **97**, 5–36.

Akerlof, G.A. and J.L. Yellen (1985), 'A near-rational model of the business cycles, with wage and price inertia', *Quarterly Journal of Economics*, **100**, 823–38.

Bartelsman, E. and M. Doms (2000), 'Understanding productivity: lessons from longitudinal micro-data', *Journal of Economic Literature*, **38**, 569–94.

Bartelsman, E., S. Scarpetta and F. Schivardi (2005), 'Comparative analysis of firm demographics and survival: evidence from micro-level sources in OECD countries', *Industrial and Corporate Change*, **14**, 365–91.

Baxter, M. and R. King (1999), 'Measuring business cycles: approximate band-pass filter for economic time series', *The Review of Economics and Statistics*, **81**, 575–93.

Benhabib, J. and M. Spiegel (1994), 'The role of human capital in economic development: evidence from aggregate cross-country data', *Journal of Monetary Economics*, **34**, 143–73.

Blanchard, O. (2009), 'The state of macro', *Annual Review of Economics*, **1**, 209–28.

Caballero, R.J. (1999), 'Aggregate investment', in J. Taylor and M. Woodford (eds), *Handbook of Macroeconomics*, Amsterdam: Elsevier Science.

Canova, F. (2008), 'How much structure in empirical models?', in T. Mills and K. Patterson (eds), *Palgrave Handbook of Econometrics Volume 2: Applied Econometrics*, Basingstoke, UK and New York: Palgrave Macmillan.

Castaldi, C. and G. Dosi (2008), 'The patterns of output growth of firms and countries: scale invariances and scale specificities', *Empirical Economics*, **37**(3), 475–95.

Caves, R. (1998), 'Industrial organization and new findings on the turnover and mobility of firms', *Journal of Economic Literature*, **36**, 1947–82.

Ciarli, T., A. Lorentz, M. Savona and M. Valente (2008), 'Structural change of production and consumption: a micro to macro approach to economic growth and income distribution', LEM Papers Series 2008/08, Laboratory of Economics and Management (LEM), Sant'Anna School of Advanced Studies, Pisa, Italy.

Colander, D., P. Howitt, A.P. Kirman, A. Leijonhufvud and P. Mehrling (2008), 'Beyond DSGE models: toward an empirically based macroeconomics', *American Economic Review*, **98**, 236–40.

Dawid, H. (2006), 'Agent-based models of innovation and technological change', in L. Tesfatsion and K. Judd (eds), *Handbook of Computational Economics vol. II*, Amsterdam: North-Holland.

Dawid, H., S. Gemkow, P. Harting, K. Kabus, M. Neugart and K. Wersching (2008), 'Skills, innovation, and growth: an agent-based policy analysis', *Journal of Economics and Statistics*, **228**, 251–75.

Del Boca, A., M. Galeotti, C.P. Himmelberg and P. Rota (2008), 'Investment and time to plan and build: a comparison of structures vs. equipment in a panel of Italian firms', *Journal of the European Economic Association*, **6**, 864–89.

Di Guilmi, C., M. Gallegati and P. Ormerod (2004), 'Scaling invariant distributions of firms' exit in OECD countries', *Physica A: Statistical Mechanics and its Applications*, **334**, 267–73.

Dinopoulos, E. and P. Segerstrom (1999), 'A Schumpeterian model of protection and relative wages', *American Economic Review*, **89**, 450–72.

Doms, M. and T. Dunne (1998), 'Capital adjustment patterns in manufacturing plants', *Review of Economic Dynamics*, **1**, 409–29.

Dosi, G. (1998), 'Sources procedures and microeconomic effects of innovation', *Journal of Economic Literature*, **26**, 126–71.

Dosi, G. (2007), 'Statistical regularities in the evolution of industries. A guide through some evidence and challenges for the theory', in F. Malerba and S. Brusoni (eds), *Perspectives on Innovation*, Cambridge, MA: Cambridge University Press.

Dosi, G., G. Fagiolo and A. Roventini (2006), 'An evolutionary model of endogenous business cycles', *Computational Economics*, **27**, 3–34.

Dosi, G., G. Fagiolo and A. Roventini (2008), 'The microfoundations of business cycles: an evolutionary, multi-agent model', *Journal of Evolutionary Economics*, **18**, 413–32.

Dosi, G., G. Fagiolo and A. Roventini (2010), 'Schumpeter meeting Keynes: a policy-friendly model of endogenous growth and business cycles', *Journal of Economic Dynamics and Control*, **34**, 1748–67.

Dosi, G., S. Fabiani, R. Aversi and M. Meacci (1994), 'The dynamics of international differentiation: a multi-country evolutionary model', *Industrial and Corporate Change*, **3**, 225–42.

Dosi, G., O. Marsili, L. Orsenigo and R. Salvatore (1995), 'Learning, market selection and the evolution of industrial structures', *Small Business Economics*, **7**, 411–36.

Eisner, R. (1972), 'Components of capital expenditures: replacement and modernization versus expansion', *The Review of Economics and Statistics*, **54**, 297–305.

Fabiani, S., M. Druant, I. Hernando, C. Kwapil, B. Landau, C. Loupias, F. Martins, T. Mathä, R. Sabbatini, H. Stahl and A. Stokman (2006), 'What firms' surveys tell us about price-setting behavior in the euro area', *International Journal of Central Banking*, **2**, 3–47.

Fagiolo, G. and A. Roventini (2012), 'On the scientific status of economic policy: a tale of alternative paradigms', *Knowledge Engineering Review*, **27**, 163–85.

Fagiolo, G., G. Dosi and R. Gabriele (2004), 'Matching, bargaining, and wage setting in an evolutionary model of labor market and output dynamics', *Advances in Complex Systems*, **14**, 237–73.

Fagiolo, G., A. Moneta and P. Windrum (2007), 'A critical guide to empirical validation of agent-based models in economics: methodologies, procedures, and open problems', *Computational Economics*, **30**, 195–226.

Fagiolo, G., M. Napoletano and A. Roventini (2008), 'Are output growth-rate distributions fat-tailed? Some evidence from OECD countries', *Journal of Applied Econometrics*, **23**, 639–69.

Farrel, J. and C. Shapiro (1988), 'Dynamic competition with switching costs', *RAND Journal of Economics*, **19**, 123–37.

Feldstein, M. and D. Foot (1971), 'The other half of gross investment: replacement and modernization expenditures', *The Review of Economics and Statistics*, **53**, 49–58.

Fitoussi, J. and F. Saraceno (2010), 'Inequality and macroeconomic performance', OFCE Working Paper.

Fogel, K., R. Morck and B. Yeung (2008), 'Big business stability and economic growth: is what's good for General Motors good for America?', *Journal of Financial Economics*, **89**(1), 83–108.

Fujiwara, Y. (2004), 'Zipf law in firms bankruptcy', *Physica A: Statistical and Theoretical Physics*, **337**(1–2), 219–30.

Fukac, M. and A. Pagan (2006), 'Issues in adopting DSGE models for use in the policy process', Working Paper 10/2006, CAMA.

Galí, J. and M. Gertler (2007), 'Macroeconomic modelling for monetary policy evaluation', *Journal of Economic Perspectives*, 21, 25–46.

Goolsbee, A. (1998), 'The business cycle, financial performance, and the retirement of capital goods', NBER Working Paper 6392, Cambridge, MA: NBER.

Gourio, F. and A.K. Kashyap (2007), 'Investment spikes: new facts and a general equilibrium exploration', *Journal of Monetary Economics*, 54, 1–22.

Greenwald, B. and J. Stiglitz (1993a), 'Financial market imperfections and business cycles', *Quarterly Journal of Economics*, 108, 77–114.

Greenwald, B. and J. Stiglitz (1993b), 'New and old Keynesians', *Journal of Economic Perspectives*, 7, 23–44.

Greenwald, B. and J. Stiglitz (2003), 'Macroeconomic fluctuations in an economy of Phelps–Winter markets', in P. Aghion, R. Frydman, J. Stiglitz and M. Woodford (eds), *Knowledge, Information, and Expectations in Modern Macroeconomics: In Honor of Edmund S. Phelps*, Princeton, NJ: Princeton University Press.

Hicks, J.R. (1937), 'Mr. Keynes and the "classics": a suggested interpretation', *Econometrica*, 5, 147–59.

Hubbard, G.R. (1998), 'Capital-market imperfections and investment', *Journal of Economic Literature*, 36, 193–225.

Kaldor, N. (1955), 'Alternative theories of distribution', *The Review of Economic Studies*, 23, 83–100.

Kirman, A.P. (2010), 'The economic crisis is a crisis for economic theory', *CESifo Economic Studies*, 56, 498–535.

Klemperer, P.D. (1987), 'Markets with customer switching costs', *Quarterly Journal of Economics*, 102, 375–94.

Klemperer, P.D. (1995), 'Competition when consumers have switching costs: an overview with applications to industrial organization, macroeconomics and international trade', *Review of Economic Studies*, 62, 515–39.

Klevorick, A.K., R. Levin, R.R. Nelson and S.G. Winter (1995), 'On the sources and significance of interindustry differences in technological opportunities', *Research Policy*, 24, 185–205.

Lane, D.A. (1993), 'Artificial worlds and economics, part I and II', *Journal of Evolutionary Economics*, 3, 89–107, 177–97.

LeBaron, B. and L. Tesfatsion (2008), 'Modeling macroeconomies as open-ended dynamic systems of interacting agents', *American Economic Review*, 98, 246–50.

Malerba, F. and L. Orsenigo (1995), 'Schumpeterian patterns of innovation', *Cambridge Journal of Economics*, 19, 47–65.

Metcalfe, J.S. (1994a), 'Competition, Fisher's principle and increasing returns to selection', *Journal of Evolutionary Economics*, 4, 327–46.

Metcalfe, J.S. (1994b), 'Evolutionary economics and technology policy', *The Economic Journal*, 104, 932–44.

Minsky, H. (1986), *Stabilizing an Unstable Economy*, New Haven, CT: Yale University Press.

Napoletano, M., A. Roventini and S. Sapio (2006), 'Are business cycles all alike? A bandpass filter analysis of the Italian and US cycles', *Rivista Italiana degli Economisti*, 1, 87–118.

Nelson, R.R. and E.S. Phelps (1966), 'Investment in humans, technological diffusion, and economic growth', *American Economic Review*, 61, 69–75.

Nelson, R.R. and S.G. Winter (1982), *An Evolutionary Theory of Economic Change*, Cambridge: The Belknap Press of Harvard University Press.

Pavitt, K. (1984), 'Sectoral patterns of technical change: towards a taxonomy and a theory', *Research Policy*, **13**, 343–73.

Phelps, E.S. and S.G. Winter (1970), 'Optimal price policy under atomistic competition', in E.S. Phelps (ed.), *Microeconomic Foundations of Employment and Inflation Theory*, New York: W.W. Norton.

Pyka, A. and G. Fagiolo (2007), 'Agent-based modelling: a methodology for neo-Schumpeterian economics', in H. Hanusch and A. Pyka (eds), *The Elgar Companion to Neo-Schumpeterian Economics*, Cheltenham, UK and Northampton, MA, USA: Edward Elgar Publishing.

Romer, P. (1990), 'Endogenous technical change', *Journal of Political Economy*, **98**, 71–102.

Rotemberg, J. (2008), 'Behavioral aspects of price setting, and their policy implications', NBER Working Paper 13754, Cambridge, MA: NBER.

Rotemberg, J. and M. Woodford (1999), 'The cyclical behavior of prices and costs', in J. Taylor and M. Woodford (eds), *Handbook of Macroeconomics*, Amsterdam: Elsevier Science.

Saviotti, P. and A. Pyka (2008), 'Product variety, competition and economic growth', *Journal of Evolutionary Economics*, **18**, 323–47.

Silverberg, G. and B. Verspagen (2005), 'Evolutionary theorizing on economic growth', in K. Dopfer (ed.), *Evolutionary Principles of Economics*, Cambridge: Cambridge University Press.

Silverberg, G., G. Dosi and L. Orsenigo (1988), 'Innovation, diversity and diffusion: a self-organization model', *The Economic Journal*, **98**, 1032–54.

Solow, R.M. (1956), 'A contribution to the theory of economic growth', *Quarterly Journal of Economics*, **70**, 65–94.

Solow, R.M. (2008), 'The state of macroeconomics', *Journal of Economic Perspectives*, **22**, 243–46.

Stiglitz, J. (1994), 'Endogenous growth and cycles', in Y. Shionoya and M. Perlman (eds), *Innovation in Technology, Industries, and Institutions. Studies in Schumpeterian Perspectives*, Ann Arbor, MI: The University of Michigan Press.

Stiglitz, J. and A. Weiss (1992), 'Credit rationing in markets with imperfect information', *American Economic Review*, **71**, 393–410.

Stock, J. and M. Watson (1999), 'Business cycle fluctuations in US macroeconomic time series', in J. Taylor and M. Woodford (eds), *Handbook of Macroeconomics*, Amsterdam: Elsevier Science.

Tesfatsion, L. (2000), 'Structure, behavior, and market power in an evolutionary labor market with adaptive search', *Journal of Economic Dynamics & Control*, **25**, 419–57.

Tesfatsion, L. and K. Judd (eds) (2006), *Handbook of Computational Economics II: Agent-Based Computational Economics*, Amsterdam: North Holland.

Verspagen, B. (2002), 'Evolutionary macroeconomics: a synthesis between neo-Schumpeterian and Post-Keynesian lines of thought', *The Electronic Journal of Evolutionary Modeling and Economic Dynamics*, 1007, available at: www.e-jemed.org/1007/index.php (accessed 20 June 2011).

Woodford, M. (2003), *Interest and Prices: Foundations of a Theory of Monetary Policy*, Princeton, NJ: Princeton University Press.

6. Booms and busts: New Keynesian and behavioural explanations

Paul De Grauwe

INTRODUCTION

Capitalism is characterized by booms and busts, by periods of strong growth in output followed by periods of declines in economic growth. Every macroeconomic theory should attempt to explain these endemic business cycle movements. How does the New Keynesian (dynamic stochastic general equilibrium – DSGE) model explain booms and busts in economic activity? And how does an alternative, behavioural model explain these features? These are the questions analysed in this chapter.

In order to answer such questions, it is useful to present some stylized facts about the cyclical movements of output. Figure 6.1 shows the movements of the output gap in the USA since 1960. We observe strong cyclical movements. They imply that there is strong autocorrelation in the output

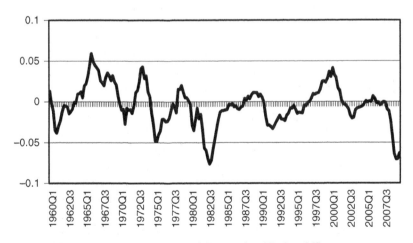

Source: US Department of Commerce and Congressional Budget Office.

Figure 6.1 Output gap for the USA, 1960–2008

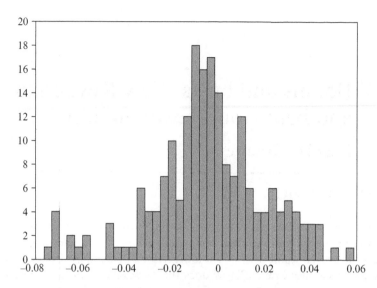

Notes: Kurtosis: 3.61; Jarque–Bera: 7.17 with p-value = 0.027.

Source: US Department of Commerce and Congressional Budget Office.

Figure 6.2   Frequency distribution of US output gap (1960–2009)

gap numbers, that is, the output gap in period *t* is strongly correlated with the output gap in period *t*−1. The intuition is that if there are cyclical movements, we will observe clustering of good and bad times. A positive (negative) output gap is likely to be followed by a positive (negative) output gap in the next period. That is what we find for the US output gap over the period 1960–2009: the autocorrelation coefficient is 0.94. Similar autocorrelation coefficients are found in other countries.

A second stylized fact about the movements in the output gap is that these are not normally distributed. The evidence for the USA is presented in Figure 6.2. We find, first, that there is excess kurtosis (kurtosis = 3.61), which means that there is too much concentration of observations around the mean to be consistent with a normal distribution. Second, we find that there are fat tails, that is, there are more large movements in the output gap than is compatible with the normal distribution. That also means that if we were basing our forecasts on the normal distribution, we would underestimate the probability that in any one period a large increase or decrease in the output gap can occur. Finally, the Jarque–Bera test leads to a formal rejection of normality of the movements in the US output gap series.

In this chapter I will contrast the rational expectations (DSGE) model with a behavioural macroeconomic model, that is, a model in which agents have cognitive limitations and do not understand the whole picture (the underlying model). I will ask the question of how these two models explain these empirical regularities.

The rational expectations model will be the New Keynesian model. Its characteristic features are price and wage inertia. It is sufficiently well known as not to require much explanation. The behavioural model is less well known, and I will spend more time developing it. Its basic assumption is that agents have cognitive limitations; in other words, they only understand small bits and pieces of the whole model and use simple rules to guide their behaviour. I will introduce rationality in the model through a selection mechanism in which agents evaluate the performance of the rule they are following and decide to switch or to stick to the rule depending on how well the rule performs relative to other rules.

The modelling approach presented in this chapter is not the only possible one for modelling agents' behaviour under imperfect information. In fact, a large body of literature has emerged attempting to introduce imperfect information into macroeconomic models. These attempts have been based mainly on the statistical learning approach pioneered by Thomas Sargent (1993) and George Evans and Seppo Honkapohja (2001). This literature leads to important new insights (see, for example, Gaspar et al., 2006; Orphanides and Williams, 2004; Milani, 2007; Branch and Evans, 2009). Nevertheless, I feel that this approach still loads individual agents with too many cognitive skills, which they probably do not possess in the real world.[1]

The purpose of this chapter is to contrast the dynamics of the DSGE model with the behavioural model, and to draw some policy conclusions. It is very much inspired by the new literature on 'agent-based macroeconomic models' (see Howitt, 2008; Tesfatsion, 2006, among others). The next section presents the behavioural model. The sections that follow it discuss the different implications that the behavioural model has when contrasted with the rational expectations model. The last section presents some empirical evidence, followed by the conclusion with a discussion of some methodological issues.

A BEHAVIOURAL MACROECONOMIC MODEL

In this section, the modelling strategy is described by presenting a standard aggregate-demand–aggregate-supply model augmented with a Taylor rule. The novel feature of the model is that agents use simple rules – heuristics – to forecast the future. These rules are subjected to an adaptive learning mechanism, that is, agents endogenously select the forecasting rules that have delivered the highest performance ('fitness') in the past. This selection mechanism acts as a disciplining device on the kind of rules that are acceptable. Since agents use different heuristics, we obtain heterogeneity. This, as will be shown, creates endogenous business cycles.

This behavioural model is contrasted with a similar model that incorporates rational expectations, and that is interpreted as a stylized version of DSGE models. This comparison will make it possible to focus on some crucial differences in the transmission of shocks, in particular, of monetary policy shocks.

The Model

The model consists of an aggregate demand equation, an aggregate supply equation and a Taylor rule.

The aggregate demand equation is specified in the standard way, that is:

$$y_t = a_1 \widetilde{E}_t y_{t+1} + (1 - a_1) y_{t-1} + a_2 (r_t - \widetilde{E}_t \pi_{t+1}) + \varepsilon_t \qquad (6.1)$$

where y_t is the output gap in period t, r_t the nominal interest rate, π_t the rate of inflation, and ε_t a white noise disturbance term. E_t is the expectations operator where the tilde above E refers to expectations that are not formed rationally. This process will be specified subsequently. I follow the procedure introduced in DSGE models of adding a lagged output to the demand equation. This is usually justified by invoking habit formation. I keep this assumption here as I want to compare the behavioural model with the DSGE rational expectations model. I will show later, however, that I do not really need this inertia-building device to generate inertia in the endogenous variables.

The aggregate supply equation can be derived from profit maximization of individual producers. As in DSGE models, a Calvo pricing rule and some indexation rule used in adjusting prices are assumed. This leads to a lagged inflation variable in the equation.[2] The supply curve can also be interpreted as a New Keynesian Philips curve:

$$\pi_t = b_1 \widetilde{E}_t \pi_{t+1} + (1 - b_1) \pi_{t-1} + b_2 y_t + \eta_t \qquad (6.2)$$

Finally, the Taylor rule describes the behaviour of the central bank:

$$r_t = c_1 (\pi_t - \pi^*) + c_2 y_t + c_3 r_{t-1} + u_t \qquad (6.3)$$

where π^* is the inflation target, which for the sake of convenience will be set equal to 0. Note that, as is commonly done, the central bank is assumed to smooth the interest rate. This smoothing behaviour is represented by the lagged interest rate in equation (6.3). Ideally, the Taylor rule should be formulated using a forward-looking inflation variable, that is, central banks set the interest rate on the basis of their forecasts about the rate of inflation. This was not done here in order to maintain simplicity in the model.

Introducing heuristics in the forecasting output
Agents are assumed to use simple rules (heuristics) to forecast the future output and inflation. I proceed as follows. I start with a very simple forecasting heuristics and apply it to the forecasting rules of future output. I assume two types of forecasting rules. The first rule can be called 'fundamentalist'. Agents estimate the steady-state value of the output gap (which is normalized at 0) and use this to forecast the future output gap. (In a later extension, it will be assumed that agents do not know the steady-state output gap with certainty and only have biased estimates of it.) The second forecasting rule is an 'extrapolative' one. It does not presuppose that agents know the steady-state output gap; they are agnostic about it. Instead, agents extrapolate the previously observed output gap into the future.

The two rules are specified as follows: the fundamentalist rule is defined by:

$$\tilde{E}_t^f y_{t+1} = 0 \tag{6.4}$$

The extrapolative rule is defined by:

$$\tilde{E}_t^e y_{t+1} = y_{t-1} \tag{6.5}$$

This kind of simple heuristic has often been used in the behavioural finance literature where agents are assumed to use fundamentalist and chartist rules (see Brock and Hommes, 1997; Branch and Evans, 2006; De Grauwe and Grimaldi, 2006). It is probably the simplest possible assumption one can make about how agents, who experience cognitive limitations, use rules that embody limited knowledge to guide their behaviour. In this sense, they are bottom-up rules. They only require agents to use information they understand, and do not require them to understand the whole picture.

Thus, the specification of the heuristics in (6.4) and (6.5) should not be interpreted as a realistic representation of how agents forecast. Rather, it is a parsimonious representation of a world where agents do not know the 'Truth' (that is, the underlying model). The use of simple rules does not mean that the agents are dumb and that they do not want to learn from their errors. I will specify a learning mechanism later in this section in which these agents continuously try to correct for their errors by switching from one rule to the other.

The market forecast is obtained as a weighted average of these two forecasts, that is:

$$\tilde{E}_t y_{t+1} = \alpha_{f,t} \tilde{E}_t^f y_{t+1} + \alpha_{c,t} \tilde{E}_t^e y_{t+1} \tag{6.6}$$

$$\tilde{E}_t y_{t+1} = \alpha_{f,t} 0 + \alpha_{c,t} y_{t-1} \tag{6.7}$$

and

$$\alpha_{f,t} + \alpha_{e,t} = 1 \tag{6.8}$$

where $\alpha_{f,t}$ and $\alpha_{e,t}$ are the probabilities that agents use a fundamentalist or an extrapolative rule, respectively.

A methodological issue arises here. The forecasting rules (heuristics) introduced are not derived at the micro level and then aggregated. Instead, they are imposed ex post on the demand and supply equations. This has also been the approach in the learning literature pioneered by Evans and Honkapohja (2001). One could argue, therefore, that my modelling technique is still not fully bottom-up. Ideally one would like to derive the heuristics from the micro level in an environment in which agents experience cognitive problems. Our knowledge about how to model this behaviour at the micro level and how to aggregate it is too sketchy, however, so I have not tried to do so.[3] Clearly, this is an area that will have to be researched in the future.

As indicated earlier, agents are rational in the sense that they continuously evaluate their forecasting performance. I apply notions of discrete choice theory (see Anderson et al., 1992; and Brock and Hommes, 1997) in specifying the procedure agents follow in this evaluation process. Discrete choice theory analyses how agents decide between different alternatives. The theory takes the view that agents are boundedly rational, that is, utility has a deterministic component and a random component. Agents compute the forecast performance of the different heuristics as follows:

$$U_{f,t} = - \sum_{k=0}^{\infty} \omega_k [y_{t-k-1} - \tilde{E}_{f,t-k-2} y_{t-k-1}]^2 \tag{6.9}$$

$$U_{e,t} = - \sum_{k=0}^{\infty} \omega_k [y_{t-k-1} - \tilde{E}_{e,t-k-2} y_{t-k-1}]^2 \qquad (6.10)$$

where $U_{f,t}$ and $U_{e,t}$ are the forecast performances (utilities) of the fundamentalists and extrapolators, respectively. These are defined as the mean squared forecasting errors (MSFEs) of the optimistic and pessimistic forecasting rules; ω_k are geometrically declining weights.

Applying discrete choice theory, the probability that an agent will use the fundamentalist forecasting rule is given by the expression (Anderson et al., 1992; Brock and Hommes, 1997):

$$\alpha_{f,t} = \frac{\exp(\gamma U_{f,t})}{\exp(\gamma U_{f,t}) + \exp(\gamma U_{e,t})} \qquad (6.11)$$

Similarly the probability that an agent will use the extrapolative forecasting rule is given by:

$$\alpha_{e,t} = \frac{\exp(\gamma U_{e,t})}{\exp(\gamma U_{f,t}) + \exp(\gamma U_{e,t})} = 1 - \alpha_{f,t} \qquad (6.12)$$

Equation (6.11) says that as the past forecasting performance of the fundamentalists improves relative to that of the extrapolators, agents are more likely to select the fundamentalist rule about the output gap for their future forecasts. As a result, the probability that agents will use the fundamentalist rule increases. Equation (6.12) has a similar interpretation. The parameter γ measures the 'intensity of choice'. It parametrizes the extent to which the deterministic component of utility determines actual choice. When $\gamma = 0$, utility is purely stochastic. In that case, agents decide to be fundamentalist or extrapolator by tossing a coin, and the probability to be fundamentalist (or extrapolator) is exactly 0.5. When $\gamma = \infty$, utility is fully deterministic and the probability of using a fundamentalist rule is either 1 or 0. The parameter γ can also be interpreted as expressing a willingness to learn from past performance. When $\gamma = 0$, this willingness is zero; it increases with the size of γ.

Note that this selection mechanism is the disciplining device introduced in this model on the kind of rules of behaviour that are acceptable. Only those rules that pass the fitness test remain in place. The others are weeded out. In contrast with the disciplining device implicit in rational expectations models, implying that agents have superior cognitive capacities, we do not have to make such an assumption here.

It should also be stressed that although individuals use simple rules in forecasting the future, this does not mean that they fail to learn. In fact, the fitness criterion used should be interpreted as a learning mechanism based on 'trial and error'. When observing that the rule they use performs less well than the alternative rule, agents are willing to switch to the better performing rule. Put differently, agents avoid making systematic mistakes by constantly being willing to learn from past mistakes and to change their behaviour. This also ensures that the market forecasts are unbiased.

The mechanism driving the selection of the rules introduces a self-organizing dynamic into the model. This dynamic goes beyond the capacity of understanding of any one individual in the model. In this sense it is a bottom-up system. It contrasts with the mainstream macroeconomic models in which it is assumed that some or all agents can take a bird's eye view and understand the whole picture. These agents not only understand the whole picture, but also use this whole picture to decide on their optimal behaviour. Thus, there is a one-to-one correspondence between the total information embedded in the world and the individuals' brains.

Introducing heuristics in forecasting inflation

Agents also have to forecast inflation. A similar simple heuristics is used as in the case of output gap forecasting, with one rule that could be called a fundamentalist rule and the other an extrapolative rule (see Brazier et al., 2006, for a similar set-up). The fundamentalist rule is based on the announced inflation target, that is, agents using this rule have confidence in its credibility and use it to forecast inflation. The extrapolative rule is used by agents who do not trust the announced inflation target. Instead they extrapolate inflation from the past into the future.

The fundamentalist rule will be called an 'inflation targeting' rule. It consists in using the central bank's inflation target to forecast future inflation, such that:

$$\tilde{E}_t^{tar} = \pi^* \tag{6.13}$$

where the inflation target π^* is normalized to be equal to 0.

The 'extrapolators' are defined by:

$$\tilde{E}_t^{ext}\pi_{t+1} = \pi_{t-1} \tag{6.14}$$

The market forecast is a weighted average of these two forecasts, such that:

$$\tilde{E}_t\pi_{t+1} = \beta_{tar,t}\tilde{E}_t^{tar}\pi_{t+1} + \beta_{ext,t}\tilde{E}_t^{ext}\pi_{t+1} \tag{6.15}$$

or

$$\tilde{E}_t \pi_{t+1} = \beta_{tar,t} \pi^* + \beta_{ext,t} \pi_{t-1} \qquad (6.16)$$

and

$$\beta_{tar,t} + \beta_{ext,t} = 1 \qquad (6.17)$$

The same selection mechanism is used as in the case of output forecasting to determine the probabilities of agents who trust the inflation target and those who do not and revert to extrapolation of past inflation, such that:

$$\beta_{tar,t} = \frac{\exp(\gamma U_{tar,t})}{\exp(\gamma U_{tar,t}) + \exp(\gamma U_{ext,t})} \qquad (6.18)$$

$$\beta_{ext,t} = \frac{\exp(\gamma U_{ext,t})}{\exp(\gamma U_{tar,t}) + \exp(\gamma U_{ext,t})} \qquad (6.19)$$

where $U_{tar,t}$ and $U_{ext,t}$ are the weighted averages of past squared forecast errors of using targeter and extrapolator rules, respectively. These are defined in the same way as in (6.9) and (6.10).

This inflation forecasting heuristics can be interpreted as a procedure of agents to find out how credible the central bank's inflation targeting is. If this is very credible, using the announced inflation target will produce good forecasts, and as a result, the probability that agents will rely on the inflation target will be high. If, on the other hand, the inflation target does not produce good forecasts (compared to a simple extrapolation rule), the probability that agents will use it will be small.

The solution of the model is found by first substituting (6.3) into (6.1) and rewriting in matrix notation. This yields:

$$\begin{bmatrix} 1 & -b_2 \\ -a_2 c_1 & 1 - a_2 c_2 \end{bmatrix} \begin{bmatrix} \pi_t \\ y_t \end{bmatrix} = \begin{bmatrix} b_1 & 0 \\ -a_2 & a_1 \end{bmatrix} \begin{bmatrix} \tilde{E}_t \pi_{t+1} \\ \tilde{E}_t y_{t+1} \end{bmatrix}$$

$$+ \begin{bmatrix} 1 - b_1 & 0 \\ 0 & 1 - a_1 \end{bmatrix} \begin{bmatrix} \pi_{t-1} \\ y_{t-1} \end{bmatrix} + \begin{bmatrix} 0 \\ a_2 c_3 \end{bmatrix} r_{t-1} + \begin{bmatrix} \eta_t \\ a_2 u_t + \varepsilon_t \end{bmatrix}$$

or

$$A Z_t = B \tilde{E}_t Z_{t+1} + C Z_{t-1} + b r_{t-1} + v_t \qquad (6.20)$$

where bold characters refer to matrices and vectors. The solution for Z_t is given by

$$Z_t = A^{-1}[B\tilde{E}_t Z_{t+1} + C Z_{t-1} + b\, r_{t-1} + v_t] \qquad (6.21)$$

The solution exists if the matrix A is non-singular, that is, if $(1 - a_2 c_2)$ $a_2 b_2 c_1 \neq 0$. The system (6.21) describes the solution for y_t and π_t given the forecasts of y_t and π_t. The latter have been specified in equations (6.4) to (6.12) and can be substituted into (6.21). Finally, the solution for r_t is found by substituting y_t and π_t obtained from (6.21) into (6.3).

My research strategy consists in comparing the dynamics of this behavioural model with the same structural model (aggregate demand equation (6.1), aggregate supply equation (6.2) and Taylor rule equation (6.3)) under rational expectations, which I interpret as a stylized DSGE-model.

The model consisting of equations (6.1) to (6.3) can be written in matrix notation as follows:

$$\begin{bmatrix} 1 & -b_2 & 0 \\ 0 & 1 & -a_2 \\ -c_1 & -c_2 & 1 \end{bmatrix} \begin{bmatrix} \pi_t \\ y_t \\ r_t \end{bmatrix} = \begin{bmatrix} b_1 & 0 & 0 \\ -a_2 & a_1 & 0 \\ 0 & 0 & 0 \end{bmatrix} \begin{bmatrix} E_t\pi_{t+1} \\ E_t y_{t+1} \\ E_t r_{t+1} \end{bmatrix}$$

$$+ \begin{bmatrix} 1 - b_1 & 0 & 0 \\ 0 & 1 - a_1 & 0 \\ 0 & 0 & a_3 \end{bmatrix} \begin{bmatrix} \pi_{t-1} \\ y_{t-1} \\ r_{t-1} \end{bmatrix} + \begin{bmatrix} \eta_t \\ \varepsilon_t \\ u_t \end{bmatrix}$$

$$\Omega Z_t = \Phi E_t Z_{t+1} + \Lambda Z_{t-1} + v_t \qquad (6.22)$$

$$Z_t = \Omega^{-1}[\Phi E_t Z_{t+1} + \Lambda Z_{t-1} + v_t] \qquad (6.23)$$

This model can be solved under rational expectations using the Binder–Pesaran (1996) procedure.

Calibrating the Model

I proceed by calibrating the model. In the Appendix, the parameters used in the calibration exercise are presented. The model was calibrated in such a way that the time units can be considered to be months. A sensitivity analysis of the main results to changes in some of the parameters of the model will be presented. The three shocks (demand, supply and interest rate) are independent and identically distributed (i.i.d.) with standard deviations of 0.5 per cent.

ANIMAL SPIRITS, LEARNING AND FORGETFULNESS

In this section simulations of the behavioural model in the time domain are presented and interpreted. The upper panel of Figure 6.3 shows the time pattern of the output gap produced by the behavioural model. A strong cyclical movement in the output gap can be observed. The lower panel of Figure 6.3 shows a variable called 'animal spirits'.[4] It represents the evolution of the fractions of the agents who extrapolate a positive output gap. Thus when the curve reaches + 1, all agents are extrapolating a positive output gap; when the curve reaches 0, no agents are extrapolating a positive output gap. In fact, in that case they all extrapolate a negative

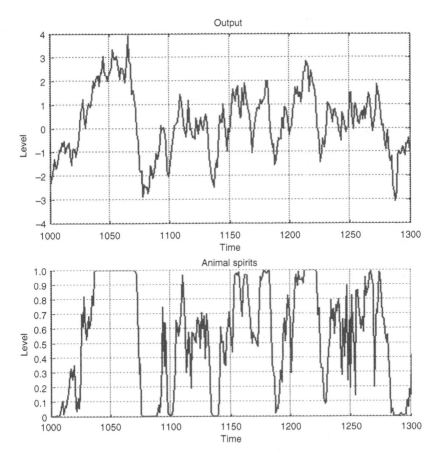

Figure 6.3   Output gap in behavioural model

output gap. The curve thus shows the degree of optimism and pessimism of agents who make forecasts of the output gap.

Combining the information of the two panels in Figure 6.3, it can be seen that the model generates endogenous waves of optimism and pessimism. During some periods optimists (that is, agents who extrapolate positive output gaps) dominate, and this translates into above-average output growth. These optimistic periods are followed by pessimistic ones when pessimists (that is, agents who extrapolate negative output gaps) dominate, and the growth rate of output is below average. These waves of optimism and pessimism are essentially unpredictable. Other realizations of the shocks produce different cycles with the same general characteristics.

These endogenously generated cycles in output are made possible by a self-fulfilling mechanism that can be described as follows. A series of random shocks creates the possibility that one of the two forecasting rules – say the extrapolating one – delivers a higher pay-off, that is, a lower mean squared forecast error (MSFE). This attracts agents that were using the fundamentalist rule. If the successful extrapolation happens to be a positive extrapolation, more agents will start extrapolating the positive output gap. The 'contagion effect' leads to an increasing use of the optimistic extrapolation of the output gap, which in turn stimulates aggregate demand. Optimism is therefore self-fulfilling. A boom is created. At some point, negative stochastic shocks and/or the reaction of the central bank through the Taylor rule make a dent in the MSFE of the optimistic forecasts. Fundamentalist forecasts may become attractive again, but it is equally possible that pessimistic extrapolation becomes attractive and therefore fashionable again. The economy turns around.

These waves of optimism and pessimism can be understood to be searching (learning) mechanisms of agents who do not fully understand the underlying model but are continuously searching for the truth. An essential characteristic of this searching mechanism is that it leads to systematic correlation in beliefs (for example, optimistic extrapolations or pessimistic extrapolations). This systematic correlation is at the core of the booms and busts created in the model. Note, however, that when computed over a significantly long period of time, the average error in the forecasting goes to zero. In this sense, the forecast bias tends to disappear asymptotically.

The results concerning the time path of inflation are shown in Figure 6.4. The lower panel of Figure 6.4 shows the fraction of agents using the extrapolator heuristics, that is, the agents who do not trust the inflation target of the central bank. One can identify two regimes. There is a regime in which the fraction of extrapolators fluctuates around 50 per cent, which also implies that the fraction of forecasters using the inflation target as

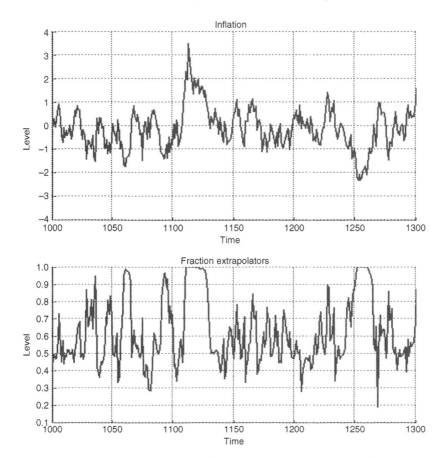

Figure 6.4   Inflation in behavioural model

their guide (the 'inflation targeters') is around 50 per cent. This is sufficient to maintain the rate of inflation within a narrow band of approximately + or −1 per cent around the central bank's inflation target. There is a second regime, though that occurs when the extrapolators are dominant. During this regime, the rate of inflation fluctuates significantly more. Thus, the inflation targeting of the central bank is fragile. It can be undermined when forecasters decide that relying on past inflation movements produces better forecasting performances than relying on the central bank's inflation target. This can occur unpredictably as a result of stochastic shocks in supply and/or demand. I will return to the question of how the central bank can reduce this loss of credibility.

The simulations reported in the previous section assumed a given set

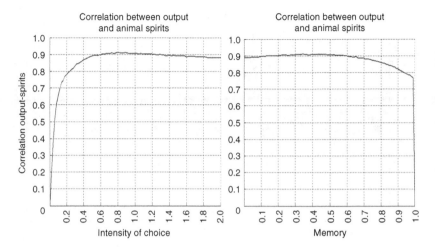

Figure 6.5   Correlations between output gap and fraction of optimists

of numerical values of the parameters of the model. It was found that for this set of parameter values, animal spirits (measured by the movements in the fraction of optimistic extrapolators) emerge and affect the fluctuations of the output gap. The correlation coefficient between the fraction of optimists and the output gap in the simulation reported in Figure 6.3 is 0.86. One would like to know how this correlation evolves when one changes the parameter values of the model. I concentrate on two parameter values here: the intensity of choice parameter, γ, and the memory agents have when calculating the performance of their forecasting. The latter is represented by the parameter ω_k in equations (6.9) and (6.10), and is a series of declining weights attached to past forecasting errors. I define $\omega_k = (1 - \rho)\rho^k$ (and $0 \leq \rho \leq 1$). The parameter ρ can then be interpreted as a measure of the memory of agents. When $\rho = 0$, there is no memory, meaning only last period's performance matters in evaluating a forecasting rule; when $\rho = 1$, there is infinite memory, meaning all past errors, however far in the past, obtain the same weight.

The results of the sensitivity analysis are shown in Figure 6.5. The left-hand panel shows the correlation between the output gap and the fraction of optimistic extrapolators (animal spirits) for increasing values of the intensity of choice parameter, γ. It can be seen that when γ is zero (that is, when the switching mechanism is purely stochastic), this correlation is zero. The interpretation is that in an environment in which agents decide purely randomly – in other words, they do not react to the performance of their forecasting rule – there are no systematic waves of optimism and pessimism (animal spirits) that can influence the business cycle. When γ increases, the correlation increases sharply. Thus, in an environment in which agents learn from their mistakes, animal spirits arise. One thus needs a minimum level of rationality (in the sense of a willingness to learn) for animal spirits to emerge and to influence the business cycle. Figure 6.3 shows that this is achieved with relatively low levels of γ.

The right-hand panel shows the correlation between the output gap and the fraction of optimists for increasing values of the memory parameter ρ. It can be seen that when ρ = 1 the correlation is zero. This is the case where agents attach the same weight to all past observations, however far in the past they occurred. Put differently, when agents have infinite memory, they forget nothing. In that case animal spirits do not occur. Thus one needs some forgetfulness (which is a cognitive limitation) to produce animal spirits. Note that the degree of forgetfulness does not have to be large. For values of ρ below 0.98, the correlations between output and animal spirits are quite high.

Having presented the main features of the behavioural model, I will now proceed to show how this model leads to a view of macroeconomic dynamics that contrasts greatly with the one obtained from the rational-expectations DSGE models. I will concentrate on two areas. The first one has to do with the business cycle theories implicit in the behavioural and the rational expectations models. The second one focuses on the implications for monetary policies.

TWO DIFFERENT BUSINESS CYCLE THEORIES

Are the behavioural and the New Keynesian models capable of mimicking these empirical regularities? Let us first focus on the behavioural model presented in the previous section. Figure 6.3 presented a typical simulation of the output gap obtained in that model. The autocorrelation coefficient of the output gap obtained in Figure 6.3 is 0.95, which is very close to 0.94, that is, the autocorrelation of the output gap in the USA during 1960–2009 (see the introduction). In addition, my behavioural macroeconomic model produces movements of output that are very different from the normal distribution. I show this by presenting the histogram of the output gaps obtained from Figure 6.3. The result is presented in Figure 6.6. The frequency distribution of the output gap deviates significantly from a normal distribution. There is excess kurtosis (kurtosis = 4.4), meaning there is too much concentration of observations around the mean for the distribution to be normal. In addition, there are fat tails. This means that there are too many observations that are extremely small or extremely

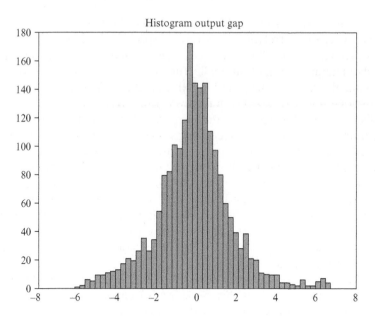

Notes: Kurtosis = 4.4, Jarque–Bera = 178.4 (p-value = 0.001).

Figure 6.6   Frequency distribution of simulated output gap

large to be compatible with a normal distribution. I also applied a more formal test of normality, the Jarque–Bera test, which rejected normality. Note that the non-normality of the distribution of the output gap is produced endogenously by the model, as I feed the model with normally distributed shocks.

This result is not without implications. It implies that when we use the assumption of normality in macroeconomic models, we underestimate the probability of large changes. In this particular case, assuming normal distributions tends to underestimate the probability that intense recessions or booms will occur. The same is true in finance models that assume normality. These models greatly underestimate the probability of extremely large asset price changes. In other words, they underestimate the probability of large bubbles and crashes. To use the metaphor introduced by Nassim Taleb, there are many more Black Swans than theoretical models based on the normality assumption.

It is fine to observe this phenomenon. It is even better to have an explanation for it. My model provides such an explanation. It is based on the particular dynamics of 'animal spirits', illustrated in Figure 6.7, which shows the frequency distribution of the animal spirits index (defined

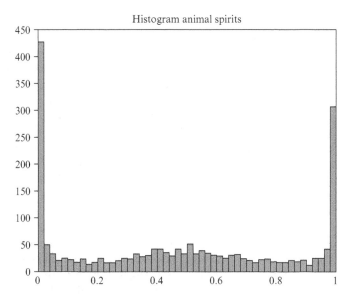

Figure 6.7   Frequency distribution of simulated animal spirits

earlier). This index is associated with the frequency distribution of the output gap obtained in Figure 6.6. From Figure 6.7, we observe that there is a concentration of the animal spirits at the extreme values of 0 and 1 and also in the middle of the distribution (but more spread out). This feature provides the key explanation of the non-normality of the movements of the output gap.

When the animal spirits index clusters in the middle of the distribution, we have tranquil periods. There is no particular optimism or pessimism, and agents use a fundamentalist rule to forecast the output gap. At irregular intervals, however, the economy is gripped by either a wave of optimism or of pessimism. The nature of these waves is that beliefs get correlated. Optimism breeds optimism; pessimism breeds pessimism. This can lead to situations where everybody has become either optimistic or pessimistic. These periods are characterized by extreme positive or negative movements in the output gap (booms and busts).

From the previous discussion, it follows that my behavioural macroeconomic model has a strong prediction about how the movements of the output gap are distributed. These movements should be non-normal. This is also what one observes in reality.

How well does the New Keynesian (DSGE) model perform in mimicking the empirical regularities about the business cycle? I simulated the Rational Expectations version of equations (6.1) to (6.3) (the New Keynesian model) using the same calibration. I show the movements of the simulated output gap in Figure 6.8. The upper panel shows the output gap in the time domain and the lower panel in the frequency domain. The autocorrelation in the output gap is 0.77, which is significantly lower than in the observed data (for the USA, I found 0.94). In addition, these output gap movements are normally distributed (see lower panel). We cannot reject that the distribution is normal.

The next step in making this model more empirically relevant consists in adding autocorrelation in the error terms. This is now the standard procedure in DSGE models (see Smets and Wouters, 2003). I have done the same with my version of the New Keynesian model and assumed that the autocorrelation of the error terms in equations (6.1) to (6.3) is equal to 0.9. The result of this assumption is shown in the simulations of the output gap in Figure 6.9. We now obtain movements of the output gap that resemble real-life movements. The autocorrelation of the output gap is now 0.98, which is very close to the observed number of 0.94 in the post-war US output gap. We still cannot reject normality though (see the Jarque–Bera test). This is a problem that DSGE models have not been able to solve.

Thus, in order to mimic business cycle movements, the New Keynesian (DSGE) model builders have had recourse to introducing autocorrelation in the error terms (the shocks that hit the economy). This trick has allowed DSGE models to closely fit observed data (see Smets and Wouters, 2003). This success has been limited to the first and second moments of the movements of output, but not to the highest moments (kurtosis, fat tails). The latter failure has the implication that in order to explain a large movement in output (for example, a deep recession, or a strong boom), DSGE models have to rely on large unpredictable shocks.

There are two problems with this theory of the business cycle implicit in the DSGE models. First, business cycles are not the result of endogenous dynamics. They occur as a result of exogenous shocks and slow transmission of those shocks. Put differently, the DSGE models picture a world populated by rational agents who are fully informed. In such a world, there would never be business cycles. The latter arise because of exogenous disturbances and of constraints on agents' ability to react instantaneously to these shocks. A given shock will thus produce ripple effects in the economy, that is, cyclical movements.

The second problem is methodological. When the New Keynesian model is tested empirically, the researcher finds that a lot of the output dynamics are not predicted by the model. These unexplained dynamics are then found in the error term. Everything is fine up to this point. The next

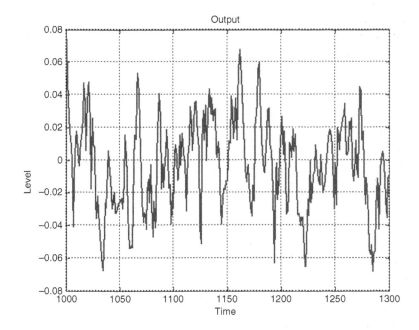

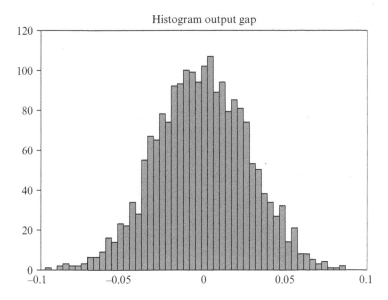

Note: Kurtosis: 2.9; Jarque–Bera: 1.03 with p-value = 0.5.

Figure 6.8   Simulated output gap in extended New Keynesian model

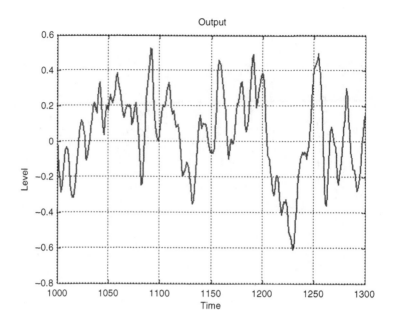

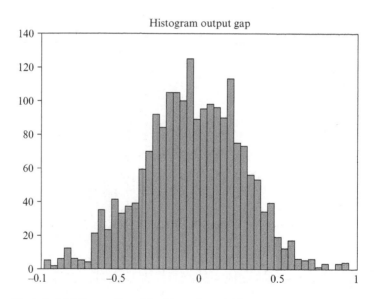

Note: Kurtosis: 3.16; Jarque–Bera: 3.2 with p-value = 0.17.

Figure 6.9   Simulated output gap in extended New Keynesian model and autocorrelated errors

step taken by DSGE modellers is to conclude that these errors (typically autocorrelated) should be considered as exogenous shocks.

The problem with this approach is that it is not scientific. When the DSGE modeller finds dynamics that are not predicted by the model, he or she decides that the New Keynesian model must nevertheless be right (because there can be no doubt that individual agents are rational), and thus that the deviation between the observed dynamics and those predicted by the model must come from outside the model.

THE ROLE OF OUTPUT STABILIZATION

Modern macroeconomics in general, and DSGE models in particular, have provided the intellectual foundation of inflation targeting. Until the eruption of the financial crisis in 2007, inflation targeting strategies had become the undisputed policy framework modern central banks should adopt. And most did. The official holders of macroeconomic wisdom declared that this step towards inflation targeting constituted a great victory of macroeconomics as a science (Woodford, 2009). From now on, we would be living in a more stable macroeconomic environment – a 'Great Moderation'. How things can change so quickly.

Inflation targeting, of course, does not imply that there is no role for output stabilization. DSGE modellers who have put a New Keynesian flavour into their models have always stressed that wage and price rigidities provide a rationale for output stabilization by central banks (see Clarida et al., 1999; and Galí, 2008). This idea has found its reflection in 'flexible' inflation targeting (Svensson, 1997; Woodford, 2003). Because of the existence of rigidities, a central bank should not attempt to keep inflation close to its target all the time. When sufficiently large shocks occur that lead to departures of inflation from its target, the central bank should follow a strategy of gradual return of inflation to its target. The rationale is that in a world of wage and price rigidities, overly abrupt attempts to bring back inflation to its target would require such high increases in the interest rate as to produce overly strong declines in output.

Output stabilization in the DSGE world, however, is very much circumscribed. The need to stabilize arises because of the existence of rigidities in prices that makes it necessary to spread out price movements over longer periods. The limited scope for output stabilization is based on a model characterized by a stable equilibrium. There is no consideration of the possibility that the equilibrium may be unstable or that fluctuations in output have a different origin than price rigidities. Should the scope for output stabilization be enlarged? In order to shed some light on this issue, I will now derive the trade-off between output and inflation variability in the context of the behavioural model, and formulate some policy conclusions.

The trade-offs are constructed as follows. The model was simulated 10000 times, and the average output and inflation variabilities were computed for different values of the Taylor rule parameters. Figure 6.10 shows how output variability (Panel a) and inflation variability (Panel b) change as the output coefficient (c_2) in the Taylor rule increases from 0 to 1. Each line represents the outcome for different values of the inflation coefficient (c_1) in the Taylor rule.

Panel a, showing the evolution of output variability exhibits the expected result: as the output coefficient (c_2) increases (inflation targeting becomes less strict), output variability tends to decrease. One would now expect that this decline in output variability resulting from more active stabilization comes at the cost of more inflation variability. This, however, is not found in Panel b. We observe that the relationship is non-linear. As the output coefficient is increased from zero, inflation variability first declines. Only when the output coefficient increases beyond a certain value (in a range from 0.6–0.8) does inflation variability start to increase. Thus, the central bank can reduce both output *and* inflation variability when it moves away from strict inflation targeting ($c_2 = 0$) and engages in some output stabilization without overdoing it. Too much output stabilization reverses the relationship and increases inflation variability.

Figure 6.10 makes it possible to construct the trade-offs between output and inflation variability. These are shown in Figure 6.11 for different values of the inflation parameter c_1. Take the trade-off AB. This is the one obtained for $c_1 = 1$. Start from point A on the trade-off. In point A, the output parameter is $c_2 = 0$ (strict inflation targeting). As output stabilization increases, it first moves downwards. Thus, increased output stabilization by the central bank reduces output and inflation variability. The relation is non-linear, however. At some point, with an overly high output stabilization parameter, the trade-off curve starts to increase, becoming a 'normal' trade-off: a lower output variability is obtained at the cost of increased inflation variability.

How can we interpret these results? Let us start from the case of strict inflation targeting, that is, the authorities set $c_2 = 0$. There is no attempt at stabilizing output at all. The ensuing output variability intensifies the waves of optimism and pessimism (animal spirits), which in turn feed back into output volatility. These large waves lead to higher inflation variability. Thus, some output stabilization is good; it reduces both output and inflation variability by preventing overly large swings in animal spirits. With no output stabilization at all ($c_2 = 0$), the forces of animal spirits are

Panel a

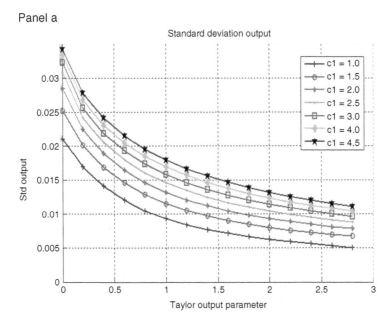

Panel b

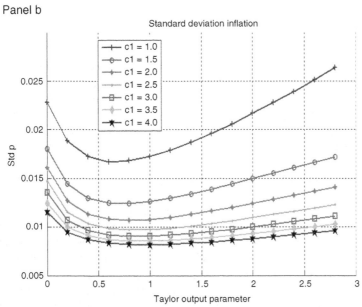

Figure 6.10   Output and inflation variability

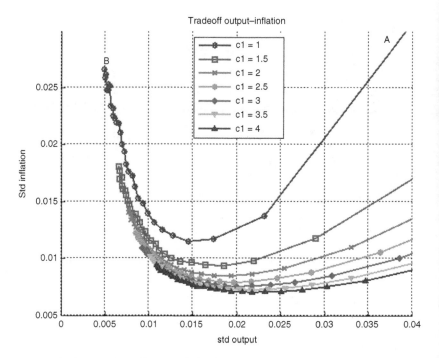

Figure 6.11   Trade-offs in the behavioural model

so high that the high output variability also increases inflation volatility through the effect of the output gap on inflation (supply equation). Too much output stabilization, however, reduces the stabilization bonus provided by a credible inflation target. When the central bank attaches too much importance to output stabilization, it creates more scope for better forecasting performance of the inflation extrapolators, leading to more inflation variability.

Figure 6.11 also tells us something important about inflation targeting. We note that increasing the inflation parameter in the Taylor rule (c_1) has the effect of shifting the trade-offs downwards, in other words, the central bank can improve the trade-offs by reacting more strongly to changes in inflation.[5] The central bank achieves this improvement in the trade-off because by reacting more intensely to changes in inflation, it reduces the probability that inflation extrapolators will tend to dominate the market. As a result, it reduces the probability that inflation targeting will lose credibility. Such a loss of credibility destabilizes both inflation and output. Thus, maintaining credibility of inflation targeting is an important source of macroeconomic stability in my behavioural model.

FISCAL POLICY MULTIPLIERS: HOW MUCH DO WE KNOW?

Since the eruption of the financial crisis in 2007–08, governments of major countries have applied massive policies of fiscal stimulus. This has led to a heated debate about the size of the fiscal policy multipliers. This debate has revealed (once more) how divergent economists' views are about the size of these multipliers (see Wieland, Chapter 2 in this volume). The estimates of the short-term multipliers vary from 0 to numbers far exceeding 1. There has been a lot of soul-searching about the reasons for these widely divergent estimates.

An important source of these differences is to be found in the use of different models that embody different priors. For example, in mainstream macroeconomic models that incorporate agents with rational expectations (both New Classical and the New Keynesian), fiscal policy multipliers are likely to be very small, as these models typically have Ricardian equivalence embedded in them. That means that agents who anticipate future tax increases following a fiscal stimulus (budget deficit) will start saving more (consuming less) so that one dollar of government spending is offset by one dollar of less private spending. In these models, the fiscal policy multiplier is close to zero. In Keynesian models, there is scope for a net stimulatory effect of fiscal policies. Thus, the different estimates of fiscal policy multipliers are not 'neutral estimates', but reflect theoretical priors and beliefs that have been put in these models in the construction stage.

My behavioural model makes it possible to shed some additional light on the uncertainty surrounding the effects of fiscal policies. I will do this by studying how a positive shock in aggregate demand produced by a fiscal expansion affects output. I will not give an exhaustive analysis of fiscal policies. The model does not give sufficient detail of government spending and taxation to be able to do that. I will model a fiscal policy shock just as a shock in the demand equation. The model then allows me to establish the nature of uncertainty surrounding such a shock, even in an extremely simple model.

I assume the fiscal policy expansion to occur under two different monetary policy regimes. In the first regime, I assume that the central bank uses the standard Taylor rule as specified in equation (6.3). Thus, under this regime, the fiscal policy expansion will automatically lead the central bank to raise the interest rate. This follows from the fact that the demand stimulus produces an increase in output and inflation to which the central bank reacts by raising the interest rate.

In the second regime, I assume that the central bank does not react to the stimulus-induced expansion of output and inflation by raising the

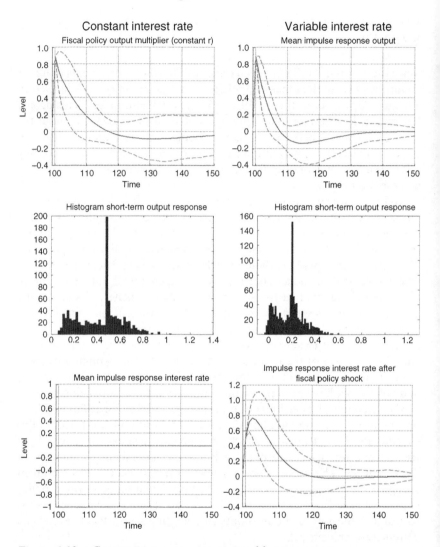

Figure 6.12   Constant interest rate vs. variable interest rate

interest rate. I do this, not because it is realistic, but rather to estimate the pure Keynesian multiplier effect of a fiscal stimulus. The Keynesian multiplier is usually estimated under the assumption of a constant interest rate so that crowding-out does not occur.

The results of this fiscal policy stimulus under the two monetary policy regimes are presented in Figure 6.12. The upper two panels show the impulse responses under the two monetary policy regimes. The instantaneous effects of the fiscal stimulus are the same under the two regimes. Under the variable interest rate regime, however, the positive effects of the fiscal stimulus decline faster and undershoot in the negative region more than under the constant interest regime. This is not surprising, as under the variable interest rate regime we see that the interest rate is raised substantially (see bottom panel), leading to a quick crowding-out.

A second important difference concerns the degree of uncertainty about the size of the output effects of a fiscal stimulus. As the upper panels show, the divergence in the impulse responses is larger in the constant interest rate regime than in the variable interest rate regime. This is also illustrated in the second panels. These show the frequency distribution of the short-term output responses under the two regimes. We observe a wider spread of these short-term output responses under the fixed interest rate regime. The reason is to be found in the fact that animal spirits behave differently under the two monetary regimes. The interest rate response under the variable interest rate regime tends to reduce the impact of animal spirits on the transmission mechanism, thereby reducing the volatility in this transmission. Put differently, when, as a result of the fiscal expansion, the central bank raises the interest rate, it lowers the expansionary effect of this expansion, making it less likely that positive animal spirits will enhance the fiscal policy stimulus.

These results make clear that there is likely to be a great amount of uncertainty about the size of the output effects of fiscal policies. This uncertainty is even more pronounced in the Keynesian scenario of a constant interest rate. This is also the scenario usually associated with the occurrence of a liquidity trap (a horizontal LM-curve). This is the assumption that tends to make fiscal policies most effective. In my model, it is also the assumption that makes the uncertainty about the size of these effects all the greater.

These differences are also made clear from a comparison of the long-term fiscal policy multipliers obtained from the same simulations as in Figure 6.12. The fiscal policy shock underlying the previous simulations is a one-period increase in demand (by one standard deviation). (The closest example of such a shock is the 'Cash for Clunkers' car-buying stimulus programmes introduced in many European countries and in the USA in 2009.) This temporary increase then produces the impulse responses as given in Figure 6.12. In order to obtain the long-term multipliers, I add up all the output increases (and declines) following this temporary fiscal policy shock. These long-term fiscal policy multipliers are presented in Figure 6.13 under the two monetary policy regimes.

Two results stand out. First, as expected, the long-term fiscal policy multipliers are higher under the constant interest rate rule than under

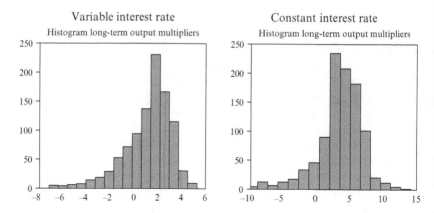

Figure 6.13   Long-term fiscal policy multipliers: frequency distribution

the variable interest rate rule. Second, the uncertainty surrounding these long-term multipliers is considerable. And this uncertainty is the most pronounced under the constant interest rate rule. It should be stressed again that the nature of the uncertainty here is not the uncertainty surrounding the parameters of the model. I assume exactly the same parameters in all these simulations. Put differently, it is not the uncertainty produced by the use of different models with different prior beliefs about the effectiveness of fiscal policies that yields uncertainty. The uncertainty is due to differences in initial conditions (market sentiments). These differences in market sentiments have a pronounced effect on how the same fiscal policy shock is transmitted in the economy.

CONCLUSION

Capitalism is characterized by booms and busts; in other words, economic activity is often subjected to strong growth followed by sharp declines. As a result, the frequency distribution of the output gap (and output growth) is non-normal, exhibiting excess kurtosis and fat tails. The latter means that if we are basing our forecasts on the normal distribution, we will tend to underestimate the probability that in any one period a large increase or decrease in the output gap can occur.

In this chapter, I used two alternative models to explain this empirical regularity. One model is the DSGE model, which assumes rational expectations. The other is a behavioural model. The latter is a model in which agents experience cognitive limitations. These limitations force agents to use simple rules to forecast output and inflation. Rationality is introduced into this model by assuming a learning mechanism that allows for the selection of those rules that are more profitable than others.

In the DSGE model, large booms and busts can only be explained by large exogenous shocks. Price and wage rigidities then lead to wavelike movements of output and inflation. Thus, booms and busts are explained exogenously. The fat tails observed in the frequency distribution of the output gap arise because there are large shocks hitting the economy.

My behavioural model provides a very different explanation. The behavioural model creates correlations in beliefs, which in turn generate waves of optimism and pessimism. Such waves produce endogenous cycles, which are akin to the Keynesian animal spirits. Occasionally this correlation of beliefs leads to extreme optimism (explaining booms) followed by extreme pessimism (explaining busts). The behavioural model thus provides for an endogenous explanation of business cycle movements.

In both models, the inflation targeting regime turns out to be of great importance for stabilizing the economy. In the behavioural model, this follows from the fact that credible inflation targeting also helps to reduce correlations in beliefs and the ensuing self-fulfilling waves of optimism and pessimism. Nevertheless, and this is where the behavioural model departs from the rational expectations model, strict inflation targeting is not an optimal policy. Some output stabilization (given a credible inflation target) also helps to reduce the correlation of biased beliefs, thereby reducing the scope for waves of optimism and pessimism to emerge and to destabilize output *and* inflation.

The behavioural model proposed in this chapter can be criticized for being 'ad hoc'. There is no doubt that the model has ad hoc features, that is, assumptions that cannot be grounded on some deeper principle, and therefore have to be taken for granted. In defence of this 'ad hocness', the following should be stressed. Once we leave the comfortable world of agents who experience no limits to their cognitive abilities, ad hoc assumptions are inevitable. This is due to the fact that we do not fully comprehend the way individuals with cognitive limitations process information. In contrast, there is no secret in how the superbly informed individuals in the rational expectations world process information. They understand the model, and therefore there is only one way to write down how they form their expectations. This feature may give the model builder intellectual satisfaction, but it is unclear whether such a model is useful in understanding a world in which agents' cognitive capacities are severely restricted.

An important shortcoming of the behavioural model presented in this chapter is that it does not introduce financial markets and the banking sector. Financial markets have been shown to be gripped by movements of optimism and pessimism, leading to bubbles and crashes. It will be interesting to extend the model to incorporate these features and to see how they interact with the animal spirits analysed here.

NOTES

1. See the fascinating book by Gerd Gigerenzer and Peter Todd (1999) on the use of simple heuristics as compared to statistical (regression) learning.
2. It is now standard in DSGE models to use a pricing equation in which marginal costs enter on the right-hand side. Such an equation is derived from profit maximization in a world of imperfect competition. It can be shown that under certain conditions the aggregate supply equation (6.3) is equivalent to such a pricing equation (see Galí, 2008; and Smets and Wouters, 2003).
3. Psychologists and brain scientists struggle to understand how our brain processes information. There is as yet no generally accepted model we could use to model the micro-foundations of information processing. There have been some attempts, however, to provide micro-foundations of models with agents experiencing cognitive limitations. See, for example, Kirman (1993) and Delli Gatti et al. (2005).
4. The *locus classicus* is Keynes (1936). See also Farmer (2006) and the recent book by George Akerlof and Robert Shiller (2009).
5. A similar result on the importance of strict inflation is also found in Gaspar et al. (2006), which uses a macromodel with statistical learning.

REFERENCES

Akerlof, G. and R. Shiller (2009), *Animal Spirits. How Human Psychology Drives the Economy and Why it Matters for Global Capitalism*, Princeton, NJ: Princeton University Press.

Anderson, S., A. de Palma and J-F. Thisse (1992), *Discrete Choice Theory of Product Differentiation*, Cambridge, MA: MIT Press.

Binder, M. and M.H. Pesaran (1996), 'Multivariate rational expectations models and macroeconomic modeling: a review and some results', in M.H. Pesaran and M. Wickens (eds), *Handbook of Applied Econometrics: Macroeconomics*, Oxford: Blackwell Publishers.

Branch, W. and G. Evans (2006), 'Intrinsic heterogeneity in expectation formation', *Journal of Economic Theory*, **127**, 264–95.

Branch, W. and G. Evans (2009), 'Monetary policy with heterogeneous expectations', mimeo, Stanford University.

Brazier, A., R. Harrison, M. King and T. Yates (2006), 'The danger of inflating expectations of macroeconomic stability: heuristic switching in an overlapping generations monetary model', Working Paper 303, Bank of England, August.

Brock, W. and C. Hommes (1997), 'A rational route to randomness', *Econometrica*, **65**, 1059–95.

Clarida, R., J. Gali and M. Gertler (1999), 'The science of monetary policy, a new Keynesian perspective', *Journal of Economic Literature*, **37**, 1661–707.

De Grauwe, P. and M. Grimaldi (2006), *The Exchange Rate in a Behavioural Finance Framework*, Princeton, NJ: Princeton University Press.

Delli Gatti, D., C. Di Guilmi, E. Gaffeo, G. Giuloni, M. Gallegati and A. Palestrini (2005), 'A new approach to business fluctuations: heterogeneous interacting agents, scaling laws and financial fragility', *Journal of Economic Behavior and Organization*, **56**, 489–512.

Evans, G. and S. Honkapohja (2001), *Learning and Expectations in Macroeconomics*, Princeton, NJ: Princeton University Press.

Farmer, Roger E.A. (2006), 'Animal spirits', in L. Blume and S. Durlauf (eds), *Palgrave Dictionary of Economics*, Basingstoke: Palgrave Macmillan.

Galí, J. (2008), *Monetary Policy, Inflation and the Business Cycle*, Princeton, NJ: Princeton University Press.

Gaspar, V., F. Smets and D. Vestin (2006), 'Adaptive learning, persistence and optimal monetary policy', Working Paper Series 644, European Central Bank.

Gigerenzer, G. and P.M. Todd (1999), *Simple Heuristics that Make Us Smart*, New York: Oxford University Press.

Howitt, P. (2008), 'Macroeconomics with intelligent autonomous agents', in R. Farmer (ed.), *Macroeconomics in the Small and the Large: Essays on Microfoundations, Macroeconomic Applications and Economic History in Honor of Axel Leijonhufvud*, Cheltenham, UK and Northampton, MA, USA: Edward Elgar Publishing.

Keynes, J.M. (1936), *The General Theory of Employment, Interest and Money*, London: Macmillan.

Kirman, A. (1993), 'Ants, rationality and recruitment', *Quarterly Journal of Economics*, **108**, 137–56.

Milani, F. (2007), 'Learning and time-varying macroeconomic volatility', mimeo, University of California, Irvine.

Orphanides, A. and J. Williams (2004), 'Robust monetary policy with imperfect information', Board of Governors of the Federal Reserve System.

Sargent, T. (1993), *Bounded Rationality in Macroeconomics*, Oxford: Oxford University Press.

Smets, F. and R. Wouters (2003), 'An estimated dynamic stochastic general equilibrium model', *Journal of the European Economic Association*, **1**, 1123–75.

Svensson, L. (1997), 'Inflation forecast targeting: implementing and monitoring inflation targets', *European Economic Review*, **41**, 11–46.

Tesfatsion, L. (2006), 'Agent-based computational economics: a constructive approach to economic theory', in L. Tesfatsion and K. Judd (eds), *Handbook of Computational Economics, Volume 2: Agent-Based Computational Economics*, Handbooks in Economics Series, the Netherlands: North-Holland/Elsevier, Spring, pp. 831–80.

Woodford, M. (2003), *Interest and Prices: Foundations of a Theory of Monetary Policy*, Princeton, NJ: Princeton University Press.

Woodford, M. (2009), 'Convergence in macroeconomics: elements of the new synthesis', *American Economic Journal: Macroeconomics*, **1**(1), January, 267–97.

APPENDIX: PARAMETER VALUES OF THE CALIBRATED MODEL

Heuristic Model

pstar = 0;	% central bank's inflation target
$a1$ = 0.5;	% coefficient of expected output in output equation
$a2$ = −0.2;	% a is interest elasticity of output demand
$b1$ = 0.5;	% $b1$ is coefficient of expected inflation in inflation equation
$b2$ = 0.05;	% $b2$ is coefficient of output in inflation equation
$c1$ = 1.5;	% $c1$ is coefficient of inflation in Taylor equation
$c2$ = 0.5;	% $c2$ is coefficient of output in Taylor equation
$c3$ = 0.5;	% interest smoothing parameter in Taylor equation
β = 1;	% fixed divergence in beliefs
δ = 2;	% variable component in divergence of beliefs
gamma = 1;	% intensity of choice parameter
sigma1 = 0.5;	% standard deviation shocks for output
sigma2 = 0.5;	% standard deviation shocks for inflation
sigma3 = 0.5;	% standard deviation shocks for Taylor equation
rho = 0.5;	% rho measures the speed of declining weights in mean squares errors (memory parameter)

Rational Model

pstar = 0;	% central bank's inflation target
$a1$ = 0.5;	% coefficient of expected output in output equation
$a2$ = −0.2;	% a is interest elasticity of output demand
$b1$ = 0.5;	% $b1$ is coefficient of expected inflation in inflation equation
$b2$ = 0.05;	% $b2$ is coefficient of output in inflation equation
$c1$ = 1.5;	% $c1$ is coefficient of inflation in Taylor equation
$c2$ = 0.5;	% $c2$ is coefficient of output in Taylor equation
$c3$ = 0.5;	% interest smoothing parameter in Taylor equation
sigma1 = 0.5;	% standard deviation shocks for output
sigma2 = 0.5;	% standard deviation shocks for inflation
sigma3 = 0.5;	% standard deviation shocks for Taylor equation

7. The economics of the laboratory mouse: where do we go from here?

Xavier Ragot

Very few economists foresaw the economic and financial crisis that broke out in 2007 and which has turned into the deepest world recession since 1929. Even worse, the field of economics may have prevented observers from perceiving the first movements – the steady accumulation of economic and financial fragility – of this extremely grave turbulence. It is thus time to reassess the usefulness of current economic theory, but how far should we go? How should a researcher in economics approach the subject if he has come to perceive his work as being much like that of a laboratory mouse? How can he advance his discipline, and therefore the understanding of economics? And once the experimenters outside the cage have placed the cheese, in which direction should he then search? What needs to be changed in the research process of the discipline of economics?

The purpose of this chapter is primarily to identify what exactly needs to be reconsidered in economics. The task consists in addressing the problem for numerous rival research programmes: the exploration of the role of rationality, financial imperfections and their nature, the importance of comparison to the data, and so on. Beyond this diversity, we must seek the principles of common methods to define the mainstream in economics. The question we then face is this: can the reform of economic thought be achieved through modifying the dominant approach, or do we have to search much farther afield?

Where will the new light come from to illuminate those obscure mechanisms that have brought economies to the brink of ruin? If we knew the answer to that question, research would no longer be research, and we would have already understood the crisis. So we have little alternative but to compare the different research programmes, in other words, to observe the mice and choose the best adapted. This, however, is still far from providing a solution to the problem, as we shall see. The selection criteria of research programmes are themselves under debate: should they be able to reproduce past historical data, make better predictions than the others, or make fewer mistakes? And over what time horizon?

The first part of this chapter seeks to define the dominant current, the mainstream. I define the mainstream, in brief, as the hypotheses of equilibrium and absence of arbitrage opportunities, since recent works show that the concept of rationality is becoming too narrow even for the mainstream. Equilibrium does not necessarily mean stability. On the contrary, the multiplicity of equilibria is considered a sign of instability. On the basis of this definition, one can attempt to identify recent works that lie outside the mainstream. The second part of the chapter presents the author's research programme as an example of the endeavour to evolve economic thought.

A REPRESENTATION OF THE DYNAMICS OF ECONOMIC RESEARCH PROGRAMMES: THE STANDARD PARADIGM

It is important to distinguish between the standard paradigm and the *world view* of the profession. The latter attached central importance to certain results – such as stability or efficiency. This was to the detriment of other works showing the instability or inefficiency of market economies, which were treated as theoretical curiosities. I start with a description of the world view held by the majority of economists, before defining the mainstream. I will then give some examples of very different research programmes that can be placed in the mainstream.

In early 2007, the most widely held economic view, as expressed in journals, conferences and speeches, could be summed up as follows. The market economy is stable and remarkably resistant to macroeconomic shocks. The more developed the mechanisms of the market are, the more resistant the economy is to shocks. In particular, the development of capital markets has made it possible to divide up risk between different securities, so that each agent only bears a small share of the risk, making the economy more stable. In more practical terms, the massive securitization of US mortgages allowed banks to sell credit claims that were evaluated by the discipline of the market. One of the vehicles of this securitization was the infamous subprimes, the details of which I will not go into here. More market means more stability. Moreover, allocation by the market is generally efficient. Neo-Keynesian and neoclassical economists disagreed about the inefficiencies of economies: should the central bank intervene to stabilize economies? Should fiscal policy be proactive? Sometimes they should, sometimes not. The problem then lies in the qualification of 'sometimes'. Two different currents clearly emerged, associated with identifiable policy options, but the models used in each case were very similar and the methods were the same: the dynamic stochastic general equilibrium model (DSGE).

Dynamic Stochastic General Equilibrium Models: a Genealogy

The DSGE models are largely inherited from the rational expectations revolution of the early 1980s. The names associated with this change of paradigm include Robert Lucas (1988), Thomas Sargent (Lucas and Sargent, 1978), Finn Kydland and Edward Prescott (1977). This research programme was based on a radical and forthright position. Starting with the hypotheses that the economy functions perfectly and that the market economy is efficient, what can one explain about economic fluctuations? This approach was named real business cycle theory (RBC). It had spectacular success as it greatly simplified the modelling strategy. With the hypotheses of efficiency, the dynamics of the economy can be represented by the choices of a representative agent who maximizes his or her utility; he/she is capable of using all the resources of the economy but limited by technological constraints. This research programme only gradually established itself in economics, since many theorists found this view of the world too simplistic, because it ignored the central question of aggregation. It reduced macroeconomics to microeconomics, with one sole agent and one good. The success of the RBC programme can be explained retrospectively by the new relationship between theory and data. The economists working on this research programme rigorously derived the implications for all the economic variables of the models in order to test them econometrically. Inside the RBC research agenda, a general movement has taken place in the macroeconomic profession to confront the model rigorously with the data using sophisticated econometric methods.

If nothing else, this shift of focus towards the data has shown the extent to which the basic RBC model has been a spectacular scientific failure. The basic model did not explain fluctuations in employment and asset prices or the dynamics of inflation. In fact, it is difficult to give an example of what the model explains in the data. All the anomalies were considered as enigmas, stimulating research programmes that sought to improve the match with the data by introducing additional frictions. Technological frictions, strange preferences and diverse externalities were all introduced into the model, but without ever really questioning the idea of a representative agent and of econometric comparison with the data using the appropriate filter.

One friction that enjoyed particular success was sticky prices. The original RBC models (Cooley and Hansen, 1989) addressed the monetary question on the basis of monetarist hypotheses. These models again met with failure, leading to the introduction of monopolistic competition and sticky nominal prices. This monetary dimension was all the more significant since central banks had become important, if not the leading players in macroeconomic stabilization. Developing theories likely to help central banks in choosing their monetary policy became a very active field of research.

The introduction of nominal rigidities into DSGE models was accompanied by another communication success – the rewording of the theoretical tool as a New Keynesian model: a representative agent allocates the economy's resources between consumption and saving on the one hand, and work and leisure on the other, in the face of price rigidities. The term 'Keynesian' is always open to debate when applied to these models. The basic New Keynesian models exclude involuntary unemployment and possess perfect capital markets – two hypotheses that could hardly be qualified as Keynesian. Can such models reproduce the observed dynamics of the economy with reasonable parameters? The answer is far from certain. A large number of additional hypotheses are introduced – what are called 'bells and whistles' – to test these models, and the results are sometimes good, sometimes very bad, especially in the financial part. These models cannot explain the evolution of asset prices and exclude, by hypothesis, any financial disequilibrium.

In 2007, the New Keynesian model had become the main tool of central banks, international economic organizations, and even public administrations. The approach to data, with devices such as Bayesian estimation, is very sophisticated, which makes this tool very technical, although in itself that is no guarantee of suitability. Nevertheless, this tool has become an important part of the standard paradigm, used as an interface between theoretical macroeconomics and empirical validation.

Faced with the ballooning number of additional hypotheses needed to account for the data, economists have sought to define a central method to impose some degree of intellectual discipline on the exercise. Lucas highlighted two constraints: equilibrium and rationality. In DSGE models, economies are always in equilibrium and agents always behave rationally.

These DSGE models are now being condemned, but without really being replaced by any new tools. The 'initial' New Keynesian models adopted the hypothesis of perfect capital markets – a hypothesis at the least exaggerated. The financial crisis did not call into question the models themselves, but only this particular hypothesis about the functioning of capital markets. Today, numerous works in central bank student research programmes aim to 'incorporate financial frictions into the DSGE model'. Models of financial imperfection built in the 1990s, which had met with some academic success within the standard paradigm while remaining somewhat marginal, are now being used. The models of Nobuhiro Kiyotaki and John H. Moore (1997), of Bengt Holmstrom and Jean Tirole (1998), and others are now introduced into DGSE models. The hypotheses of equilibrium and rationality are maintained, and financial frictions are added in to match the model to the data.

This endeavour to improve DSGE models is the most active research programme in macroeconomics, perhaps because of the importance of central banks in the promotion of economic research. It is always difficult to predict the success of this research programme or the nature of its possible successors. One a priori criticism that does appear legitimate, however, is that this programme restricts itself to incremental modifications of existing models, and does not, therefore, allow for radical innovations, such as the changing of models or more fundamental hypotheses. Very different research programmes have developed within the standard paradigm, gradually moving away from the hard core of hypotheses described above. Each of these programmes existed before the crisis, which has altered their scientific orientation and their relative importance within the academic world.

Trade and Labour Market Frictions

The most important model, in terms of academic recognition, is probably that developed in the works of Peter Diamond (1982a, 1982b), Dale Mortensen (Mortensen and Pissarides, 1994) and Christopher Pissarides (2000). One of the origins of this model is the desire to understand market exchange in more realistic representations of the market, notably with decentralized transactions. At the heart of these models lies the assumption that exchanges are bilateral operations conducted by agents who meet at random on the market. The prices are fixed by the agents, once they have met. For example, they may negotiate the price as a function of their bargaining power. This model has been applied to markets for goods and services and capital markets, but it is above all through its application to the labour market that it has become an essential tool. It is fair to say that it has even become the central model in that field, largely because it can take into account involuntary (frictional) unemployment, which does not exist in the so-called New Keynesian model. Criticisms have emerged that call into question some of the standard hypotheses of this literature (Shimer, 2005; Hall, 2005), but it appears that the central role of this model in labour economics has not been affected by the crisis. It has gradually been incorporated into macroeconomics (Merz, 1995; Andolfatto, 1996; Trigari, 2009), resulting in very complex models. Other attempts to introduce involuntary unemployment into macroeconomics are currently being developed.

Information

A set of very dynamic works are presently exploring the economic information that agents use in making their choices. In their simple version, rational expectations constitute a very strong hypothesis about the information available to agents. Everyone has the same information and uses that information optimally. At least four currents of research have called this hypothesis into question. The first stems from the hypothesis of information asymmetry, associated with the names of George Akerlof (2007) and Joseph Stiglitz (2009), among others. These authors show that if economic agents do not possess the same information, and in particular if one agent has more information than another, then the market is prone to failure and government intervention can improve the functioning of the economy. The macroeconomic importance of information asymmetries is difficult to assess. It appears to have had considerable influence on the understanding of one market in particular: the credit market. To simplify, the borrower generally has more information about the quality of his or her projects than the lender does. He/she can use that information asymmetry to negotiate a contract to his/her advantage, for example to obtain financing for poor-quality projects that are purely for his/her personal satisfaction. The lender, aware of this risk, will limit the volume of credit. Consequently, credit rationing is a structural element in the functioning of the credit market, justifying systematic public aid for small businesses, for instance. But it is difficult to reconcile this view of the credit market with the financial crisis, associated with an excess of credit.

A second current of research on information does not address the asymmetry of information between agents but the dispersion of information across a large number of agents. Agents possess private information and observe public information, which depends on the actions of others – as in the case of share prices, for example. Each agent therefore tries to figure out what the other agents expect, which in turn depends on what the other agents think that each agent expects, and so on. These 'higher order expectations' go back to John Maynard Keynes and the beauty contest of chapter 12 of his work, *General Theory of Employment, Interest and Money*, (1936 [1964]). These works have assumed special theoretical importance with Stephen Morris and Hyun Song Shin (Allen et al., 2006), and have been applied to the study of economic fluctuations.

A third line of research concerns the cost of gathering and processing information. If acquiring information is costly, agents may make a rational choice not to acquire it, and therefore to accept a form of 'rational inattention' (Sims, 2005).

A fourth approach to information focuses on the learning process. Economic agents do not know the correct model of the economy (but the economist who built the model does), and they gradually learn about the environment in which they interact. The formation of economic expectations is then dependent on the agents' past history, for they can be 'mistaken' over a long period of time.

These representations of the acquisition of information are important, because they lay the foundations for many other frictions. On the labour market, one can think of the constraints on unemployment benefits. Should they be conditional, and if so, on what information? Our understanding of the functioning of capital markets is also highly dependent on the way we represent informational problems.

Informational constraints have been incorporated into macroeconomics essentially through the introduction of credit constraints. Some research programmes seek to show how informational constraints can have a major influence, through different channels, but as yet this research does not appear to have been applied quantitatively.

A Definition of the Standard Paradigm

The previous section has described the diversity of research carried out within the standard paradigm. From the variety of these works, we can attempt to characterize the boundaries of the standard paradigm. Two key concepts emerge.

The first is the idea of the absence of trade-off opportunities for characterizing the behaviour of agents. This hypothesis is not as strong as that of rational expectations, which defined the standard economics of the 1980s. The hypothesis of rational expectations posits that agents make optimal use of the information available to them. This hypothesis is relaxed in works on rational inattention, which show that it can be 'rational' not to use all the information when gathering or processing the information is too costly. In such works, the volume of information processed is endogenous, and there are no trade-off opportunities: no individual could be substantially better off by processing a different quantity of information (otherwise they would do so).

Today, the hypothesis of rationality has therefore been weakened: it now consists in imposing the following discipline. If the economist builds a theory or a model in which the agents fail to do something that it is in their interest to do, then the economist must justify why they did not do it; in other words, the economist must explain agents' rationality. In this sense, the choices of economic agents are micro-founded.

A second hypothesis related to the absence of trade-off opportunities is that agents can make economic predictions: in the language of economists, this is the hypothesis of the formation of expectations. It is also subject to the absence of trade-off opportunities, but more importantly, forming expectations about the future requires some kind of equilibrium of the economy. The definition of a concept of equilibrium is therefore essential. This concept may vary from one article to another, but it remains central. The first constraints on equilibria are of an accounting nature, and they are always verified in the real world. If somebody sells something, then somebody must buy something. This kind of relation is always true. Other hypotheses on equilibria concern the interaction between individuals and the degree of sophistication in their choices.

To sum up, standard economics can be defined by an absence of trade-off opportunities and a concept of equilibrium. Not all macroeconomics meets this definition. Research in the field of behavioural economics, known as 'agent-based modelling', lies outside this framework. This includes works by Giovanni Dosi (see Chapter 5 in this volume), Paul De Grauwe (see Chapter 6 in this volume) and Willi Semmler (Chiarella et al., 2009). They build models based on the assumption that economic agents, households, firms or governments follow equations of behaviour that are fixed a priori. The agents are then left to interact, statistically, to observe how the economy evolves. So the aim is to simulate a virtual economy with pre-defined behaviour. The behaviours that are chosen are derived from the observation of real behaviour. The criticism levelled at standard economics is that agents have every interest in adapting their behaviour in response to changes in the environment, buying or selling less, employing more, and so on. In other words, agents do not actually behave like economic agents. The extent to which economic agents are rational remains a central issue in economics. The battle of methods rages: the behavioural approach and the standard economic approach throw a different light on every subject. This can be considered a good thing, but in terms of policy prescriptions, these approaches lead to different conclusions and are therefore often incompatible.

The profession of economists is largely dominated by standard economics. The current crisis has nevertheless brought the battle of methods to the fore. The issues of the stability of market economies and the existence of financial bubbles have led economists to reconsider the rationality of individual behaviour. The questions are not new, and neither, unfortunately, are the answers.

Never Mind the Bottle . . .

The aim of this first section has not been to discuss critically the hypotheses of the different research programmes; economics has suffered enough from methodological quarrels. So instead of discussing only the hypotheses, it is more instructive to discuss the results and compare them to the data or experimental results. As Xavier Timbeau points out (see Chapter 1 in this volume), the latter affirmation is somewhat naive, since there is no consensus in economics about what 'comparison to the data' really means. But for the researcher, this is what makes economics so fascinating.

AN EXAMPLE RESEARCH PROGRAMME: THE RISK OF UNEMPLOYMENT

This second section presents the research programme of the author as an example of the path followed by a laboratory mouse, to return to the imagery of the introduction. Before describing the hypotheses of the research programme, here is the substance. The aim is to present the economic mechanisms or causalities before moving on to describe the method.

Representation of Risks in Macroeconomics

In macroeconomics, the risks faced by agents are often represented in a simplistic manner. Most research works assume that households can insure themselves against all possible risks and that the insurance market functions perfectly. This hypothesis entails that households as a whole only react to aggregate risks, such as movements of inflation, overall growth, and so on.

To appreciate the extremely constraining nature of this hypothesis, one need only look at the risk of unemployment. The hypothesis of a perfect insurance market implies that households can (and want to) buy perfect insurance against the risk of unemployment. This means that when their status changes from employed to unemployed, their income should stay at the same level, because their insurance should compensate for the loss of wages. Consequently, the agents' consumption should not decrease when they become unemployed. This hypothesis of perfect insurance does not correspond, however, to observations of the labour market. Admittedly, state insurance mechanisms (the compensation rate varies between 40 and 90 per cent depending on the country and for a fixed period) and, sometimes, private insurance, make up for the absence of earned income in the case of a lay-off. Nevertheless, the compensation is far from perfect, and household income falls in the event of unemployment. Empirical estimations indicate a fall in consumption when agents lose their jobs (see Carroll, 1992, for example).

Risks like that of unemployment concern individual agents, and they can only be partly insured against. Economists call them 'uninsurable idiosyncratic risks', because of the incomplete nature of insurance markets. In addition to unemployment, health risks are also important in some countries. In France, for example, the public health system provides almost perfect insurance against the more serious health risks. In the United States, where health care must be largely paid for by the patient's household, the risks of poor health are very serious, and one of the leading causes of household bankruptcy (Chatterjee et al., 2007). Economists sometimes consider uninsurable family risks, depending on the country. In this case, 'risk' could mean having an unplanned child or divorcing, which represents a net transfer to the lawyers.

Out of these different risks, unemployment is the most important for two reasons. First, it is the most frequent risk causing a substantial loss of income. Second, unemployment is endogenous to economic activity and a natural subject of attention for the public authorities: by pursuing countercyclical policies or by modifying unemployment allowances, the public authorities can easily alter the unemployment risk.

The risk of unemployment, like all uninsurable idiosyncratic risks, gives rise to precautionary behaviour on the part of agents. When they expect a rise in unemployment, they tend to consume less and to postpone the purchase of durable goods in order to set aside some savings in case of need. This fall in consumption can have a negative impact on production because of the fall in aggregate demand. In turn, the fall in production causes a rise in unemployment, creating a multiplier effect on the initial rise in unemployment. This mechanism can be qualified as Keynesian in the broadest sense: the rise in unemployment is caused by a fall in aggregate demand (rather than effective, in this case) and an increase in uncertainty.

Precautionary saving is therefore a mechanism related to a financial imperfection, namely the absence of perfect insurance. This mechanism is missing from most macroeconomic models, which assume the hypothesis of perfect capital markets, allowing them to consider a representative agent. There is a stream of research, however, that focuses on the role of self-insurance, known as the macroeconomics of incomplete markets or the macroeconomics of heterogeneous agents (because the hypothesis of the representative agent no longer holds in these models). A third appellation is the Bewley–Hugget–Aiyagari model, after three of the main contributors. These works stand out first by their complexity: they call for intensive computing, and the methods used to solve such models, when all the individual behaviours have to be aggregated, continue to be a subject of debate. Another reason for the low popularity of these models is the relative uncertainty as to their importance for macroeconomics. Per Krusell and Anthony A. Smith (1998) have shown that in some cases, during average fluctuations in economic activity, the role of precautionary saving appears to be negligible, and the hypothesis of a representative agent is therefore valid.

Nevertheless, precautionary saving does seem to play an important role during deep recessions when the risk of unemployment increases perceptibly (Challe and Ragot, 2011). On US data, we can identify a noticeable fall in aggregate consumption due to precautionary saving. In addition, simple tools can be developed to study precautionary saving in macroeconomics.

If the works mentioned above focus on precautionary saving in households, recent research investigates the behaviour of companies faced with an increase in uninsurable uncertainty (Bloom, 2009; Arellano, 2008; Arellano et al., 2011). In such cases, the rise in uncertainty leads firms to reduce investment and postpone recruitment, thus contributing to the rise in unemployment. The rise in precautionary saving also appears to have affected financial intermediaries who have maintained large amounts of liquidity with the central bank. Precautionary saving can therefore help to explain the fall in private-sector credit. These mechanisms probably played an important role in the financial crisis, and more precisely in its impact on the real economy. Quantification of this impact and precise discussion of the crisis lie outside the scope of this chapter, however.

Precautionary Saving in Incomplete Markets and Standard Economics

So the causalities proposed to explain the mechanism of precautionary saving are based on agents' expectations, on their rationality (they choose to self-insure), and on the role of the equilibrium on the goods markets. If consumption falls, so must the production of consumption goods, unless stocks are to rise. The above research programme thus comes within the domain of standard economics, encapsulated by the absence of trade-off opportunities and by the concept of equilibrium. The author of these lines, endeavouring to formalize Keynesian intuitions (in collaboration with Edouard Challe, in many cases), thus finds himself at the heart of standard economics with mathematical formalizations that are sometimes very unwieldy.

Non-standard formalizations of precautionary savings can be made. For example, one can introduce, arbitrarily, a savings rate that increases with the rate of unemployment. By exploring in more detail the relation between precautionary saving and the incompleteness of insurance markets, we can better explain how unemployment benefits can limit precautionary saving, or how the level of wage inequality influences the aggregate effect of the rise in household risk. Precise analysis of the behaviour of microeconomic agents (assumed to be rational) extends the range of possible experiments. The data appear to show that agents can make mistakes in the evaluation of their idiosyncratic risk (of becoming unemployed, for example). Consequently, the introduction of deviations from rational expectations can be used to analyse the effects of over-optimistic and over-pessimistic expectations.

CONCLUSION

The aim of this chapter is to shift the focus of the debate from the tools to the theories and mechanisms. What are the fundamental mechanisms lacking from economic understanding? From the answer to this preliminary question, we can derive the tools and the (inevitably simplistic) hypotheses required. The chapter started by seeking to define standard economics before moving on to describe the author's research programme. It turns out that the latter lies within the bounds of standard economics, which is neither good nor bad; it is simply not relevant.

The profession of economists is waiting for the understanding of new mechanisms. There has been an effervescence in the work produced by economists since the crisis, but the novelty of the work does not appear to be on a par with the intellectual issues currently at stake. A new research programme, or even a new paradigm, is needed. The question of what tools it will use and how far they will rely on mathematics and computer simulations remains entirely open. The only yardstick for the comparison of research programmes is the relevance of the mechanisms brought to light and their capacity to explain the data, although there will always be disagreements about the nature of the relevant data. This affirmation is above all normative, before being positive. In a nutshell, epistemology is the revenge of the living cheese on the dead mouse.

REFERENCES

Akerlof, George (2007), 'The missing motivation in macroeconomics', *American Economic Review*, **97**(1), 5–36.
Allen, F., S. Morris and H.S. Shin (2006), 'Beauty contests and iterated expectations in asset markets', *Review of Financial Studies*, Oxford University Press for Society for Financial Studies, **19**(3), 719–52.

Andolfatto, D. (1996), 'Business cycles and labor market search', *American Economic Review*, **86**, 112–32.

Arellano, C. (2008), 'Default risk and income fluctuations in emerging economies', *American Economic Review*, **98**(3), 690–712.

Arellano, C., Y. Bai and P. Kehoe (2011), 'Financial markets and fluctuations in uncertainty', Federal Reserve Bank of Minneapolis Working Paper.

Bloom, N. (2009), 'The impact of uncertainty shocks', *Econometrica*, **77**(May), 623–86.

Carroll, C.D. (1992), 'The buffer-stock theory of saving: some macroeconomic evidence', Brookings Papers on Economic Activity, **1992**(2), 61–156.

Challe, E. and X. Ragot (2011), 'Fiscal policy in a tractable liquidity-constrained economy', *Economic Journal*, **121**(551), 273–317.

Chatterjee, S., D. Corbae, M. Nakajima and J.-V. Ríos-Rull (2007), 'A quantitative theory of unsecured consumer credit with risk of default', *Econometrica*, **75**(6), 1525–89.

Chiarella, C., P. Flaschel, H. Hung and W. Semmler (2009), *Business Fluctuations and Long-phased Cycles in High Order Macrosystems*, New York: Nova Publishers.

Cooley, T.F. and G.D. Hansen (1989), 'The inflation tax in a real business cycle model', *American Economic Review*, **79**(4), 733–48.

Diamond, P. (1982a), 'Demand management in search equilibrium', *Journal of Political Economy*, **90**, 881–94.

Diamond, P. (1982b), 'Wage determination and efficiency in search equilibrium', *Review of Economic Studies*, **49**, 217–27.

Hall, R.E. (2005), 'Employment fluctuations with equilibrium wage stickiness', *American Economic Review*, **95**(1), 50–65.

Holmstrom, B. and J. Tirole (1998), 'Private and public supply of liquidity', *Journal of Political Economy*, **106**(1), 1–40.

Keynes, J.M. (1936 [1964]), *General Theory of Employment, Interest and Money*, Orlando, FL: First Harvest/Harcourt Inc.

Kiyotaki, N. and J. Moore (1997), 'Credit cycles', *Journal of Political Economy*, **105**(2), 211–48.

Krusell, P. and A.A. Smith Jr (1998), 'Income and wealth heterogeneity in the macroeconomy', *Journal of Political Economy*, **106**(5), 867–96.

Kydland, F.E. and E.C. Prescott (1977), 'Rules rather than discretion: the inconsistency of optimal plans', *Journal of Political Economy*, **85**(3), 473–91.

Lucas, R.E. (1988), 'What economists do', *Journal of Applied Economics*, May, pp. 1–4.

Lucas, R. and T. Sargent (1978), 'After Keynesian macroeconomics', in Federal Reserve Bank of Boston, *After the Phillips Curve: Persistence of High Inflation and High Unemployment*, proceedings of conference held in June 1978, The Federal Reserve Bank of Boston Conference Series, no. 19, pp. 49–72.

Merz, M. (1995), 'Search in the labor market and the real business cycle', *Journal of Monetary Economics*, **36**(2), 269–300.

Mortensen, D. and C. Pissarides (1994), 'Job creation and job destruction in the theory of unemployment', *Review of Economic Studies*, **61**, 397–415.

Pissarides, C. (2000), *Equilibrium Unemployment Theory*, 2nd edn, Cambridge, MA: The MIT Press.

Shimer, R. (2005), 'The cyclical behavior of equilibrium unemployment and vacancies', *American Economic Review*, **95**(1), 25–49.

Sims, C. (2005), 'Rational inattention: a research agenda', Deutsche Bundesbank, Research Centre, Discussion Paper Series 1: Economic Studies no. 2005, 34.
Stiglitz, Joseph E. (2009), 'The current economic crisis and lessons for economic theory', *Eastern Economic Journal*, **35**(3), 281–96.
Trigari, A. (2009), 'Equilibrium unemployment, job flows, and inflation dynamics,' *Journal of Money, Credit and Banking*, **41**(1), 1–33.

8. Round table discussion: where is macro going?

Wendy Carlin, Robert J. Gordon and Robert M. Solow

Robert M. Solow (MIT) A round table about the current state or the future of macroeconomics should not start from the opposition of good and bad models. Even the simplest fundamentalist dynamic stochastic general equilibrium (DSGE) models contain a certain amount of ordinary common-sense economics that no one would be against in principle. In response to criticism, the naive versions of that kind of model have been fixed up with some financial intermediation, with sticky prices, with what are now called 'rule-of-thumb' consumers. It is better not to try to take positions for or against the whole school of modelling, which has good things and bad things about it, but to try to be careful about what characteristics of that modelling style one likes or doesn't like.

What particularly sets my teeth on edge is the prominent role that gets played by forward-looking, relatively unconstrained consumer-worker-owners. I don't know whether the New Keynesian Phillips curve is new, but it's certainly neither Keynesian nor a Phillips curve, but I guess that's pretty good, as far as nomenclature goes. I suspect that nearly all consumers are rule-of-thumb consumers and rule-of-thumb labour suppliers, not necessarily because they're liquidity constrained, but for various reasons: because they're boundedly rational, or they don't care, or they do what their parents did, and so on. I thought it was interesting to see what Paul De Grauwe [Chapter 6] can do with such a simple version of rule-of-thumb consumers. I think the key reason why I baulk at the forward-looking, relatively unconstrained consumer-worker-owner is because that device imposes more intertemporal coherence on economic time series than we have any reason to suspect economic time series to have. Even if individual consumers obey Euler equations (although there is no empirical evidence of anyone ever obeying a Euler equation), there is absolutely no reason to believe that aggregate consumption would obey such an equation. So that's my particular irritation, and remember what I said at the

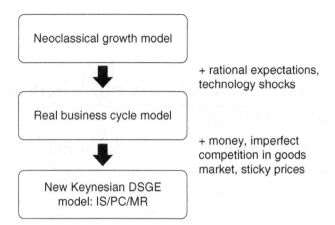

Figure 8.1   Mainstream macroeconomics pre-crisis: narrow version

beginning: a lot in those models is perfectly acceptable and is just ordinary economics.

We have two contributors in the discussion: Wendy Carlin of University College London and Bob Gordon of Northwestern University. After their presentations, we will open up the debate.

Wendy Carlin (University College London)   The subject of my presentation is 'Macroeconomic paradigms, policy regimes and the crisis: the origins, strengths and limitations of Taylor Rule macroeconomics'. Bob [Solow] provided a nice introduction to the themes I want to develop. I'd like to start with the point that Bob has made about how we should characterize the mainstream macro model and the policy regime before the crisis, and I'll refer to both narrow and broad versions of what I'm going to call 'Taylor Rule macro'. In the second part I will look at where Taylor Rule macroeconomics came from, since it's the focus around which many of the contributions to this volume have centred. To do that, I want to draw a connection between the rather rare events of global economic crisis, macro models, or paradigms, and policy regimes. The third part will focus specifically on the Taylor principle and stabilization so as to highlight some good and bad things in Taylor Rule macro. I will use three examples: the eurozone, the causes of the global crisis, and the issue of post-crisis management. I'll finish with a point or two about where we go from here.

Figure 8.1 is the narrow version of mainstream macro that Bob was referring to. It's a very linear structure. We start with the neoclassical growth model, and then add rational expectations and technology shocks

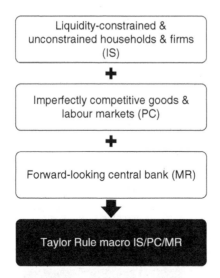

Figure 8.2   Mainstream macroeconomics pre-crisis: broad version

with a particular kind of structure, which Paul De Grauwe brought out very clearly in his contribution [Chapter 6]. This produces the real business cycle (RBC) model. Next, we add money, imperfect competition in goods markets and sticky prices, and we get the canonical New Keynesian DSGE model, with the three famous equations: the Euler equation form of the (IS), the Phillips curve (PC) – recognizable or not, as Bob says – and the monetary rule (MR). So that's the narrow version.

The broad version of mainstream macro is depicted in Figure 8.2. It can be thought of as comprising three blocks: a demand block, with liquidity-constrained and unconstrained households and firms; a supply block with imperfectly competitive goods and labour markets; and a policy block with a forward-looking central bank. Once again, we've got the three-equation structure: the IS, the PC and the MR. The associated macroeconomic policy regime has come to be known as Taylor Rule macro because of the central role on the policy side played by the Taylor Rule.

We can see in Figure 8.3 that narrow and broad versions of Taylor Rule macro come from different 'lineages'. Paul De Grauwe [Chapter 6] develops the broad version using very different behavioural assumptions, but with the same blocks. This is a way of thinking about a wide variety of models in the mainstream and close to the mainstream, of the sort that Volker Wieland [Chapter 2] has included in his large set for model comparison. So what's wrong with this? Obviously the big problem is that irrespective of whether you have the broad or the narrow version, these

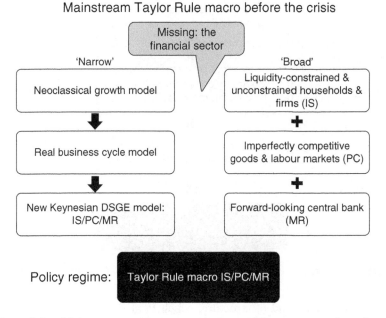

Figure 8.3   Mainstream macroeconomics pre-crisis: narrow vs. broad

mainstream models were unable to provide a good explanation for the crisis that we faced – never mind being able to predict it! Both versions omitted the financial sector. So let me use that to lead into the question of where a rules-based policy regime centred on the Taylor principle came from.

Global crises are very rare events. After each of the two global crises of the Great Depression and the Great Stagflation, a new macroeconomic paradigm emerged, associated with a new policy regime and followed by a couple of decades of satisfactory performance (see Figure 8.4). Then, what I call 'inattention' developed, and another global crisis occurred. We are familiar with that pattern in relation to the Great Depression: Keynes developed his General Theory of Employment to account for persistent involuntary unemployment, within which the voluntary-only unemployment equilibrium could be nested as a special case. A new macro policy regime, both at the national and international levels, developed and the decades of the Golden Age followed. This model and policy regime, however, didn't pay proper attention to what was going on below the surface of good macro performance during the Golden Age, and it was inattentive to supply shocks and to the role of expectations. So, once the inflationary shocks emerged, the existing policy regime gave the

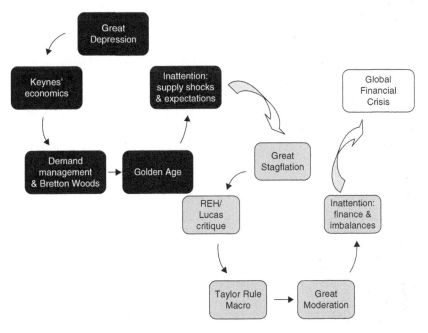

Figure 8.4   From the Great Depression to the global financial crisis

wrong signals, and we ended up with the next crisis, which was the Great Stagflation of the 1970s and early 1980s.

Going through the same steps, we can see that in the aftermath of the Great Stagflation there was a shift in thinking. A new paradigm emerged centred on rational expectations and the Lucas critique, and out of that came the new policy regime – Taylor Rule macro. This was followed by good performance and the Great Moderation. Yet once again, something was building up beneath the surface of tranquillity. We can think of it in terms of what was happening in the financial sector and in the build-up of imbalances of various kinds – both private-sector imbalances and imbalances between countries. Then the global financial crisis came. If we put these two cycles together, we can ask whether the improved macroeconomic performance on the back of each new policy regime didn't contain the seeds of a new source of instability that had the potential to incubate the next global crisis.

This brings to the fore the question of whether a process is underway of moving to a new macroeconomic paradigm and policy regime, and if so, whether it will contain the seeds of the next crisis. A lot of the contributions to this volume focus on macroeconomic modelling at business cycle

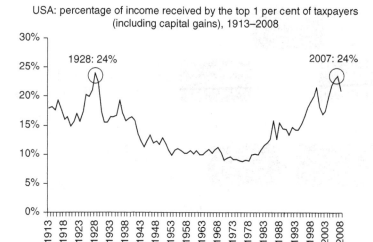

Source: The World Top Incomes Database available at
http://g-mond.parisschoolofeconomics.eu/topincomes/ (accessed 22 August 2011).

*Figure 8.5   USA: percentage of income received by the top 1 per cent of
             taxpayers*

frequency. Is there a link between a business cycle orientation, which
characterized both the Keynesian paradigm and the Taylor Rule paradigm, and the cycle of global crisis–new paradigm–new policy regime–
satisfactory performance–next crisis?

Figure 8.5 shows a U-shaped pattern from just before the Great
Depression to just before the global financial crisis in the share of income
received by the top 1 per cent of taxpayers in the USA (Saez and Piketty,
2003). In 1928, 24 per cent of income was in the hands of 1 per cent of
taxpayers in the USA; the share fell to a trough in 1975–76, and then rose
until it was back to 24 per cent in 2007. Shifts in distribution happen at
much lower frequency than the business cycle and may be important for
understanding crises.

Figure 8.6 is taken from the work of Thomas Philippon and Ariell
Reshef (2009) and reveals another big U-shaped pattern of this kind for
the USA. The solid line captures an index of financial regulation: there
was an increase in regulation from the 1930s – the bottom of the U-shape
occurred during the Golden Age – and then financial deregulation began
from the early 1980s. The line with markers is the ratio of wages in the
financial sector to average wages in the economy. We can see that the
financial sector became very boring during the Golden Age: there was no

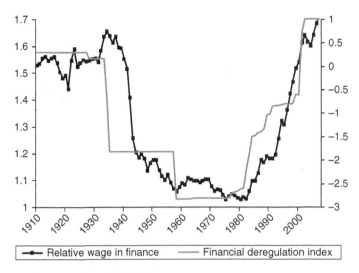

Source: Philippon and Reshef (2009).

Figure 8.6 Relative wages in the financial sector and financial deregulation, USA

wage premium for working there. But with financial deregulation, that premium re-emerged, and by the mid-2000s had returned to the level of the 1920s.

For the Golden Age and after, Figure 8.7 shows the evolution of the share of labour in GDP (workers' compensation corrected for changes in self-employment) for the USA and for 15 other OECD countries. The wage share rose through the Golden Age, peaked during the Great Stagflation, and then declined in the run-up to the global financial crisis. In the lower panel of Figure 8.7, the stagnant level of real wages in the bottom part of the labour market in the USA is shown. Measured in 2009 US dollars, the minimum wage peaked in 1968. The average real wage of production workers increased to $22 per hour in 1978 and was about the same level in real terms in the 2000s.

Is there a connection between these low-frequency changes in distribution and the kinds of crisis that we have experienced? In the run-up to the Great Stagflation, there was a shift in bargaining power towards workers – this was an important component of the supply-side shocks that produced high inflation and the sharp recessions of the early 1980s. We have seen the reverse happening in the period since the early 1980s.

The idea that shifts in distribution could be linked to financial fragility

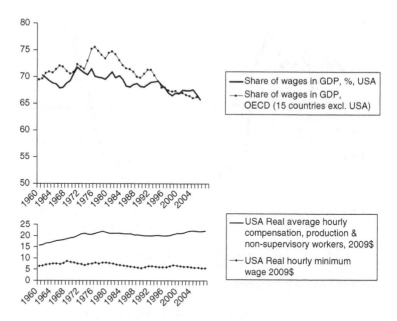

Sources: Data on real average compensation and real hourly minimum wages are from Economic Policy Institute (EPI) http://www.stateofworkingamerica.org/files/files/Wages_minwage.xlsx adjusted to 2009$ and http://www.stateofworkingamerica.org/files/files/3B_hourly_wage_and_comp_growth.xlsx; Wage shares from Glyn (2009).

Figure 8.7　The wage squeeze in the USA and OECD, 1960–2007

in the run-up to the global financial crisis was discussed by Raghuram Rajan (2010) and formalized in a recent paper by Michael Kumhof and Romain Rancière (2010). A shift in bargaining power and in between-group inequality is crucial to generating financial fragility in their model; we should think about how to include this mechanism in our macroeconomic framework. The shock is a shift in wage inequality, as illustrated in the stylized facts in the earlier figures. More detailed data show that in the USA, consumption inequality rose less than income inequality and that debt-to-income ratios outside the top 5 per cent of households increased. This suggests that there was a nascent weakness of aggregate demand caused by the distributional shift, for which the solution required workers' indebtedness to rise.

In this way, we can see a possible connection between the big shifts in income distribution, the growth of credit and the link to financial fragility. By connecting the wage squeeze, as I've called it, to financialization, credit growth and the leverage cycle, we have an explanation for the so-called

'Greenspan Put': low interest rates were required in order to stabilize domestic demand. This relates to Taylor's argument that the US Board of Governors of the Federal Reserve System (the Fed) failed to increase interest rates in the early 2000s in line with his rule. If, however, an underlying weakness of aggregate demand (associated with the distributional effects) had lowered the neutral interest rate, then the Fed may have been justified in keeping rates low to encourage households to borrow and spend within a Taylor-rule macro framework.

As the Taylor Rule has played a part in most of the contributions to this volume, I will take three examples to suggest its role in macroeconomic models and policy in the future. I want to talk very briefly about the eurozone crisis. I will argue that Taylor Rule macro had something to contribute, but was largely ignored. Ireland and Spain had negative real interest rates for most of the eurozone's first decade. There was no Taylor principle equivalent in place in the member countries' national policy regimes to promote stabilization.

Take the example of a very simple, country-specific inflation shock occurring in one eurozone country. Before turning to the case of a eurozone member, think first of all of what would happen under flexible exchange rates: with a positive inflation shock, the central bank and the foreign exchange market forecast the output contraction that's required to get back to target inflation. So the central bank raises the interest rate, the exchange rate appreciates, a negative output gap emerges and the economy is guided back to equilibrium with target inflation; all real variables are unchanged. This is just the optimal Taylor Rule. Now think of the same temporary, country-specific inflation shock in a eurozone member. Let's assume that a fiscal policy rule was used to implement exactly the same Taylor Rule optimal output and inflation path back to target – that is, the eurozone inflation target – as under flexible exchange rates. Once we're back at equilibrium, however, the home country's real exchange rate has appreciated due to higher inflation along the path back to equilibrium. Consumption and investment are unchanged, the real interest rate is back at the eurozone real interest rate, but net exports are lower, so the fiscal balance must have deteriorated. This very simple example shows that fiscal imbalance in this case arises not because of any 'profligacy', but due to implementing the same optimal policy rule as chosen by a flexible exchange rate central bank. But even *that* version of the Taylor Rule was not used by member countries in the eurozone.

The rule for stabilization for a member country requires something more than just getting back to eurozone target inflation. Policy makers have to deliver output at equilibrium, inflation at the eurozone target *and* a real exchange rate consistent with primary fiscal balance. That's a much

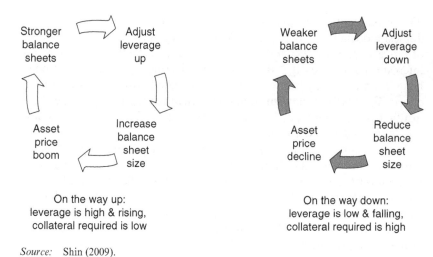

Source: Shin (2009).

Figure 8.8   The leverage cycle

harder job than just replicating the Taylor Rule path. One interpretation of what happened is that policy makers in member countries were implicitly relying on a real exchange rate channel to stabilize shocks of this kind, while ignoring the destabilizing real interest rate channel highlighted in the Walters' critique. This was an important source of pre-crisis divergence among eurozone members, which was exacerbated by the leverage cycle. But it is really a story about the failure to apply the lessons of Taylor Rule macro. The equivalent in fiscal policy for a member of a common currency area was missing, and as I've said, it would have to be more sophisticated than an ordinary Taylor Rule.

Leaving the eurozone and turning to my second example, if policy makers rely on the Taylor principle as their stabilization mechanism, then they may neglect the upswing of a leverage cycle. John Geanakoplos's work (Geanakoplos, 2009) and Hyun Song Shin's work (Shin, 2009) provide very nice ways of formalizing a leverage cycle by introducing two different kinds of investor – passive investors and value-at-risk investors. In these models, there is an asset price boom that comes from outside, which improves the balance sheets; this leads the value-at-risk investor to adjust leverage upwards because of the gap in the balance sheet that is created. We therefore have an upwards-sloping demand curve for risky assets, which generates instability (see Figure 8.8).

This whole process was outside the Taylor Rule paradigm. In the aftermath of the crisis, there have been long debates about what policy can and

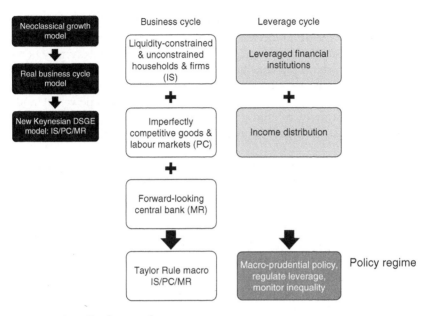

Figure 8.9 The future of macroeconomics

can't do. It obviously depends on how we characterize the crisis. This is my final example. Is this a 'balance sheet' recession or is it a much more 'normal' kind of recession? And there's no reason why the answer should be the same across different countries. It depends very much on the conditions that different countries were in before the crisis, and, therefore, the way in which the shock actually affected them. If the economy is characterized by a balance sheet recession, then that would be a reason for thinking that fiscal multipliers would be larger under these circumstances than they would under normal conditions. It might also suggest that there could be perverse effects of standard supply-side policies if such policies were successful in reducing expected inflation: some curious perversities arise if the state of the world really is characterized by a balance sheet recession and a serious possibility of deflation.

Figure 8.9 gives a forward-looking perspective of the landscape of macroeconomics.

If we take the broad interpretation of the mainstream, then we can see Taylor Rule macro as incorporating many insights of Keynesian economics, but combining it with much better models of equilibrium unemployment, proper attention to credibility, the role of expectations, and dynamics, and sensitivity to the Lucas critique. It is necessary, however, to augment Taylor Rule macro with a model of the leverage cycle and connect this way of thinking about macro with income distribution. In Figure 8.9, the DSGE model has shrunk a bit up into the left-hand corner. This is not to say that this work and methodology are not extremely powerful and important, but that it should be at the service of building and improving the macroeconomic framework and policy regime. It shouldn't dictate or define those things; it should simply be seen as a powerful modelling tool. We need to build good models of the leverage cycle, and to incorporate distributional effects of the kinds I have suggested.

Robert J. Gordon (Northwestern University) Throughout my presentation, I will take an American perspective for two reasons: first, because American authors have dominated the development of business cycle theory over the last 50 years, and, second, because we all agree that the worldwide crisis started in 2007 with the American subprime mortgage market and the debacle of US financial markets. Exclusively, I'm going to be talking about closed-economy, business-cycle macro, excluding international macro and long-run growth issues.

For me, the basic unanswered questions are: why are some slumps long and intractable while other downturns are quickly reversed? Do the answers clarify the co-existence in our history of the Great Depression, the Japanese Lost Decade (now becoming two decades), and the Great Moderation followed by the Great American Slump?

I'm going to focus on what we can learn from history about shocks and propagation mechanisms, and then move on to modern macro, which is largely the DSGE models. I will then try to convince you that not only do the DSGE models have the wrong set of shocks, or at least an incomplete list of shocks, but they also miss many of the propagation mechanisms that are essential to explaining the history with which I begin.

The emphasis on shocks is highlighted by the debate among US economists. Up until three years ago, all that anybody talked about was, 'What was the source of the Great Moderation? Was it diminished shocks or better behaviour by the Fed?' This debate was summarily ended by the post-2007 crisis, because 'poof!', the Great Moderation went away. But the emergence of the crisis highlighted the fact that Alan Greenspan – unlike the name that had been given to him by the famous journalist Bob Woodward in his book on Greenspan called 'Maestro' (Woodward, 2000) – far from being a maestro, was just plain lucky. He was particularly lucky that his term ran out in January 2006 at the height of the bubble, leaving poor hapless Ben Bernanke to come in and clean up what Greenspan had left behind. There wasn't any great performance by the Fed in the 20 years before 2007. It was the same old Fed; it just benefited from 20 years of reduced shocks. The Fed fuelled the housing bubble by deviating from

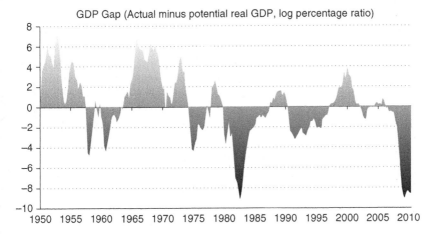

Figure 8.10   GDP gap

Taylor's Rule (and I agree with John Taylor's very insistent, repeated claims to that effect), but also by defaulting on its own duty to regulate financial institutions, again partly because of Greenspan's doctrinaire opposition to regulation.

Figure 8.10 displays the output gap for the United States since 1950. It looks almost identical to the graph in Paul De Grauwe's contribution [Chapter 6]. The only difference is that in his graph, the recent output gap only went down to about −6 per cent, and here it goes down to −8 per cent. That's not because of a different measurement technique; it's because the GDP data were revised in July 2010 to show a substantially steeper decline in US GDP over 2008–10 than in the earlier data. This graph shows that the economy can be both overheated and ice-cold, with all the gradations in between. Let me point out some of the things you see here: we had an overheated economy during the Vietnam War, which is well-known – that's when the great acceleration of inflation occurred – and a similarly overheated economy in the Korean War era. The recent great crisis and recession in the USA looks about the same in its maximum negative output gap as in 1982. The big difference, however, is when you look at how fast that gap was eliminated in 1983–84 as compared to 2009–10.

A traditional taxonomy of shocks distinguishes three different types: private-sector demand shocks, government-created demand shocks, and then the supply shocks, which have been almost entirely neglected in the literature of the last 20 years by the so-called New Keynesian Phillips curve. It's helpful to divide up, initially, the private-sector demand shocks into the four categories of expenditure on GDP, consumption, investment, government spending and net exports. This first list of shocks is adequate to understand most of the post-war period, but it is certainly not enough to understand either 1929–33 or post-2007. Direct shocks to consumption are minor. Consumption behaviour is better categorized as a propagation mechanism, particularly the role of consumption in responding to wealth bubbles or changes in real wealth, including the effect of changes in household liabilities in the aftermath of wealth bubbles. This goes back to Franco Modigliani's life-cycle hypothesis, which formally introduced wealth effects into Keynesian macro. The heart of instability in the private sector is unstable investment, particularly for residential and non-residential structures. It's part of the Keynesian heritage, based on the central concepts of coordination failures and long slumps following overbuilding.

One may ask if the problem is overbuilding or over-indebtedness. The two things go together: in a cycle of overbuilding such as in the late 1920s, structures are financed by debt, and the economy is left with see-through vacant office buildings and a hangover of debt. The residential construction instability was aggravated by the peculiar US financial market regulations before 1980 that made residential construction a sort of residual afterthought of financial markets. Residential construction would collapse through quantitative rationing whenever tight money was introduced. Government military spending created a lot of instability between 1940 and 1973, but then it became too small to matter, and even the Iraq and Afghanistan wars have not caused enough variation in government spending share of GDP even to notice. At times net exports matter, mainly as a propagation mechanism, particularly in 1980 to 1985, when tight money and fiscal easing caused a dollar appreciation and a collapse in net exports.

Residential and non-residential structures are at the centre of old-fashioned, traditional Keynesian macro. Structures are inherently subject to overbuilding because of long gestation lags. Different people get the uncoordinated idea that it would be great to build an office building at the corner of Wacker and Madison in Chicago. Except four people get the same idea, and they each manage to convince banks to finance them, when only one building is needed. And all four eventually get built and wind up vacant. The developers may fail, and the buildings may be sold for half of their construction costs, and the economy is left with this hangover of vacant buildings and over-indebtedness. This happened not just in the 1920s, but in the last few years. *The Wall Street Journal* reported in 2010: 'In Las Vegas numerous multi-billion-dollar casino-hotel projects have halted construction midway'; 'Hotel rooms are wildly overbuilt'; and 'There won't be another casino property built in Las Vegas for a decade'. There was no tall building of any kind built in Chicago or New York during the entire decade of the 1930s, and the tallest building in Chicago was the Board of Trade from 1930 until 1957. The tallest building in New York was the Empire State Building from 1931 until 1973 when the World Trade Centre was built.

Let's move on to the second main source of shocks, government-created demand shocks. We had volatile military spending in World War Two, and in the Korean and Vietnam wars. This ties in with the Barro paradox, as I call it, about estimating fiscal multipliers: we only get variation in government spending in wartime when we have capacity constraints, and we don't get much variation that we can see in periods when the economy has a lot of excess capacity, as it does now. We should also add to the list of sources of government-caused instability demand shocks caused by tight money when the Fed decides to fight inflation. That also means that we need an inflation model to explain the sources of inflation that become in turn the motivation for tight money. The history of the Phillips curve is well known, and I have a recent survey paper on it (Gordon, 2011). There was the dilemma, so well described by Paul Samuelson and Robert Solow in 1959: how come inflation started taking off in the mid-1950s in the USA before it appeared that full capacity had been reached? The initial Phillips curve, as it was christened by Samuelson and Solow in the American Economic Association (AEA) meetings in 1959, involved a negative trade-off, and they were rightly sceptical, even then, that this would be permanent or could be exploited. But the formal destruction of the permanent, negatively-sloped Phillips curve, which was actually taken seriously – particularly by the Democratic administration in the 1960s – was achieved by the natural rate hypothesis of Milton Friedman (1968) and Edmund Phelps (1968): they both argued that there may be a short-run negative trade-off, but in the long run unemployment is independent of inflation. Then followed the first supply shock in 1973–75. Very rapidly a theoretical framework was developed into a model that took price-inelastic commodity demand, namely for oil, and put it together with sticky wages and prices in the non-oil sector. The new model produced two insights: first, that unemployment and inflation could be either positively or negatively correlated, and second, that policy makers can't do anything about it. In the language of the Taylor rule, you've got one instrument and two targets, which is OK if it's a demand shock, because the output gap and the inflation rate tend to move in the same direction. When it's a supply shock, however, output and inflation tend to move in opposite directions and the central bank is stymied; it can't reach both goals.

Figure 8.11 is a scatter plot of 4-quarter moving average inflation rates from 1961 to 1980, and the years are labelled. From 1961 to 1969, we have a nicely sloped Phillips curve, and then all hell breaks loose! We had a

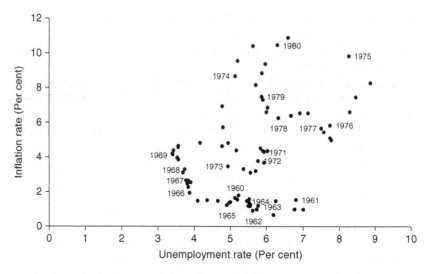

Figure 8.11   Inflation rate vs. the unemployment rate (%)

spiral from 1972 to 1975, and then a second spiral. In looking at it, you say, 'well, it's not really a zero correlation; it looks like it's a positive correlation'. That is what was explained by the new supply-shock model back in 1975.

So as I view traditional macro, it reached a complete set of explanations around 1978. The Keynesian fixed-price IS–LM macro had been joined together with the dynamic aggregate-supply/aggregate-demand framework for inflation. The twin peaks for inflation in the 1970s (see Figure 8.12) were linked to explicit measures of supply shocks: changes in the relative price of food and oil and in exchange rates; major changes in productivity trends, and the particular American nuance of the Nixon-era price controls. These were imposed in 1971 and lifted in 1974, just when the oil price shock was hitting hardest. The theory was validated not just by the 'twin peaks' of inflation and unemployment in 1974–75 and 1979–81, but also two decades later when we had a 'valley', a simultaneous drop in inflation and unemployment, in the late 1990s. A set of beneficial shocks included the post-1995 productivity revival, the appreciation of the dollar, and the period of declining oil prices. Theory can explain not only the twin peaks of inflation (dashed line) in the 1970s, but also the fact that inflation leads unemployment in that period.

It's not just the old-fashioned Phillips curve where the output gap or the unemployment gap pushes inflation gradually to adjust. When you have an oil shock, the causation is reversed and the lags are reversed. In

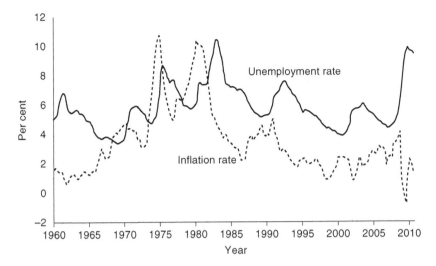

Figure 8.12   Unemployment and inflation rates (1960–2010)

the late 1990s, beneficial supply shocks prevented accelerating inflation, despite the fact that unemployment went down almost as much as it did in the 1960s.

Now, what does this have to do with understanding the sources of business cycles? Here's an interesting way of showing the connection. Let's take a 20-quarter rolling standard deviation of output changes and inflation and plot them next to each other (see Figure 8.13).

The solid line is standard deviation of changes in real GDP, and the dashed line is the same thing for inflation. We thus notice a very strong contribution of inflation volatility to output volatility in that mid-1970s to mid-1980s period, followed by virtually no connection after that. If that doesn't have something to do with the Great Moderation, I would be very surprised. Notice how in the 1950s and 1960s, there is a lot of output volatility without much contribution from inflation volatility. That was the period of volatile residential construction due to financial regulation and also the big swings in military spending, which back in 1955 was something like 10 per cent of GDP.

There is another way of looking at the role of explicit supply shock variables: taking my model of inflation, we can run a simulation of the model, feeding back the effect of lagged, backward-looking inflation, feeding back the effect of the actual unemployment rate, but suppressing the role of the explicit supply shock variables (see Figure 8.14).

The simulation with the supply shock variables is the dashed line with

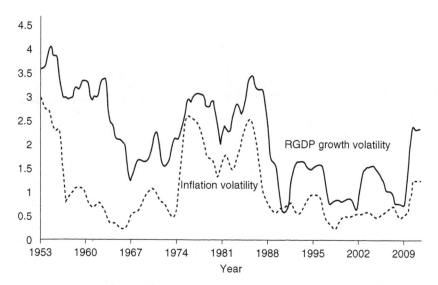

*Figure 8.13   Inflation volatility and real GDP growth volatility
               (1953–2009)*

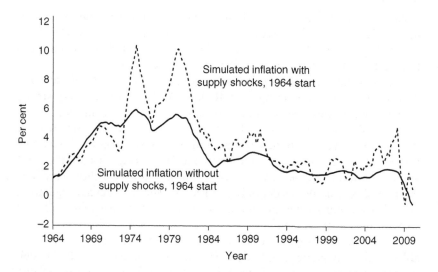

*Figure 8.14   Simulated inflation with and without supply shocks
               (1964–2009)*

the twin peaks and the valley around 1998. The solid line shows that we get much more of a standard Phillips curve story if we take out the supply shocks: the Vietnam excess demand pushed up inflation leading to more excess demand in 1973, and then the big Volcker disinflation, which boosted unemployment and brought inflation down. After that, nothing much happened until the great post-2007 crisis. The model's coefficients are not set in stone, and there are two things that appear to be changing. The effect of oil prices on overall inflation has definitely been less in the last ten years than it was back in the 1970s, and there are some good reasons for that; second, it looks like this model is tending to over-predict a movement into deflationary territory in the 2009–10 recovery period. It is not surprising that over 50 years' time the coefficients might gradually evolve, and I think that's happening, but within the same framework.

How do we explain the Great Moderation? Supply shocks dominated from 1973 to 1981; beneficial supply shocks helped explain how we got so much prosperity in the late 1990s without inflation, and reduced demand shocks helped further to explain the Great Moderation. The biggest sources of reduced demand shocks were (1) the diminished share of military spending, (2) financial deregulation that temporarily suspended the instability of residential construction, and (3) the role of computers in improving inventory management. Remember back in the 1982 recession, there were enormous, whipsaw changes in inventory accumulation that did not happen to the same extent recently.

But something's missing. What I've described so far is a pretty good story about the post-war era from 1950 to about 2007, but we don't get much insight about the years that follow. To achieve that, we have to bring in the role of asset bubbles and 'post-bubble hangovers', which help to elucidate not just the contemporary crisis, but also the Great Depression and Japan's malaise. The key ingredient in an asset bubble is leverage, or excessive growing leverage. Wendy emphasized that with a very nice layout of paradigms. In the 1920s, the leverage problem was centred on a 10 per cent margin or down-payment requirement for equities in the stock market. You could borrow the remaining 90 per cent. So, when the stock market began to fall, there were all these frantic margin calls; people were forced to sell their stock, because they had no more money to add more equity, and the house of cards came tumbling down. Something similar happened in Japan after 1989, where the bubble was in real estate, and the Ginza area of Tokyo was worth more than the entire state of California. With the bubble in the US after 2001, these bubbles shared in common a collapse in asset values that in turn led to tightened credit standards, a demand for increased collateral as the leverage ratio came back down.

Particularly important was the lack of regulated down-payment requirements in the US residential housing bubble of 2001 to 2006, similar to low margin requirements in the stock-market bubble of the late 1920s. It explains why the stock market bubble that we had in the late 1990s, which looks almost the same as the 1920s in a graph, did not lead to a major recession – that is because it was not financed by leverage. We had a 50 per cent margin requirement for people who bought stocks directly, but a vast amount of equities was being bought through mutual funds where there was no leverage at all. People actually put up the money, through retirement funds and otherwise, to buy stocks purely for cash. The housing bubble was built on ever-decreasing down-payments and increasing financial sector leverage: from Alan Blinder, I learned that leverage of the major banks and non-banks went from something like 12 to 1 to something like 33 to 1. John Geanakoplos's name has been mentioned several times, and I would like to endorse his recent paper (Geanakoplos, 2009) with its endogenous model of leverage. He begins by saying: 'Variations in leverage cause wild fluctuations in asset prices. This leverage cycle can be damaging to the economy and should be regulated'. And we know that it was not.

The bubble of 1927 to 1929 evokes additional comparisons. Leverage in corporate finance in the late 1920s had similar effects to the mortgage-backed securities in the recent crisis: the major part (of new equity issues), particularly from 1926 on, seems to have gone into erecting a financial superstructure of holding companies, investment trusts, and other forms of inter-corporate security holdings that was to come crashing down in the 1930s. Also similar in the 1920s and in the current decade were large profits by investment bankers and a stimulus to consumer demand, which took the form of capital gains on equities that were largely untaxed in the 1920s and by home mortgage credit withdrawals in the most recent episode.

Why are there bubbles in some places and not in others? We've heard a lot about Iceland and Ireland moving beyond the traditional banking model where loans equal deposits into a new world in which loans are much bigger than deposits, with the difference financed by bank borrowing, often in foreign currencies. We also have a contrast between Canada and the United States. There was caution and tight regulation in Canada, with much less of a bubble and much less of a hangover than in the USA. But I think the least known and most fascinating story is the contrast between the state of Texas and the United States. The state of Texas has an amazing constitution that requires minimum 20 per cent down-payments on residential housing and prohibits cash-out equity withdrawal. I would never even have known that, except that my home-town *Chicago Tribune* wrote a story about why Texas had escaped most of the fallout of the financial crisis. With such a stark contrast between these cases, can there

be any doubt that institutions matter? I think we don't give enough attention to Wendy's story about the increased demand for collateral by financial institutions. Consider a story from a friend of mine who is a mortgage
broker. A mortgage broker in the United States tries to convince people
to finance or refinance their mortgages and then goes and tries to sell this
application to a mortgage institution actually to provide the financing.
This friend says that five years ago only 5 per cent of his deals were turned
down by the lending institutions. Today, 80 per cent are turned down. If
you wonder why the US housing market has been so slow to recover, why
prices are still falling, why there are so many foreclosures, part of it is the
simple lack of availability of credit. So here is another case of rationing to
add to all the others.

Let's move on from shocks to propagation mechanisms in traditional
macro. There was the Friedman permanent-income hypothesis: the short-
run marginal propensity to consume is lower than in the long run. The
Modigliani life-cycle theory formally introduced a role for assets as a
determinant of consumption and saving. We have Dale Jorgenson's neoclassical theory of investment, which built on the traditional, old-fashioned
accelerator that had no prices in it, and combined an effect of changes in
output and also the use of cost of capital in determining investment. And
behind the scenes we had James Tobin, William Baumol and Milton
Friedman working out a better, more complete version of the demand for
money. The models of Friedman and Tobin, in particular, used money
as a substitute for other assets and helped to explain why velocity was so
unstable after financial deregulation in 1980. Ironically, Friedman's own
theory helped to undermine monetarism because of that instability of
velocity. There was mention earlier about the rejected theories of Robert
Clower, Don Patinkin, Robert Barro, Sanford Grossman, Jean-Pascal
Bénassy and Axel Leijonhufvud, which tried to develop the formal interplay between price stickiness and its implication that markets no longer
cleared. In the Barro–Grossman model, as in IL–SM, the price level is not
just sticky but absolutely fixed, and so any change in nominal demand
automatically translates into a change in output. In this world, any change
in output alters constraints – those faced by households trying to work the
number of hours they wish, and those faced by firms attempting but failing
to sell the profit-maximizing amount of output.

In 1956, Patinkin introduced the distinction between Marshallian
'notional' demand curves and constrained – what he called 'effective'
– demand curves for labour. In Patinkin's world, there is a downward-
sloping labour demand curve and an upward-sloping labour supply curve
that cross at the long-run equilibrium. But a short-run decline in output
shifts the vertical effective labour demand curve to the left, as if it were

a vertical brick wall that prevents workers from attaining the amount of employment given by the crossing point of notional demand and supply. That means that the marginal rate of substitution is no longer equal to the real wage, which is no longer equal to the marginal product. The essential truth of this paradigm was evident in almost every country in the world in 2009 when we ask, 'does each member of the labour force have the free choice of working the desired number of hours at the going wage and price?', and 'does each firm find it possible to sell the optimal level of production at the current wage and price?' Traditional macro answers 'no' and understands why.

Why was the Great Depression so deep and why did it last so long? It was a post-bubble hangover aggravated by unit banking, a world without deposit insurance and the collapse of the money supply. Unlike Milton Friedman and Anna Schwarz, who treated it as exogenous, the money supply was partly endogenous as a result of bank failures and the lack of Federal Reserve action. Friedman and Schwarz failed to realize that much of the decline in money supply was caused by output rather than the other way around. The New Deal fiscal stimulus was too small, but in contrast to the Obama stimulus, there was direct federal employment of all those workers at the WPA,[1] the CCC[2] and the other alphabetical agencies. Michael Darby reminded us, more than 30 years ago, that the effect of direct federal employment was to lower the unemployment rate in the late 1930s by a full 3.5 per cent, something the Obama stimulus came nowhere close to doing. We all know and often hear from everybody from Allan Meltzer to Bob Lucas to Harold Cole and Lee Ohanian that the New Deal tried to push up wages and prices, interfering with the normal self-correcting properties.

Traditional macro also has an answer to the second question: why was the recovery from the 1980–82 recession – the *previous* most serious recession – so fast, and why is the recovery now so slow? That's a bit of a no-brainer. The 1980–82 recession was caused by tight money, the Volcker disinflation, designed to fight inflation with brutally high interest rates. When money was eased in 1982, the economy took off like a rocket. Just to give you an idea of what that rocket was like, the S&P 500 average of American stock prices went up by a factor of 5 between 1982 and 1995, and by another factor of 3 in the five years after that. Since the post-2007 crisis was not caused by tight money, it can't be cured by loose money. We've got this post-bubble hangover with no obvious policy fixes.

Modern macro, as Wendy and Robert Boyer have shown, began with the real business cycle model. Only supply shocks mattered; there were no prices and no money. Oil shocks and crop failures had already been incorporated into traditional macro, so the new and unique element in the real business cycle models was the idea that you could have negative technology shocks, in other words, forgetfulness. It made no sense to many of us, but the RBC model had its decade when people took it seriously. With no demand or prices, the original RBC framework was forced to interpret the Great Depression as a massive bout of forgetfulness. Some of the elements of the RBC model have been merged together with the DSGE New Keynesian theories that we've heard so much about in the other contributions, based, as Wendy pointed out in her acronym, on IS, PC and MR: these are a very special IS, a very special PC, and I think a relatively uncontroversial monetary reaction function.

Let's turn to the problems with the Euler consumption function and the New Keynesian Phillips curve. I refer here to Olivier Blanchard's very interesting and partly-correct, partly-misleading paper called, 'The state of macro' (2009). Aggregate demand combines a Euler first-order condition for consumers that leads to a consumption function in which only the real interest rate and future expected consumption enter. There is no other source of demand in the simplest DSGE model, no fixed investment, no inventory investment, no military spending and no foreign sector. Since the earliest DSGE models, individual papers have introduced some of these elements, often one at a time. There was mention earlier about rule-of-thumb consumers, which also partially breaks through the Euler equation framework. But the basic DSGE model does not allow consumption to depend on current income, and thus allows no role for non-market clearing and constraints. Naturally, I would object to the New Keynesian Phillips curve, including the nomenclature: it makes inflation a function of expected future inflation instead of backward-looking expectations.

The New Keynesian Phillips Curve (NKPC) literature is split in the additional variable introduced besides future expectations – sometimes the output gap, sometimes the unemployment gap, and sometimes marginal cost, often proxied by changes in labour's share. There is no role for backward-looking inertia and, in particular, no role for supply shock variables, which I have argued here are essential to explaining the twin peaks of inflation in the 1970s. Blanchard's own evaluation is that the benefit of this DSGE framework is formalism in the ability to make welfare statements, and the costs are that the first two equations are patently false. But I don't think he quite gets the essence of why they're patently false. The problem with the consumption or IS equation is the lack of constraints, and the problem with the NKPC is the lack of supply shocks. We know from basic specification bias that if you leave out a variable that is possibly correlated with inflation, and you're estimating only a term that is supposed to be negatively correlated with inflation – namely the unemployment gap – you're going to end up biasing the coefficient on the unemployment gap towards zero, and that's exactly what happened. There have been some excellent critiques of these NKPC showing that their Phillips curves are essentially insignificant. What's my complaint about the shocks? Well, let's take a brand-new paper by my colleague Larry Christiano (Christiano et al., 2010). His paper has three shocks: a generalized technology shock (shades of RBC); something called 'investment-specific technology shock' – that's like saying, 'Oh we forgot how to make laptops, we'll have to go back and use mainframes again'; and the third is a shock term in the Taylor Rule equation. People often interpret, for example, the low interest rates of 2002 and 2003 as an aberration by the Fed from what they should have been doing according to the Taylor Rule. The wide variety of demand shocks that I mentioned and listed before are missing, as are the asset market hangovers. How then can these models help us understand all these big questions of macro?

What's missing in the propagation mechanisms? There is an absence of channels from financial meltdown to the real economy. There is no channel from current income to current consumption. There are no wealth effects on consumption, no liquidity effects of credit tightening, no multiplier-accelerator mechanism to explain the instability of demand for consumer durables or investment, and except in very special individual applications, no role for either destabilizing military spending or stabilizing fiscal policy. The failure to introduce rationing and constraints right from the beginning is a central fault, and you've got to wonder about these Euler-equation consumers. It's very clear from Christiano's latest paper: basically a Euler-equation consumer just hates to work! That disutility of work makes you wonder why unemployment has got such a bad name. It's because these consumers would really just like to be sitting around the house if it weren't necessary to earn a living. Blanchard's own characterization of ritual obedience to the rules of DSGE research is wonderfully entertaining, and I would like to repeat some of it. Blanchard laments the herd mentality in modern macro, in which an article today often follows what he calls 'strict, haiku-like rules'. According to Blanchard, the problem with these repetitive articles in the DSGE tradition is the introduction of an additional ingredient in a benchmark model already loaded with questionable assumptions, and little or no independent validation for the added ingredient. He longs for the lifting of the haiku-like doctrinaire approach to macro and hopes for 'the re-legalization of shortcuts and of simple models'. Unfortunately, his conclusion says almost nothing about the basic flaws: the contradiction between market clearing and price stickiness and the inability of the NKPC to explain why inflation and unemployment are sometimes negatively, sometimes positively, correlated. So here is my last line: modern macro has too much micro and too little macro.

Individual representative agents assume complete and efficient markets and market clearing. Models ignore the basic macro interactions implied by price stickiness, including macro externalities (of which that 'supply shock inflation creates recession' is a classic example, originally suggested by the late Arthur Okun) and coordination failures. In an economy-wide recession, most agents are not maximizing unconditional utility functions (as in DSGE models), but subject to binding income and liquidity constraints. DSGE models do not leave room for the full set of channels by which post-bubble hangovers reduce spending through capital losses, overbuilding, over-indebtedness and credit constraints.

Solow   I sometimes take the line that the popularity of the kind of model that Bob Gordon was just decrying, comes from a fondness for neatness. And a criticism that could be made of the Gordon presentation here is that it is 'not neat'. It is not parsimonious. To which I think the proper reply was given by no less an economist than Albert Einstein, who said once that every model should be as simple as possible, but not more so. And the case that you've heard from Wendy as well is that it's not possible, though it's all too tempting, to be a little too parsimonious when you're talking about economic fluctuations, macroeconomic fluctuations. I would rather not hear comments which say, 'Oh well, Gordon, you've got an answer for everything, but what we really want is the *same* answer for everything', because I don't think that's a good principle here. But if that's what anybody wants to assert, of course, go ahead.

Gordon   One thing I would like to hear from the group is that I was parsimonious enough not to bring up inequality, which was one of Wendy's main themes. I would love to hear from people, especially since the French have maintained a much more equal income distribution than the Americans. Is that really a key part of understanding macro over the last decade?

From the floor   Do we really need to understand shocks better? Should we not completely remove the idea of shock from the macroeconomic model and return to an endogenous theory of business cycle? The old-fashioned Keynesian theory was an endogenous theory of business cycle, and so was the Minskian theory, where the economy builds up the next recession during the expansion phase.

Gordon   If there was a contest between 'shocks' and 'no shocks', a good thing to do would be to go back to the original Samuelson multiplier-accelerator model, which is a purely mathematical model. It's a second-order difference equation with a knife-edge property that you only get steady cycles with one set of parameters, and without them you either get explosion or dying out, and so it's no longer a business cycle. John R. Hicks wrote a book about the trade cycle (Hicks, 1950), in which he introduced ceilings and floors to get around the problem of the explosive case. We know, just trivially, that changes in military spending, along with some of these other shocks that I've mentioned, were big enough to perturb that Samuelson cycle so it could never possibly die out. So we don't get very far with a shockless environment. The intellectual device of a shock is extremely important in understanding the Great Moderation. I don't think it's even worth a metaphysical crisis about why we went 20 years without any really substantial shocks. We had a big stock market bubble, and we had a lot of dramatic things happen in the 1990s, and it worked out pretty well, or seemed to.

Robert Boyer (CEPREMAP) [from the floor]   What correlation do you make between inequalities and financial deregulation?

Carlin   If you think about the USA as the epicentre of the global financial crisis – and this also relates to what may be a point of disagreement about what was going on in terms of Greenspan and the Taylor Rule in the early 2000s – then the question is, 'why was there such a low real interest rate, not conforming with the simple Taylor Rule?' Taylor was right, they didn't follow the simple Taylor Rule, but the question is, why not? And my answer to that question is, 'because the alternative would have been a recession'. And since there was no inflationary problem, then the question is, 'why would there have been a recession?' And the answer is, 'because there was inadequate demand'. And so what was the problem? Given the build-up of the effects of the big distributional shifts, capital owners could have invested in physical capital, which would have increased the capital stock, increased wages, and we wouldn't have had such a problem. They could have increased their consumption, which no doubt they did, but there's some limit to that. Or they could have increased their acquisition of financial assets, which is exactly a part of the leverage cycle. Financial deregulation made possible a solution to the weakness of fixed investment through increased lending to households outside the top part of the income distribution. That was the connection I was trying to make.

Jean-Louis Beffa (Cournot Centre, Banque Lazard) [from the floor]   Following Robert Gordon's presentation, I want to stress that many countries have accepted a wide view – which was sustained by the OECD and many international organizations, including, of course, the

European Commission – that liberalizing the financial markets was the way to ensure the optimum growth of countries and absolute efficiency. They added that large-scale financial innovation was a plus to the real economy. That is completely wrong. It has produced nothing but problems for the real economy. It is shown by the difference between continental Europe and the two countries that have become the pre-eminent centres of speculation approved by governments. It is the influence of the United States and the United Kingdom on the overall world attitude of regulating the financial sector that brought on the disaster. Their view is, 'Leave us alone; you can't understand; let us self-regulate'. The problem is the financial sector's failure to self-regulate. When Germany and others tried to regulate, the British and US governments opposed it, on grounds of modernity. That modernity did *nothing* for the real economy, in my view.

Gordon There's an interesting link between these two comments. On the one hand, we have increased inequality – much of it concentrated in the financial sector, including those gigantic incomes at the top – and on the other the widely discussed fact that in the United States the median wage and the median household income were flat, didn't grow at all, during the period of 2000 to 2007. It's also been pointed out that despite the appearance that unemployment was relatively low, there was a slow erosion of the labour-force participation rate. The employment-to-population ratio was actually lower in 2007 than it was in 2001, in the recession. A lot of people dropped out of the labour force. A startling fact is that if today we had the same employment-to-population ratio as in the year 2000, the United States would have 14 million more jobs, of which 9 million would be due to a lower unemployment rate, and the other 5 million would be due to the higher participation rate of 2000. That shows how big a hole we've fallen into. There's an interesting point to be made on the financial compensation. We had this enormous share of GDP, value-added that was contributed by the financial sector. There are two extreme interpretations of that. One was that these financial salaries were actually doing something real, so that the real share in GDP and value-added was going up. The other view is that it was entirely inflation of compensation, that they weren't producing anything real, and that it should have all been deflated away in the price indexes. They don't deflate it away, and so we have a phoney increase in productivity in the financial sector due to what is ultimately an arbitrary decision about how to deflate.

On Jean-Louis's comment, there's an interesting connection with Wendy's idea that we have a crisis, then we have a new paradigm, then inaction and lack of attention for 20 years. What we had in the United

States was a set of financial deregulations at the end of the 1970s that eliminated arbitrary borders between savings and loan banks and commercial banks, eliminated regulated interest ceilings on savings and deposits, and allowed people to write cheques on a broader range of deposits. That was widely accepted as a good thing. Then, in the Wendy analogy, we had 20 years in which nothing bad seemed to happen, and so it seemed that maybe more financial deregulation would be a good thing. But then we went into the abolition of the Glass–Steagall Act and the opening up of the 'wild west' of finance through unregulated shadow banking. I don't want to retell the story of all this because we all know it, but if the regulations had kept up with the deregulations and controlled rigorously not just the shadow banks but these down-payments that you were talking about, much of this problem would not have happened. Remember the state of Texas, because that is a remarkable demonstration of all the things we've been saying.

Solow   I want to endorse a little more strongly the point that Jean-Louis Beffa made. In all of our discussions of the financial sector and the financial crisis, we tend to ignore – I won't say necessarily lose sight of – the fact that God made a financial sector to improve the efficiency of the real economy, not for the enjoyment of hedge fund managers. If you look at the evolution not only of compensation but of the use of resources, particularly human resources, in the financial sector, it is impossible to believe that it contributes anything to the efficiency of the real economy. It essentially promotes speculation and inflates compensation. Paul Volcker made this wonderful joke that he thought the most important financial innovation of the last 50 years was the automatic teller machine. So I do think that we pay inadequate attention to the question as to whether we have a financial system of even remotely near optimal size, if we look at its effects on the real economy. There is a question on which I would like the opinion of more expert people (Robert and Wendy): it's fashionable to dump on Alan Greenspan these days – and sometimes for good reason. Greenspan, however, had a notion that was perhaps wrong but not unintelligent, and I would like to know if anyone has any insights into this. He thought, and said at one point, that participants in the shadow banking explosion were not 'babes in the woods'; they were experts, they disposed of large sums of money, they were not fools, and their self-interest as creditors to financial institutions should have led them to discipline the activities of financial institutions a bit more. That didn't happen, and I don't know how one could assign reasons for this. There are various possibilities. One is that in this competition for high compensation, nobody wants to pull the plug until the last possible minute, and if you wait until the last possible minute, you may pull the plug *after* the last possible minute. Some of it may have been that expensively educated and well-compensated financial people are subject to herd behaviour, just like anyone else. What one cannot credit is suicide, a suicidal impulse. So something went wrong; it was not a wholly stupid thought on Greenspan's part.

Gordon This is the contrast between the macro and the micro. We have all of these people maximizing what they see as their self-interest, and according to Adam Smith, that should make everything OK. But go back to my analogy of the four different developers who all want to build skyscrapers on the same street corner where only one is needed. Each of those is an independent, rational agent. It may be because of information imperfections that somehow they get far enough along without realizing that there are others like them . . . It's an information failure and a coordination failure. I think the same thing is true of the financial sector. Each of these people is in their niche, and they don't see the system-wide dangers. Who among us, besides Nouriel Roubini, Bob Shiller and a few savants, really could honestly say that they were sitting there in 2004, 2005, realizing that the values of our homes were all about to go down, and we'd better make careful plans for the next ten years to anticipate all this, back at the height of the bubble?

Solow I think there is something to that, but I would put it a little differently. There really is something to the extraordinary complexity of log-scale financial transactions in the world of the high-speed computer. So the demands are very great on the participant who is supposed to be disciplining the financial process. He or she has to worry not only about the balance sheet of his or her debtors, but also the creditors to those debtors and the creditors of the creditors and all that. It may simply be that the complexity of the whole thing both made it impossible to discipline and created an enormous uncertainty at the beginning of the collapse, which tended to magnify the whole thing.

Beffa [from the floor] If you take, today, the head of Citigroup, the head of Lehman Brothers, or the head of Bernstein . . ., are they ruined, or are they still enormously rich? I think those people played a game, where they knew well the risks they were taking, and they protected themselves. They made sure to avoid any negative impact on their personal wealth in the future. They heavily lobbied regulation agencies and governments. That is absolutely clear. These were very intelligent people just playing the casino, for pleasure, and protecting themselves. In a regulated world, if something goes wrong, they won't receive their bonuses; part of the bonuses will be paid in stock. This is a big change and would help to regulate better that kind of attitude. Frankly, it's a game where if it goes wrong, I don't lose, and if it goes right, I make even more money.

Solow   I think there is something to that: the stories of the 1929 crash involved many stockbrokers leaving their offices by way of the window, 30 or 40 storeys up. One hears less of that, these days. I want to add one further comment on the question of endogenous and exogenous shocks. What Bob said was quite right; one could add a little more – some technical and some non-technical. In the first place, anyone who can successfully endogenize what we had thought yesterday to be an exogenous shock: good luck! One is for that. That is the way economics can make progress. The technical thing is: the necessity for shocks comes in part from our ability to deal mainly with linear models. A linear model – this was Bob's point – needs shocks in order for the fluctuations it generates not to die out. A non-linear model need not have that characteristic. Knut Wicksell made this wonderful analogy to a rocking horse. A rocking horse is an essentially non-linear oscillatory mechanism, but what it needs is a child to keep hitting it so that it keeps rocking. If you leave it alone, it will become stationary. So the division – the separation between propagation mechanisms and shocks – is not something that is given once and for all. A shock is something that we don't now know how to explain, so we have to treat it as a tangent.

Carlin   I have one comment on that. A striking aspect of DSGE models is the shock structure, where much of the dynamics comes from the assumptions about the shock itself. That really downplays the idea that you have to have an economic propagation mechanism, which seems to be an Achilles heel in terms of modelling the economics of the process. What Paul De Grauwe (Chapter 6) does is something different: he says we should have just random shocks, and we should have a propagation mechanism, however simple. So I think some serious attention has to be given to these issues in modelling.

Gerhard Illing (Ludwig Maximilian University of Munich) [from the floor]   First a comment on Bob's presentation. I liked your pointing out of some of the weaknesses of the DSGE models and the modelling of the shocks – the great vacation shock or the great forgetfulness shock. I agree that this is a really weird concept. But I was a bit surprised that you claim that the New Keynesian model doesn't have aggregate supply shocks. That would mean this serious forgetting of technological progress.

But there are actually aggregate demand shocks, aggregate supply shocks and mark-up shocks, so there are three types of shocks in addition to the framework that you praised.

A comment or question for Wendy: I found your comment appealing that we are always fighting the last war, so the next generation of macro models will include leverage cycles, credit constraints, and then we can explain why these financial crises happened. But we are pretty bad, presumably, at explaining the next big shock. So my question is: in what way should we go to avoid the next big shock? One way would be to include more about heterogeneity and inequality, which may be a big problem in the future.

Giovanni Dosi (Sant'Anna School of Advanced Studies, Pisa) [from the floor]   It is much easier to have an endogenous dynamic if one takes fully on board heterogeneous interacting agents, as in agent-based modelling. Let me make a related remark: when we were talking qualitatively earlier about what happened during the crisis, one tells the story of interacting agents: coordination, herd behaviour, lack of coordination . . . . When one moves to the formal part – even with those who don't believe in DSGE – there is a sort of anthropomorphism of the macro, in which there is an agent who reacts to shocks in different ways. The qualitative story, in contrast, is one in which there is no isomorphism between what the agents do and the macroeconomic dynamics. This is, of course, an advocacy for agent-based modelling, but there might be other ways to deal with that, in the way that Alan Kirman does, for example, where the model has very little phenomenology inside; still, he has a multitude of agents and non-linear dynamics in their aggregate interactive behaviour.

I also have a question for all three panellists. What do you think are the most important transmission mechanisms from the financial to the real side, in general and in this crisis in particular?

Gordon   The point has been made that there are already shocks in the DSGE models. I'm arguing that they are the wrong kinds of shocks. In particular, to label something a technology shock and treat it as an IID[3] process implies that there is some substantive way in which technology – which is inherently forward-moving over time and involves the building of knowledge – could possibly move backwards in time and involve the forgetting of knowledge. That's just a fundamental economic point. And I don't think that by technology shocks they're thinking about oil prices; if they are, then let them say that. They don't have it in their Phillips curve, so why should it matter? So I don't see that aggregate supply shocks make sense, and using Christiano's paper as an example: they don't really have any aggregate demand shocks except the Taylor Rule error term, and that differs very significantly from the traditional paradigm that I offered, where you get a shock even if the Fed is exactly carrying out the Taylor Rule. If you have some source of inflation, you're going to get higher interest rates, and that's going to potentially cause a recession, cause a decline in aggregate demand, but it is not an *error* in the Taylor Rule; it could be carrying out the Taylor Rule perfectly. And that brings us then to this question of where are these transmission shocks from monetary policy? And there we have traditional downward-sloping demand curves for global goods with respect to interest rates; we have asset prices and liabilities working through the Modigliani-type consumption function, and then we have institutional arrangements that can lead to credit constraints. We've learned from the leverage cycle and from Wendy's nice link here that the collapse of an asset bubble automatically leads to increased demand for collateral, which is partly the story of my mortgage broker and one of the reasons why so many of his deals get turned down. So we've got at least four channels there between financial markets and the real economy.

Carlin	Gerhard had a nice question on what we should be doing if we are going to prepare ourselves for the next global crisis, and whether a focus on heterogeneity and distribution is a core issue. One response is rather like what Ricardo Caballero (2010) said in a recent article, where he talked about the dangers of the pretence of knowledge in macroeconomics. He argued that we should now be in broad exploratory mode rather than in narrow fine-tuning mode. That captures what I think is important. There has been a lot of new work on the Great Depression, for example, and on Japan. These things are all enlightening, but do they help us in a forward-looking way? I think we need to be working in macroeconomics in the two following directions. One is bringing into macroeconomics and properly taking account of the race between skills and technology. This interaction between skills-biased technical progress and the ability of the economy to generate human capital is very much at the core of the inequality story, and it has macroeconomic consequences that are not going to go away, irrespective of how we come out of this crisis. That leads to the second point, which also touches on Giovanni's [Dosi] transmission mechanisms (see Chapter 5), which we've hardly talked about at all, and that's the question of really taking seriously what it means when the dynamic of growth in the world economy shifts from being driven by the advanced economies to being driven by China. It relates to the recycling of surpluses – the point that came up earlier that even though China has such an enormous investment share, it has an even higher savings share, so that those surpluses have to be recycled. The question of how that recycling takes place points the finger at the role of the financial system, and whether the financial system is playing its role in allocation or playing a role in generating another bubble. I don't have any special insight into what the next kind of crisis will be, of course, but I think these are the core issues that macroeconomics has got to get to grips with.

Gordon   I'd like to talk about the next crisis. The potentially possible next crisis is one that all of us would think of initially – the eurozone. If there is enough contagion in the eurozone, starting in the periphery and moving towards the centre, the problem could become too big for the body politic in France and Germany to be willing to continue to finance. A crisis of that kind could lead to the dissolving of the euro or some sort of permanent recession or great depression in some of the countries that are most vulnerable. In the case of the United States, I would worry most about a long, slow erosion, closely related to Jean-Louis's comment earlier about the problems of his company in competing with the emerging markets and how sophisticated they are getting in making all the stuff that used to be the comparative advantage of the rich countries.

In my story, there are four causes of increased inequality in the United States for the bottom 90 per cent. The four at the bottom are the decline of the unions, the decline of minimum wage, and the globalization pair of immigration and imports, which are very nicely characterized by Richard Cooper in the Cournot Centre's volume, *The Shape of the Division of Labour* (2010). If you go back to Heckscher–Ohlin, you would predict that globalization and the linking together of the Indian and Chinese labour markets with the rich countries is going to inevitably push down the wages of the low-skilled in the rich countries. On top of that, you've got these 14 million lost jobs in the United States, and everybody who is getting a job, who was previously employed, most are taking enormous cuts in wages. That is going to further cause measured inequality to rise, because you're going to have minimal, if not negative, income growth in the bottom 70, 80, 90 per cent of the income distribution. A possible outcome, which is Ned Phelps' current mantra, is that we can never get below 7 per cent unemployment again; there are too many people in the workforce who are going to lose their skills, almost like the insider/outsider story that has been told about Europe for the last 20 years. This means a loss of potential output and what happened in Europe starting in 1985: this long, slow erosion meant that there was not enough capital stock, not enough investment, to fully employ the people that used to be working at the peak. If 14 million people aren't working for ten years, some of the capital they work with is going to depreciate, and there's no incentive to replace it. So you end up with lower potential output and a permanent slowdown in economic growth. I see that kind of long, slow erosion, sort of Japanese-style outcome, as more likely than the lightning bolt of a crisis.

NOTES

1. Works Progress Administration.
2. Civilian Conservation Corps.
3. Independent and identically distributed random variables.

REFERENCES

Blanchard, O. (2009), 'The state of macro', *Annual Review of Economics*, **1**, 209–28.
Caballero, R.J. (2010), 'Macroeconomics after the crisis: time to deal with the pretense-of-knowledge syndrome', *Journal of Economic Perspectives*, **24**(4), 85–102.
Christiano, L.J., M. Trabrandt and K. Walentin (2010), 'Involuntary unemployment and the business cycle', Working Paper Series 238, Sveriges Riksbank (Central Bank of Sweden).
Cooper, R.N. (2010), 'How integrated are Chinese and Indian labour into the world economy?', in R.M. Solow and J-P. Touffut (eds), *The Shape of the Division of Labour: Nations, Industries and Households*, Cheltenham, UK and Northampton, MA, USA: Edward Elgar Publishing, pp. 101–21.
Friedman, Milton (1968), 'The role of monetary policy', *American Economic Review*, **58**, 1–17.
Geanakoplos, J. (2009), 'The leverage cycle', *NBER Macroeconomics Annual 2009*, Vol. 24, Cambridge, MA: MIT Press, pp. 1–65.
Glyn, A. (2009), 'Functional distribution and inequality', in W. Salverda, B. Nolan and T. Smeeding (eds), *The Oxford Handbook of Economic Inequality*, Oxford: Oxford University Press, pp. 101–26.
Gordon, Robert J. (2011), 'The history of the Phillips Curve: consensus and bifurcation', *Economica*, **78**, January, 10–50.
Hicks, J.R. (1950), *A Contribution to the Theory of the Trade Cycle*, Oxford: Clarendon.
Kumhof, M. and R. Rancière, (2010), 'Inequality, leverage and crises', IMF Working Paper 10268.
Phelps, Edmund S. (1968), 'Money-wage dynamics and labor-market equilibrium', *Journal of Political Economy*, **76**, 678–711.
Philippon, T. and A. Reshef (2009), 'Wages and human capital in the US financial industry: 1909–2006', NBER Working Paper 14644, January.
Rajan, R. (2010), *Fault Lines*, Princeton, NJ: Princeton University Press.
Saez, E. and T. Piketty (2003), 'Income inequality in the United States, 1913–1998', *Quarterly Journal of Economics*, **118**(1), 1–39.

Shin, H. (2009), 'Comment' on Geanakoplos (2009) *NBER Macroeconomics Annual 2009*, **24**, Cambridge, MA: MIT Press, pp. 75–84.

Woodward, Bob (2000), *Maestro: Greenspan's Fed and the American Boom*, New York: Simon & Schuster.

Index